Fame & $hekels

Noah John Rondeau at the Sportsmen's Shows

Life Throughout the 1950s and the 1960s in the Hermit's Own Words

William J. O'Hern

Fame & $hekels

Noah John Rondeau at the Sportsmen's Shows

Book design and typesetting created by Nancy Did It! (www.NancyDidIt.com)
Cover design by Cynthia Long Graphics

For permission to reprint selected diary entries from Noah John Rondeau's 1950, 1951, 1952, 1954, 1959, 1960, and 1966 journals, grateful acknowledgment is made to the Adirondack Experience and to Ivy Gocker, librarian at the Adirondack Experience at Blue Mountain Lake.

For permission to reprint selected diary entries from Noah John Rondeau's 1953, 1955, 1956, 1957, 1958, 1960, 1961, 1962, 1963, and 1964 journals, grateful acknowledgment is made to the Lake Placid-North Elba Historical Society and to Jennifer Tufano, administrative director/register of the collections care office at The History Museum.

For permission to use "Noah Code" typeface used in this book, grateful acknowledgment is made to David Green. (copyright David Greene, 2009)
The code is based on the encrypted entries in Rondeau's diaries.

Grateful acknowledgement is made to Richard J. Smith for the use of Noah John Rondeau's photo album. Rondeau's albums are now part of the Adirondack Experience's collection at Blue Mountain Lake.

Grateful acknowledgement to reprint "The Hermit of Cold River" by Clayt Seagears is made to the *New York State Conservationist*.

"Hermit and Hermity" by William K. Verner first appeared in *The Living Wilderness Living Wilderness* magazine, Spring 1971.

Cover photo courtesy Richard J. Smith from Noah John Rondeau's photo album

Pen-and-Ink drawings by Sheri Amsel, Adirondack Artist and Illustrator

Silhouette icon of Noah John Rondeau by Lillian G. Clarke

Epigram is taken from one of many postcards Noah had made

Dedication Photo by author

☂ The Forager Press, LLC

Camillus, NY
www.theforagerpress.com
Printed in the United States of America by The Forager Press
979-8-9992740-0-7

Distributed by Blue Line Book Exchange, Lake Placid NY 12946
www.BlueLineBookExchange.com

EPIGRAM

"We can thank Rondeau, perhaps,
for reminding us that, just as civilization needs wilderness
to provide meaningful delineation to that civilization,
so does wilderness require Civilization in order for it to achieve
its sharpest meaning for man's fruitful contemplation."
—William K. Verner

Mr. Verner was Curator of Research at the Adirondack Museum,
Blue Mountain Lake, New York. He was a board member of
the Constitutional Council for the Forest Preserve, publication
chairman of the Adirondack Mountain Club (ADK), and active
on ADK's conservation committee.

DEDICATION

To Bob Bates
or "CR" Bob (Cold River)

...to all who know Bates' passion
and extensive knowledge
of the Cold River backcountry.

"C.R." is standing on Seward bridge a short distance
from Ouluska Pass lean-to.

CONTENTS

Epigram 3
Dedication 5
Preface: Hermits and Hermitry..9
Introduction: America's Thirst for Sportsmen's Shows.........................11

Part 1: Noah's Second Act 14
Chapter 1: The Hermit of Cold River Clayt B. Seagears...........................15
Chapter 2: The Naturalist and the Hermit 21
Chapter 3: Cold River Country (1913)...23
Chapter 4: A Lesson for America and Scouting 25

Part 2: 1946-1952 30
Chapter 5: The Outside World Beats a Path to Noah's Doorstep.............31
Chapter 6: Fame and Shekels 40
Chapter 7: Sportsmen's Shows of the 1940s and '50s 43
Chapter 8: From Forest to Metro 46
Chapter 9: Notes From the Hermit's Diary 49
Chapter 10: Rondeau Relates His First Experience................................51
Chapter 11: Albany Bound and Beyond 56
Chapter 12: Widespread Fame...61
Chapter 13: Spoiled for Hermiting 69
Chapter 14: Slow Progress Away from the Wilds...................................77
Chapter 15: Richard Smith Reviews Noah's Acceptance of a Santa Job.......91
Chapter 16: A Healthy Savings Account 97
Chapter 17: Permanent Outside Life 104
Chapter 18: A Living Exhibit 111

Part 3: Life on the Outside 118
Chapter 19: Smith and Wilkins Help "Mr. Whiskers".............................119
Chapter 20: Life on the Outside 122
Chapter 21: The Hermit's Journals...123
Chapter 22: Throughout the 1950s...127
Chapter 23: 1952 133
Chapter 24: 1953 142
Chapter 25: 1954 152
Chapter 26: 1955 159
Chapter 27: 1956 167
Chapter 28: 1957 173
Chapter 29: 1958 177
Chapter 30: 1959 189
Chapter 31: Throughout the 1960s...196
Chapter 32: 1961 203
Chapter 33: 1962 209
Chapter 34: 1963 218
Chapter 35: 1964 232

Chapter 36: 1965 239
Chapter 37: 1966 248
Chapter 38: February 1967 253
Afterword 256
Appendix A: Santa's Workshop at the North Pole 258
Appendix B: Camp Seward's True Story of Greer's Bear 263
Acknowledgements 268

Hermits and Hermitry

William K. Verner, from *The Living Wilderness*, Spring 1971

Hermits and hermitry have always been a part of the Adirondack scene. The nineteenth century record includes both full-time and part-time hermits, and evokes such names as Fournier, Bourne (or Bowen), Dunning, Hathorn, Beach, and Wood. Some hermits even earned the official recognition of census takers, who recorded their way of life in the "occupation" column of their rolls. In the twentieth century the tradition faded somewhat, but not entirely. Harney, French Louie, and above all, Noah John Rondeau, kept it alive.

Rondeau fell into the category of part-time hermit; in fact, his failure even at being a full-time hermit was consistent for a man who throughout his life worked at nothing other than being himself. The son of a French-Canadian miner, he was born on Jackson Hill in Clinton County, on the northwestern fringes of the Adirondacks. His schooling was spotty at best, a fact which Rondeau always regretted. He ran away from home at age sixteen, spent three decades doing odd jobs, including some barbering and guiding, and in 1902 began going into the Cold River country, in the western Adirondack high peaks area. In 1929 he started wintering there. In the thirties he was "discovered" by a group of mountain-climbing Adirondack 46-ers from Troy, New York, and beginning in May 1943, undertook his longest single stretch away from it all at Cold River for 381 days. A profile on Rondeau which appeared in the New York State *Conservationist* in 1947 brought him to wider public attention and led to his participation in the New York Sportsmen's show and other shows, both in New York State and New England. He appeared on radio and television during the late forties and early fifties, and served a stint at an Adirondack tourist attraction or trap. In 1950 a hurricane—the "Big Blowdown"—closed access to Cold River country for five years, and Rondeau took up residence in the Lake Placid and Wilmington areas; part of his Cold River camp was moved to the Adirondack Museum [now referred to as the Adirondack Experience] in the late 1950s. On August 25, 1967, he died at the Lake Placid Hospital.

Bill White poses by the remains of the hermitage. Courtesy of Bill White

America's Thirst for Sportsmen's Shows

NOAH JOHN RONDEAU'S life was really one of nearly constant contradictions—"flip-flops" were what some close friends called it: happy memories of childhood vs. hatred of his father; antagonism toward the Conservation Department vs. happiness at being part of their shows; rejection of government vs. acceptance of welfare in his old age; a Republican, but anti-Big Business.

In the winter and spring of 1947, after four years of war, the sportsmen of New York once again had the opportunity to attend the biggest sportsmen's shows in years. These events also greatly benefited Rondeau and improved his lifestyle. The unexpected attention during sportsmen's shows of the late 1940s and early 1950s might be characterized as the hermit's "Golden Era."

Sportsmen's shows presented an array of "back-to-nature props," entertainment and the biggest array of products and exhibits seen anywhere. The large variety shows had something that appealed to every age and sex: log-choppers, sawmen, pistol experts, fencers, archers, and conservationists all gave presentations.

Exhibits included tanks of wild fish and cages of wild game.

Jacques Suzanne of Lake Placid, a personal friend of Admiral Peary, brought his team of Siberian sled dogs and told of his 20-month solo trip over the bare wasteland of Siberia.

But of greater interest to the dyed-in-the-wool hunters, fishermen, and camping enthusiasts were the products and demonstrations of the sporting goods dealers and manufacturers of equipment that was used

Courtesy New York State museum

throughout the nation.

Boats, guns, fishing tackle, and camping equipment, unavailable during World War II, were now back on the market. Sleek cabin cruisers were on display as well as swift sail boats, inboard runabouts and a wide array of fishing boats.

The old favorites in the outboard motor field were there with the newer brands, all making the sportsmen wonder why anyone would ever bother with oars and paddles when they could have a sleek, fool-proof power boat.

Rifles, pistols and ammo that users had to do without during the bleak war years were back, and such famous names as Winchester, Remington, Stevens, Colt, and Ithaca were no longer topics of conversation, but realities. Anglers also examined and tried the newest in rods, reels, lines and lures, with fishing season in the not-too-distant future.

And, seen among all the products and exhibits was Noah John Rondeau. The hermit of the Adirondacks was on hand with his backwoods display and philosophy, derived from living alone for decades in the deep forest.

Courtesy David Greene

Part I

Noah's Second Act

FAME & $HEKELS

Chapter 1

The Hermit of Cold River

Clayt B. Seagears

⊙ᴕ Ϙᴵᴕ⸜θ∘ ⁻∘ˣ⸜∘⸜⊦ᵢ ⊦⊦ᵢ θˊ∘⸜ᵢ ⊦⁻ᵢ ×θᵢᵖ ´ᵢ ⊦θ θᵀ×ᴕᵀᵢ ´ ᴛ⊦⸜⸜×θ ∘θ⸝⊦⸜ᵖˊ×
⸜ᴕ ᵖ⊦θ Ϙθ∘×⊦⸝ᵖ ᴕ Ɵᴵˣ⸜ ∘⊙⊦ˍθ∘ Ɵ×ᴵᴕθ□

All entries in Noah John Rondeau's 1946 diary originally appeared in
what he referred to as his "Fancy Writing." The now decoded journal
and any secrets it contains are revealed for everyone to read in *Noah John
Rondeau's Adirondack Wilderness Days* by William J. O'Hern (The
Forager Press, LLC, 2009).

Sun. June 16th. 1946. At Cold River City.
A nice day.
Snyder come, stay. He shot a Quill Pig.

Mon. June 17th. 1946. Handsome View.
A nice day of clouds and sunshine.
3 men called. Flora: Bunchberry, Daisy, Bluegrass, Bluets, Yarrow.
I fish 15 Frog Pond and Cold River Flow with Snyder.
Saw 1 Deer. Tracks: Deer, Otter, Bear, Mink, Muskrat.

Tue. June 18th. 1946. Hall of Records.
Rain last night, clouds and sunshine today.
Snyder go. First Robin Plantain bloom. I cremate Quilly in Town Hall.
15 Fish. I overhaul Pyramid of Giza.

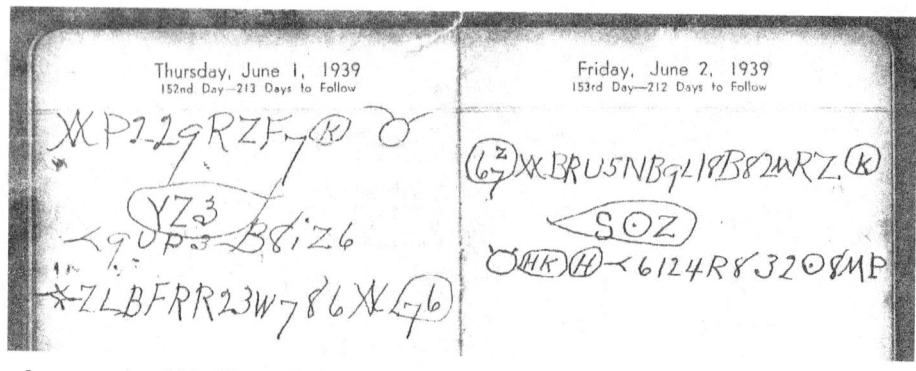

An example of Noah's early "license plate code.

* * *

Four months following Roy Snyder's visit to the hermitage, the 65-year-old hermit's picture and the story of his long life in the mountains appeared in The New York State Conservationist, *October-November 1946 issue, written by Clayt Seagears of the widely-read magazine. The story launched the hermit into the limelight of public attention.*

Seagears was the first director and writer of the Division of Conservation Education and chief architect in 1946 of its new publication. Al Bromley, a former editor of The Conservationist *said, "No one who ever heard Clayt talk...ever forgot him." Seagears, known as "Mr. Conservation," was a showman who loved the 1940s-'50s New York Sportsmen's Shows. He was admired for his prolific collection of illustrated writings, sketches, drawings, cartoons, oils and watercolors, all in the fields of natural history and conservation, as well as his* Conservationist *series, "The Inside on the Outdoors."*

Seagears described the hieroglyphics Noah used in his secret, coded writing as an "operation very closely resembling the tracks of an inebriated hen whose father was a devilish rooster and whose maternal parent could be termed foot-loose."

His article appears below.

There isn't a more bona fide hermit in the whole United States—including Sharktooth Shoal—than Noah John Rondeau, who has occupied a hole in a woodpile way the hell and gone back in the Adirondack wilderness for 33 years.

Noah John is not only the real McCoy in the hermit department; he

Courtesy *New York State Conservationist* magazine

looks like hermits are supposed to look. He lives the same way.

He has himself a Sunday suit fabricated out of a couple of deer hides and assembled with bear-tooth toggles. He hunts. He fishes. He traps. He uses the longbow. He keeps a diary in secret code and sets his calendar by the stars. He owns less household equipment than a Tenderfoot Scout would take on an overnight hike, and how he gets through a long, below-zero Adirondack winter in that layout of his is strictly a lesson in hibernation which any woodchuck would do well to look into.

Noah John is, in truth, spang out of this universe.

Perhaps we shouldn't wait to the breathless finish of this yarn to give out with a rich moral. We have a State with darned near fourteen million people in it [in 1946], the teemingest population in the nation. Yet here's a guy wanting to be a hermit who was able to be one with a minimum of outside interference, and in a peak-studded wilderness six hours by forest foot-trail from the nearest hamlet. The moral thus seems to be that (1) Noah John is one in fourteen million and (2) that despite a population density of 250 folks per square mile we still have large quantities of country for people to lose themselves in when pressed (for various reasons) for a walk in spaces very wide and very wild.

Leave us draw up a hunk of balsam stump while Noah John cooks what very well may turn out to be his whole day's "vittles"—a few flapjacks bogged down with his own brand of syrup.

This cooking function is performed (in summer) over a more or less perpetual open fire. He flaps the jacks in bear grease, rolls them up like a cigar, bites off about up to the band and then takes a healthy swig of syrup out of a bottle still ketchupy around the seams. Nuts, says Noah, to the napkin trade.

And let us gaze (withal, with awe) upon the unique living quarters of Noah John. What appear to be wooden tepees in the photo on the next page are indeed wooden tepees—but of a variety more practical than anything ever described in the Manual of Carpentry and Tinkery for Growing Boys. Noah John lives in his own woodpile. Come spring, he has burned his kitchenette, his storage vault, his front parlor and his powder room behind him. Furthermore, he has made it easy to do.

The system is this: When winter has run itself out down the mountain rivers, Noah John starts building his tepee village. He cuts long poles of efficient burning diameter. Every three feet he notches them nearly through. Then he stacks 'em up like a wigwam, leaving an interior recess large enough to stretch out in. Thus, when winter has piled the drifts high and our hermit's activity has been reduced to a minimum, the chore of keeping a fire is

Courtesy New York State Conservation Department Archives

a cinch. Noah John merely reaches out the door, removes a pole, gives it a belt with the axe head, and the notched pieces fall apart. He admits it took him a few years to figure out the proper deal for this easy-living angle, but what do a few years amount to in a pattern of life such as his?

Noah John is 63 years old. He now finds it bad news to do his main sleeping under a drafty canopy of slanted poles. So, he has a hovel made from a few boards off a long defunct lumber camp. Over the so-called door to this realm of retirement the old boy has nailed a sign, "TOWN HALL." Inside there's just room enough for a sort of bed and a crude stove. Every year the place gets smaller, due to encroachment of soot layers from the walls. On the bed is just what you'd expect to find on the bed of a better class hermit—a bear skin. The interior has touches here and there of gaudy décor—the stalagmite drippings of myriad red, yellow and white candles. There are no windows, and none are necessary, because the occupant is, perforce, always close to the door. It's as simple as that.

He has another cubbyhole for the convenience of visitors—the hikers who occasionally call on him. This jointed shelter does have a window, and more extensive decoration—the chalky shoulder blades of a dozen beavers, the antlers of bygone bucks and the skulls of two degreased bears. These rattle nicely in the breeze and add to the general cheer.

Noah John, despite his thirty-three long years of complete isolation, and despite the primitive aspects of his existence, is by no means uncouth or illiterate. By any yardstick of human behavior, he is a distinctly bright gent. It would be difficult, in fact, to find a single button missing, except on his pants. He loves to talk—picturesque hermit talk if he thinks his hiker-visitor would be made any happier by it. He reads anything he can lay hands on, but leans to books on astronomy, philosophy, and kindred subjects of the solitudes. This is quite understandable.

He likes people (if they don't crowd him), but it is suspected that he views them with some suspicion. Inherently honest himself, Noah John hints darkly that it was a sequence of sharp practices by others, when he was the youthful proprietor of a barber chair, which drove him from what he felt was a chiseling world to the honesty of open spaces.

Noah John's outdoors is built to order for a hermit. His spot is on a bluff high over the end of Cold River Flow, twelve miles as the crow flies south of Lower Saranac Lake, ten miles northeast of Long Lake Village and twenty miles west of Keene Valley. Trails maintained by the Conservation Department lead all the way—about nineteen miles of hiking in any direction, except that eleven miles can be made by canoeing to the north end of Long Lake, thence into the Raquette and then a mile or so up the Cold. Most hikers go in via Long Lake Village and Shattuck Clearing, although some prefer the hoof route via Corey's (just south of Upper Saranac) and Mountain Pond. Four miles to Noah John's east are Preston Ponds, nestling at the end of Indian Pass. He couldn't have picked a more isolated place to live with a Ouija board.

Nor could he have picked a spot of greater beauty. Towering across Noah's valley is Panther Mountain, and Santanoni and Henderson. Behind him rear Seymour, Seward and the Sawtooths. He lives on a strip of [former] lumber company holdings in the middle of a huge chunk of State land comprising about 130 square miles.

It's wild land, a stronghold of marten and fisher. Noah used to run a 40-mile trap line when he was more spry. Now he has all he can do to "come out" once a year for a packbasket of staples. Forest Rangers—like Orville Betters or Wayne Tyler—or deer hunters and hikers bring him his mail now and then, plus small supplies of food. Or Fred McLane, the Conservation Department's head plane pilot, may drop him bread and papers. Maybe the brook trout are biting in Noah John's Lost Pond or in Cold River Flow. Maybe a snowshoe rabbit rams its head against Noah John's sittin' log and conks out conveniently in time for a lonely February meal. Maybe.

The Conservation Department has a great friend in Noah John. Spry or not—if anything went wrong in the woods, he'd be out of there on all two cycles to tell the boys about it. He's a great friend of Man in General, too. For he's the magnet which lures many a hiker deep into some of the grandest country in the world, and that kind of stuff is good for what ails you.

Yep, everything considered, there's quite a guy behind all that alfalfa.

FAME & $HEKELS

Chapter 2

The Naturalist and the Hermit

JOHN BURROUGHS (April 3, 1837–March 29, 1921) was an American naturalist especially known for his collections of essays about nature. His life and that of Noah John Rondeau overlapped, and Burroughs and hermit Noah John Rondeau had some things in common. Noah also faithfully wrote observations in his journal about the natural world around him. Burroughs had a cabin where he enjoyed solitude in West Park, New York, considerably south of Noah's in the Adirondacks. Burroughs had something to say about solitude and hermits in his 1889 essay collection, *Indoor Studies*:

> "We readily attribute some extra virtue to those persons who
> voluntarily embrace solitude, who live alone in the country...in
> the woods, or in the mountains, and find life sweet...We know
> [hermits] cannot live without converse, without society of
> some sort, and we credit them with the power of invoking it
> from themselves."

Indeed, Noah spent month upon month alone, without seeing another human, yet he claimed he was never lonely. He'd share this nugget of wisdom in this way: "Of course, everyone has a lonely experience and no two are alike. I've been more lonesome waiting two hours in a railroad station that in a whole cold winter alone in the mountains. Lonesomeness isn't just when you're alone; it's when you're destitute and lost."

Perhaps he had the "fine streak" that Burroughs supposed "preserves them in solitude." Burroughs maintained that "...the finest spirits are not gregarious; they do not love a crowd. A man who retires into solitude must have a capital of thought and experience to live upon, or his soul will perish of want. This capital must be reinvested in the things around him, or it will not suffice."

This describes Noah's solitary days to a tee. He was amazingly inventive, as well as thrifty. His "capital of thought" kept him entertained—although he loved to have visitors of the right type. His "capital of experience" allowed him to live primarily off the land, and to build himself a snug home and his own little "city" to go with it.

Of course, it turned out that Noah did love a crowd—but when he first went to the woods to be alone, he intended to be just that, alone.

For most of us, it's easy to understand what Burroughs said: "But think of those long years of solitary life; the nights, the mornings, the meals, the Sundays, the weekdays, and no sound but what you made yourself!"

Courtesy C..V. Latimer Jr. M.D.

Chapter 3

Cold River Country in 1910

DEFINED BY THE VALLEY the Cold River flows through, the broadening space between the contour lines that spread out near the base of the Seward Mountains' northern slope was a place of refuge.

At first sight, the typical sportsman's woods camps looked like nothing but ramshackle log shelters. They blended into the setting of lumber slash and natural forest.

Courtesy New York State Conservation Archives

Deserted lumber camps also provided shelter for trappers, anglers and hunters.

The valley served whatever life arrived by chance or on purpose—if not wild animals, then humans. Sweet-smelling wildflowers brought butterflies; birds nested in trees and fed on seeds and insects. Below the high points of false summits were trout-filled ponds where tumbling brooks exited toward the central valley. At the summit of Ouluska and Calkins passes were avenues of travel that led to other, smaller valleys.

And beyond those valleys were thousands more acres. The land was Cold River's protection. It kept man at bay. It challenged the lumbermen, whispered to trappers, drew hardy guides and their sporting parties, and mesmerized dedicated anglers, backpackers, and mountain climbers. Without too much intervention from government regulation and game protectors, the valley's history evolved rather naturally. Wildlife reproduced, seeds grew into plants, and steel-rimmed wagon wheels cut ruts that formed rough ways for the relatively few who visited the valley.

The valley was never free of man, never quiet, never lifeless. There was the chatter of red squirrels, of trees being chopped, the susurrus of wind in withered autumn leaves. These were the sounds of contentment, of life and of ordinary disaster. A nocturnal hoot owl called out to a mate;

Courtesy New York State Conservation Archives

a rabbit cried in a fox's clasp, a sound like an injured child's scream.

This was the idyllic land where, decades ago, Noah John Rondeau, Jay Gregory and Dr. CV Latimer Sr. found the perfect getaway for themselves. It became a beloved retreat for them and for their families, the kind of place that makes the heart beat a bit faster when the snow begins to melt in the spring and vacation dates are finalized. Then there is nothing but delicious anticipation.

Vacationers' plans changed after the Big Blow on November 25, 1950. The fear that wildfire would devastate the forest caused wildlife officials to close the woods for three years, and state rangers established interior stations and jeep roads for fire protection.

Despite the destruction of thousands of acres of woodland by the 1950 hurricane, Cold River country soon recovered, and is still a fascinating land that beckons to all who love the wilderness.

Chapter 4

A Lesson for America and Scouting

CLAYTON B. SEAGEARS described Noah John Rondeau as "the nation's most [real] McCoy hermit who you'll see," in an advertising flyer hawking the New York State Conservation Department's exhibit at the April 1947 Rochester Sportsmen's Show. The hermit, he continued, "can be put down in anybody's book as one of the most unusual examples of human adaptation on record."

In 1946, the Boy Scout's Paoli Troop 1 visited the 62-year-old hermit where he had lived for 32 years in a moss-chinked log hut "just big enough for a Great Dane to wag his tail in, without getting a quick singe" on the so-called "wood-burning barrel stove," cooed Seagears in the Conservation Department's press release promoting its woodsy display of the hermit's river-top digs that was to appear at the upcoming exhibit.

Seagears continued:

"This toy structure is 19 miles in any direction (including up) from his nearest neighbor. The word 'up' is significant since our hermit's habitat nestles at the Cold River-cooled foot of towering Panther Mountain on one side, Ampersand Mountain on the other and various Adirondack Alps rivals which clutter the clouds in between. The whole region is stark spruce-studded wildness—part of New York's great Adirondack Forest Preserve—two and a half million acres of God's green grandeur which the State Constitution says, in foresighted wisdom, must remain forever wild."

Noah was a veritable part of that wilderness. When I reviewed my 1953 *Handbook for Boys* merit badge requirements, I realized that had Paoli Troop 1 wanted to name the hermit an honorary scout following their visit, they might have approved that he had mastered the requirements to earn 31 merit badges: Archery, Architecture, Art, Astronomy, Bird Study, Botany, Camping, Canoeing, possibly Citizenship in the Home, Cooking, Fishing, Forestry, Gardening, Hiking, Home Repairs, Insect Life, Journalism (had they read his autobiography or thumbed through the man's scrapbooks and poems), Leather Work, Marksmanship, Music, Nature, Personal Fitness, Pioneering, Public Speaking, Reading, Scholarship (once they learned how he returned to school at the age of twenty-six to earn an eighth-grade diploma), Soil and Water Conservation, Weather, Wildlife Management, Woodwork, and Zoology.

Noah John lived the scout motto "Be Prepared."

"Be prepared for what?" a non-scout might ask. In the "Rules of Scouting" section on the Scout handbook, the saying is defined: "The motto means that a Scout is prepared at any moment to do his duty, and to face danger, if necessary, to help others."

It would be clear to an observant scout that the hermit had learned accidents or emergencies could happen at any time, and living in the backcountry, one had to be prepared and learn what to do in all kinds of emergencies, and how to do it.

When the troop photographer was taking pictures of Noah demonstrating how and why he chopped deep notches in poles before stacking them on a wigwam, scouts would naturally see potential danger. Wherever you are, whatever you are doing, think through in advance what you ought to do. It would be too late if the hermit waited until the emergency happened and he whacked his foot with a sharp axe.

It was the hermit's duty to Be Prepared in all situations if he was going to survive.

During the time the scouts confabbed with Noah, they learned he took his game with homemade fishing tackle and with bow and arrow, also homemade. In summer he supped on brook trout. Each fall his broadhead arrows felled a buck and very often a bear. He utilized this game to the fullest for food, for clothes and for blankets. From each bear, for example, he rendered about five gallons of grease—his cooking fat, his beard-glosser, his leather softener, his fly dope.

Noah had a tiny vegetable garden. In it grew a few hills of potatoes, carrots, a few turnips, and beets. State forest rangers, hikers and hunters often brought him flour, canned foods, tea, and the like by pack basket. He kept the canned food from freezing in winter by lowering the cans into the river beneath the ice; vegetables were stored in a root cellar.

He gathered berries, "wild spinich," mushrooms, edible roots, and herbs. With these he mixed venison, bear, beaver tail, snowshoe rabbit, partridge, porcupine, trout, and red squirrel. A big pot of this sundry "Slam Bang," as he called it, would last him for days.

He retired to bed when it turned dark; he rose when it got light.

In his leisure time he read and composed poetry. There was indeed poetry in the old hermit, and although his verses were crude and lacking meter, they were interspersed in his diaries like tiny jewels among common pebbles and offered occasional flashes of beauty.

Courtesy of Richard J. Smith
from Noah's photo album

He dabbled with oil paint on canvas, both of which he was given for a birthday present. His books? The Bible, Shakespeare, H.G. Wells, philosophy, astronomy, genetics, natural history. His formal schooling? He'd quip, "I died in the fifth grade." The rest: self-taught.

Noah claimed he often spent less than $50.00 cash per year. That was the price of one good beaver pelt, when prices were normal. He was self-sufficient, utterly independent, and absolutely content. He was not antisocial, was a congenial host, and was a colorful and highly intelligent conversationalist.

True to the word, Noah fit the role of a genuine hermit. He seldom saw a human from late fall until spring; often as not, he stayed at his remote camp without coming out more than once a year; he slept 12 hours a day; his fare was simple, meager and virtually all off the land, (he was careful to balance vitamins); he would go six months without speaking one word to another human; he made much of his clothing; and he often received his Christmas mail on the Fourth of July!

Now talk about human adaptation and living the role of a hermit.

On February 12, 1947, eight months after Paoli Troop 1 had visited the

Courtesy of Richard J. Smith from Noah's photo album

FAME & $HEKELS

hermitage, the New York State Conservation Department brought Noah by helicopter from his wilderness abode to the National Sportsmen's Show in New York City.

The plan was the brainchild of Clayton Seagears. In "The Hermit at the Sportsmen's Show," in an April 1946 issue of *Boat, Rod & Gun* and in an unidentified April 1947 magazine, Seagears encouraged readers to come and meet Noah as he traveled to other shows in the state.

"Then on to the Albany Sportsmen's show, next Buffalo and then Rochester. Changed? No. He's ready to go back to his camp. He wants to go back, not because he's antisocial but simply because he loves Nature and the land and wants to live by using it wisely.

"His one lesson to America, and it's a great one: 'Use your natural resources wisely and they serve us well.'

"So, meet Noah John Rondeau at the show. Get a bit of his philosophy. Understand how he lives and why. Remember that New York State's licensed deer hunters also have increased from 68,000 to 300,000 in a little over a decade. Where do we go from here?

"Noah John can tell you. Take only what you need. Help put back more than you take. See more in hunting than just the harvest; more in the fishing than the faded spots of a dying trout; more in the nature of our outdoors than bare hills and gully scars and muddy waters.

"Shake hands with the guy. He's helping America learn something."

Part II

Noah
1946–1952

Chapter 5

The Outside World Beats a Path to Noah's Doorstep

NOAH JOHN RONDEAU is without doubt one of the Adirondack Mountains' most recognized folk characters. As Seagears put it in his article about the hermit, Noah "occupied a hole in a woodpile way the hell and gone back in the Adirondack wilderness for 33 years."

Courtesy of Ruth Prince

Steeped in woodlore and survival skills, in an outdoors life stretching back to the early 1900s, he had perfected a near flawless integration of living off the land and, after 1930, began accepting help from local forest rangers who often air dropped him food and other necessities during the winter, or from his mountain climbing, fishing, and hunting friends who supplied him with food, ammunition, socks and rubber-bottom boots, long john underwear, and money in exchange for the services he provided to sportspeople.

On Friday, September 6, 1946, amid the occasional hikers who dropped by, arrived Charles L. Mooney, city editor of *The Knickerbocker News*, and

'Round the Clock with Noah John Rondeau, Hermit of the Adirondack Wilds

GIFTS FOR NOAH—The Knickerbocker News made up a gift basket for the hermit, who is shown at right receiving his gifts. Others, left to right, are Frank T. McCue, C. L. Mooney and C. A. Smakwitz.

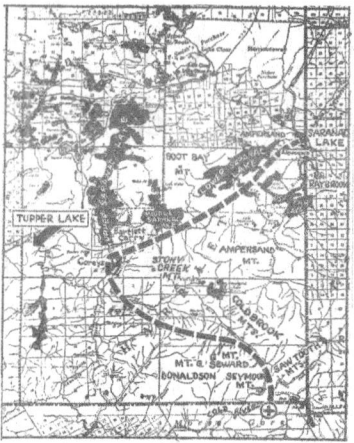

RUGGED COUNTRY—The route out of Saranac Lake to Noah's cabin winds through the wilderness shown on this map prepared by Staff Artist Archie Appio.

Courtesy *Albany-Times Union*

eight reporters and photographers from the capitol district. The Albany newspaper men thought Noah looked and lived like a hermit should. The newspaper team had learned of Noah most recently through three national magazine stories and through hearing his story on three nationwide network programs. Mooney's group was going to scoop the competition by hiking into the wilderness for a first-hand personal visit.

Somewhat to their surprise, they found a literate man who desired nothing more than to rid himself of civilization and spend his days reading and fending for himself in the loneliness of the Adirondacks.

Mooney talked about his trip two years after the fact as if it were only yesterday. "In many years of newspaper work… [I have] talked with thousands of men and women, but to this day, Noah John Rondeau remains one of the strangest, and yet one of the most interesting."

Mooney was attracted to interesting people who had an apparent weakness for living outside the typical template. Noah's difference was what endeared him to Mooney. Since Mooney had heard so much about the hermit—his aspirations to write poetry, his life as a recluse—it was quite reasonable for Mooney to resolve that he would have to climb a mountain and talk with Rondeau at his wilderness retreat.

Mooney recalled, "On the way up we had all kinds of visions of what Rondeau might be like. We wondered what his reaction might be on seeing fellows from the city advancing on his wigwam, or in whatever he might be living. World War II had ended a year and a half earlier, and we could picture ourselves bringing him the startling information, 'the war's over.' Julius Heller, city hall reporter, suggested we'd better specify which war we were talking about.

"Just as Noah was getting ready to go fishing," said Charles Mooney, "I walked into camp led by two 30-year friends of Noah's, Rangers Orville E. Betters and Wayne Tyler."

"'Hello, Noey,' said Betters, as the hermit looked out from his tiny log cabin.

"The hermit, a wisp of a man in an old, battered fedora, with a length of bag rope for suspenders, stepped out into the bright sunlight.

"'Howdy, Mr. Betters,' he said, and the ranger said: 'We brought you some folks, Noah.'"

Noah, delighted by the company, told each: "I'm glad to see you, sir—welcome to Cold River City."

"We had finally arrived...and we got a big surprise. The old fellow...then informed us we'd have to sign the guest register, a book given to him by Doc Latimer.

"We wondered whether we'd heard correctly, and said: 'Did you say a guest register?' Assured we had heard correctly, we said: 'I thought you were a hermit,' to which Rondeau retorted 'I am, but what's the use of being a hermit if you don't meet a lot of people?'

Rondeau told them about his register:

"Yes, I keep a record of my callers. Since 1940, I have a camp register. My callers are usually hikers, mountain climbers, fishermen and a few forest rangers."

"That floored us, and when he finally produced his register and we looked over the signatures, it looked like George Chelius's hotel register. This fellow's retreat, it developed, might just as well have been pitched in Times Square, for he was right plunk on a hiking trail that ran to Long Lake." The register reveals a caller from Montana, a mountain climber from Europe and two Chinese.

"Now some of my old local friends are coming back to me from the Atlantic, Pacific, Japan, Philippines, India, Australia, North Africa, British Isles and Germany," Noah observed.

Pointing to the sign tacked over the cabin door, Noah chuckled, "That's just a gag. You see, some of my friends started kidding me about being the mayor of Cold River. I figured you couldn't be a mayor without a Town Hall."

Noah was cordial. "He had a lot of homespun philosophy, this strange man of the hills," Mooney noted. "He's a good conscientious man, not a bit dangerous but rather an optimist who made no bones about saying he 'had no use for hoodlums.' Somewhere along the line Rondeau had come across the name of Al Capone.

"He must have been a pretty fresh whippersnapper, judging by the stories," Rondeau told the crew. "Good thing he never come poking around here. I'd have run him right off good and fast."

Rondeau made an advance commitment that if he ever found his way south to the capitol district of New York State he would look up Mooney. Being somewhat of an optimist, Noah figured some day he would.

The assembled group of newspapermen learned much this day. Rondeau told them a story or two and indicated they were welcome to return to talk some more. They offered him the gifts they'd brought.

That was Rondeau, the hermit of Cold River, and according to Charles Mooney—"A strange character who made good copy." (*See "Mooney's* The Knickerbocker News, *September 11, 1946, story "'Round the Clock with Noah John Rondeau, Hermit of the Adirondack Wilds" for a full accounting of this encounter.*)

Well in advance of the oncoming evening, Rangers Tyler and Betters called on their troupe of newspaper people to gather the team's overnight

HERMIT LEAVES WILDS. (AP Wirephoto)—Noah Rondeau (left), bearded 63-year-old hermit, is interviewed at the entrance to his hut in the wilderness, 22 miles from Saranac Lake, by John Wingate before coming out of his seclusion for the first time in 33 years. A helicopter plucked him out of the heart of a 3,000,000-acre Adirondack wilderness Wednesday on the first leg of his flight to New York city, where he will appear at the opening of the National Sportsmen's show.

gear, notebooks, and cameras. It was time to move out. They carried their own belongings, and Noah trekked along with the large group as far as the old dam site on Moose Creek, where he stayed overnight.

Noah had already gained some notoriety earlier that year. What this group reported furthered the Outside's knowledge of Rondeau, the man. "He has discovered he can capitalize on being a hermit with scarcely a move from the cabin he calls home," Mooney concluded. And indeed, Rondeau's notoriety was also helped by the varied character studies photographer Julius J. Heller captured on film to include with the feature story.

Noah's diary entry records the Friday, Sept. 6, 1946 meeting:

Town Hall, Cold River and Wayne Tyler. Ideal September
weather. 9 men called: photographers. 35 Dollars for Guide.

An accomplished mountain climber and Albany chapter member of the Adirondack Mountain Club (ADK), Roy Snyder had read Mooney's story.

He had known Rondeau for a decade. It was common chitchat among ADK members that increasing press coverage might change the once little known folksy woodsman.

On September 29, 1946, Snyder put his boots in motion to make his annual pilgrimage to see the hermit and climb Mount Donaldson. Years later he shared his memory.

"Noah John, as usual, was very hospitable. Leaving his painting of Santanoni, he made me at home and soon had a fire going outside the [kitchenette] wigwam. Settling into an old rocking chair, I produced food from my pack for the hermit to prepare in his own distinctive style. Had we known what was in store we certainly would have been a little more conservative of the food."

The weather "grew colder as it grew darker and we moved into the little cabin and started a fire in the stove, this time for heat. After a lengthy discussion of the technicalities of hunting bear, it was agreed that we should arise at dawn and conquer Donaldson.

"Came the dawn and we found ourselves snowbound. And when I say it snowed, I mean that it did just that, and continuously. It snowed all day, it snowed all night, and it snowed all day again, and I guess it snowed all night again, but I did not stay up to observe it. At this point I reached into my pack and touched the bottom. No more store-bought food. We ate hermit's fare—one meal—pancakes."

Less than one week later, in October 1946, Clayt Seagears' *Conservationist* article about Noah was published. Following the magazine's release, other Rondeau accounts in other periodicals appeared, all of which created a great deal of interest in the Cold River hermit.

In 1947 the New York State Conservation Department's division of education invited Noah to participate in its February New York City National Sportsmen's Show in Grand Central Palace, but at first, he declined. Two years earlier the frail woodsman had snowshoed out to Saranac under his own power for supplies. But it took him four days for the round trip and his vitality hadn't been the same since. Since the department had already started to build a replica of his Town Hall habitation at the show's New York City site, a second invitation, attached to a small parachute bundled

1/1/1974 TON PRESS 9/20/46

Rondeau, Famed Adirondack Hermit, Has Many Friends in Southern Tier

RONDEAU AND LOCAL FRIENDS—Frank C. Goodnough, left, is telling a tall fishing tale to Rondeau, right, and Dr. William B. Gregory of Owego. The three are eating in front of Rondeau's shack, near Cold River in the Adirondacks. The old hermit seems skeptical.

with a brick of butter and pound of bacon, was dropped from a plane. Noah was on hand for this special mountain-free delivery, having been standing atop his cabin waving his coat when the plane came over. The repeated invitation included an explanation that even though the snows were deep, the department would find a way to get Noah out if he agreed to take part in the show. Getting Noah's personal transportation was one thing, but the job of moving a sundry collection of the 63-year-old recluse's belongings over nineteen miles of wilderness trails buried under five feet of snow was another. Since the Division of Conservation Education had been practicing for this task with dog teams and snowmobiles, the Department remained optimistic and moved ahead with building the replica. Clayt Seagears, in charge of the Department's exhibit, was quoted as saying, "If we can't get him down to New York I'm gonna itch plenty in a beard."

Noah ultimately agreed by tramping "YES," his word of assent in the snow, visible to Bill Petty from his airplane. Petty had dropped a note asking for Noah's reply.

On February 12, a helicopter arrived to take Cold River City population one's mayor, along with four hundred pounds of Cold River relics including beaver and bear skins, deer horns, bear skulls and bones, fishing rod and reel, bear traps, snowshoes, bow, arrows and quiver, chains, hooks, pots, kettles, a handmade rocking chair, and other hermitage equipment and actual furnishings and trimmings from his camp to Saranac airport. Many trips were required.

Once landed on his first leg of an exciting new adventure, the bearded hermit, dressed in animal skins and hunting clothes, declared, "That's the easiest way I ever came out." His opinion of planes followed: "Up to now I felt flying was for the birds, but now I feel aviation is here to stay."

After Noah arrived at the Sportsmen's Show (to promote to New Yorkers the recreational facilities of the State's vast Forest Preserve, keeping the Preserve forever wild, and showing how to protect, enjoy, and live in harmony with it), he not only became a celebrity, but had no problem adapting to city life. It was reported: "He ate $3.00 steak dinners, stayed up until 2 A.M., was greeted by movie stars, spoke on fourteen radio broadcasts and on the 'We the People' television show, signed thousands of autographs, became exposed to trillions of germs, rode in big planes and small ones, made three newsreel shorts, wore store-bought clothes and talked nearly sixteen hours a day. Never once was he confused, outwardly irritated or ill."

Following the Big Apple show, Noah returned to Saranac Lake for a few days of rest before following the department's display in Albany and another big city show appearance. The high point of his Albany trip was a VIP tour of the Conservation Department's headquarters and a meeting with thirty-two state senators. In Rochester and Buffalo, he was invited to make radio broadcasts and speeches. During the following 1948 and

1949 seasons, for fees ranging from $550 to $800 per appearance, he participated in sports shows at Tahawus, Saratoga Springs, Burnt Hills, Utica, Syracuse, and Boston. In addition, he also appeared at various stores, rod, and gun clubs, at a varied assortment of organizations that ran the gamut from historical societies to church groups, scout jamborees, father and son dinners, ladies' societies, and Rotary and Lions clubs.

After four seasons of shows and being a celebrity, he returned to his Cold River digs, but wilderness life was not the same. After the November 25, 1950 "Big Blow" windstorm, which caused 10,000 acres of wind damage just in the Cold River country, and the closure to the public of the Adirondack forest for over three years, Noah, then sixty-seven, decided that he was too old to continue the life of a hermit. He ultimately settled in the Lake Placid-Wilmington area, where he lived out his remaining years.

Needless to say, Rondeau's story got around. AP and Wirephoto coverage spread the story from coast-to-coast. Frank Bruce, formerly of Saranac Lake but living in Tuscaloosa, Alabama in 1947 said, "This was probably the biggest publicity story to come out of either Tupper or Saranac in the 14 years I have been away and I was disappointed to see Saranac Lake get the date-lines, because we all know that Rondeau considers Tupper his second home…."

Noah was the last link to the original folklore greats of the Adirondack Mountains. The vibrancy and excitement of "Noah John Rondeau—live!" showed him in the latter middle part of his life— the second act—to be a colorful character who had made it through the difficulties of life's ups and downs. He successfully accomplished a real second act, welcoming sightseers to his home in the wilds. The spectators with whom he mingled and the mesmerized crowds and audiences to whom he told anecdotes and stories of the Cold River region were spellbound by the hermit—and he did it all without making any concessions to himself. He enjoyed every minute of his brief fame and fortune.

Chapter 6

Fame and Shekels

BILL PETTY, chief ranger and forester, was the pilot who dropped the second invitation to Noah from his plane, the one that Noah accepted. That acceptance ultimately changed his life. The Conservation Department would pay all Noah's expenses and pay him $100.00 for the week's appearance. That wasn't the only money he would earn for simply being his unusual and entertaining self. The coming years greatly improved his financial picture, and he would be warm, dry and well-fed while savoring the limelight.

Bill Petty's overture to draw Noah out of the mountains began out of concern for his old family pal's health and well-being, and it turned out to be a slam-bang for the Division of Conservation Education, which accomplished its purpose of acquainting New Yorkers with the recreational facilities of the state's vast Forest Preserve. Noah's presence was the main draw, but crowds were fascinated as well with the virtually exact reproduction of the spot where his real cabin stood. The foreground was designed to simulate the top of a high bluff from which he gazed down into the river valley. In the background loomed a lifelike painting and props of Seward, Seymour, the Sawtooths, Panther, Santanoni and Henderson Mountains. Two live raccoons climbed a tree stump and frolicked around.

The display drew thousands of people. Reporters elbowed for interviews; newsreels whizzed segments of Noah telling anecdotes and stories of the Cold River region; wire services zipped news of his splash to distant cities. He posed before flashing cameras and sat for hours in front of television cameras, providing information relative to the life of a bona fide hermit. The news flashes piqued the interest of new-found admirers and friends. The hermit-mayor signed innumerable autographs and relished eating and sleeping in strange surroundings and getting around in noisy cities far removed from the uninhabited wilds. Noah John Rondeau was fully equal to the situation.

When he climbed onto the helicopter at Cold River, Noah never could have imagined how each day's events would develop. On February 16, 1947, at 11:15 A.M., the waiting spectators watched Perry Duryea, New York State Conservation Commissioner, cut the tape and officially open the show. The *New York Times* reported the crowd stretched several blocks beyond the arena, "one of the largest that ever stood in line outside the Grand Central Palace... The elaborate displays plus the hundreds of booths crowded with rods, reels, tackle, guns, boats and other implements of the field sports had something to attract every visitor."

Long-time friends and supporters Maude and Jay Gregory and Doc Latimer were overawed with delight when Jay's hometown newspaper, *The Binghamton Press*, featured a picture of the hermit of Hamilton County looking dreamily skyward. The caption read: "NOAH'S LARK— Noah Rondeau finds life in New York City to his liking, especially when movie actress Arleen Whelan planted a kiss above the thick foliage on his cheek. Noah is in the big town as a feature of the Sportsmen's Show."

—Acme TELEPHOTO.

NOAH'S LARK—The hermit of Hamilton County, Noah Rondeau, finds life in New York City to his liking, especially when movie actress Arleen Whelan planted a kiss above the thick foliage on his cheek. Noah is in the big town as a feature of the Sportsmen's Show.

Courtesy Unknown 1947 newspaper

Noah's "replica exhibit" was first set up along route 3 at the Corey's Road turn off. Later moved to Willington, New York. Courtesy Dr. Adolph G. Dittmar, Jr.

Richard Smith stands at the front door of Singing Pines. A cabin he gave to Noah to live in for the remainder of his life. Courtesy of Richard J. Smith from Noah's photo album

Chapter 7

Sportsmen's Shows of the 1940s and '50s

FOR OUTDOOR-LOVING PEOPLE, sportsmen's shows throughout the 1940s were highly anticipated events. Catchy interviews and advertisements for products on the radio featured an assortment of companies. There were totally new products, improved ones, and trusted standards.

Sportsmen's shows were also defining forms of entertainment. They presumed that a person's attendance made a statement about interest in escaping the winter doldrums and getting outdoors. Audiences were excited about the variety of exhibits, and united in anticipation as they waited in line to

Courtesy Author's Photo

see favorite presenters and merchants. Neither race nor gender nor social class mattered. What did matter was that all were longing to get to their favorite place in the woods, and all were counting the weeks until they could.

Mr. and Mrs. Sportsman, boys and girls and just the curious all found Rondeau's exhibit to be one of the best attractions, and that was saying something. On display were the newest snowmobiles and sports equipment and mounted animal specimens. There were sled dogs, live trout and bald eagles, comedians and pistol experts. Spirited competitions between log-choppers and cross-cut sawmen entertained attendees. The list

Left to Right. "Mag" Dodge, Noah, Mary, Adolph and David Dittmar, meet an old friend at a April 28, 1951 sportsmen show. Courtesy Dr. Adolph G. Dittmar, Jr.

of participants seemed endless.

Rondeau might have lived primitively for thirty-three years, but he was a natural entertainer. Noah took to the crowds like a duck to water.

The Conservation Department's stated goal was to use Rondeau to acquaint New York State's folks with the vast public wilderness domain—something Noah was proud of. Who better to talk about the glitter of mountain streams, the stands of beautiful hardwoods with green canopies that made walking beneath them like being in a city park, and the beauty of towering virgin pines rising high above the aromatic balsam and spruce? Noah could imitate the unforgettable calls of the owls and loons that break the night's silence, and when he described the sputtering sounds of frying brook trout, one could almost smell them. Noah could do that and more.

Unquestionably he enjoyed the attention instant celebrity brought from adoring crowds. The Mayor of Cold River was pictured on advertising posters. The very bureaucratic establishment about which he had so long spoken harshly had laid a golden egg right in his lap, and he took quick advantage. To encourage onlookers to leave him a donation, he borrowed

FAME & $HEKELS

money from Orville Betters and Hubert Toomey, state forest rangers, who were his guardians in New York, to add to the display a false-bottomed pack basket filled with dollars and coins, so spectators got the idea to toss in a donation for a poor old bona fide hermit.

Noah was articulate, witty, and an authentic Adirondack character; the crowds loved him and his anecdotes and stories of the Cold River region, and he loved the attention. Radio shows scooped him up. His life story was a sensation.

Recognizing the potential to earn more money in a week than he had ever earned on a trap line in a year, Noah worked the crowds with the skill of an enterprising huckster. He told tales about living in the wilderness, demonstrated leather-making and validated his marksmanship with bow and arrow. He said the children who spoke to him were his greatest pleasure.

Wire services ran stories about him across the Northeast. His initial success brought him an offer from the Conservation Department to follow their exhibit of his "city" to future shows. Various groups, organizations and clubs invited him to speak about living in the wilderness—all with the offer of a meal, transportation and more than pocket change as an honorarium.

Hopped up with enthusiasm and a pocket full of dollar bills following "rest, sleep and eat" on February 26, his diary tells, "I wrote my report of Sportsmen's Show" including immediate future plans to his newspaper columnist pal at the *Essex County Republican*.

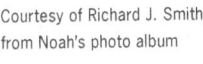

Courtesy of Richard J. Smith
from Noah's photo album

Chapter 8

From Forest to Metro

CLARENCE PETTY repeated the oft-reported way in which Chief Forester, Bill Petty, extended the invitation to bring Noah out of the mountains. "My brother flew over there in a helicopter in the winter time and dropped a message to him...to stamp out in the snow whether or not he'd come out if somebody flew in there and picked him up for the show and ... he went out on the flow and stamped on the snow YES, and that's how Bill was able to get him to come out for the show down in New York."

On February 12, 1947, the day Bill Petty arrived in a tiny helicopter Noah described as "little as a red dragon fly," the temperature was 21 degrees below zero. "...Pictures, Recorder, News Reels. 3 p.m. I fly over Ampersand Mountain. Over 200 wait for me at Saranac Lake [Air] Field. I talk with Mr. C.P. Seagears in N.Y.C. To Headquarters with W. E. Petty. Meet Mrs. Petty and daughter Marilyn," Noah recorded of his historic day, from forest to metro via helicopter and airplane. Snippets from Noah's diary offer a bit of the icing on the cake.

On Saturday, February 15, 1947, after the first day of the Sportsmen's Show, Noah noted, "John K. Rondeau and wife call on me at opening of show. Frank Rock call [and presented a] new pipe for me. Grace Hudowalski call. Mr. F.C. Stern call. Paul Arthur and wife call and They give

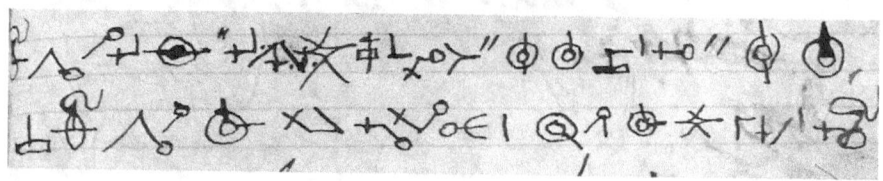

FAME & $HEKELS

Cold River's natural beauty. Courtesy C.V. Latimer, Jr. M.D.

Rondeau is greeted at the airport. Courtesy New York State Museum

Noah Rondeau, famous Adirondack guide, who is coming down from Cold River, Hamilton county, N. Y., for the Sportsmen's Show.

Hermit Sees Aviation Here to Stay

Noah Rondeau, on His Way to Sportsmen's Show, Always Had Thought Flying Was for Birds.

1947

Saranac Lake, N. Y., Feb. 13 (A. P.).—Bearded Noah Rondeau | John snowshoed out to Saranac under his own power for supplies.

me a Book. I write Autographs 5 hours and speak 4 hours to large crowds."

The following day, his diary outlines a similar scenario that included a visit from "Miss Charlotte Dittmar," who reported the two relived the day Noah came to the aid of her climbing party when they were lost in Dog Slough Swamp.

On February 17, he had interviewed for the radio and television program, *We the People.*

On February 18, his good friend Oscar Burguiere, Oscar's sister Norma and his father Henry joined the parade of well-wishers. In his illustrious secret code, Noah noted "Miss Burguiere give Hug." The New York State *Conservationist* magazine writer and director of the N.Y.S. Conservation Department's Division of Conservation Education, Clayton B. Seagears, described the hieroglyphics Noah used in his writing slightly differently this time as an "operation very closely resembling the tracks of an inebriated hen whose father was a Dervish rooster and whose maternal parent could be termed foot-loose."

Chapter 9

Notes From the Hermit's Diary

NOAH'S DIARY NOTATIONS for February 21 and 22 included seeing more old Cold River friends. Dr. Latimer, Peter Fos, Bill Patterson, Edward A. Harmes and Ed and Grace Hudowalski returned. He wrote that he enjoyed a "long talk with a lady about evolution." Gifts included three ducks, two boxes of cartridges and ice cream. And, in another hermit hieroglyphic scrawl he noted, "Miss Katherine LaVaute Marling leave lipstick on my check."

On the day he returned to the mountains Noah wrote on Wednesday, February 26: "I rest, sleep and Eat. I write 8 letters. At 8 P.M. I speak for 30 minutes to HiY club at Saranac Lake High School."

Former high school students remember bits and pieces of Noah's presentation. The hermit made an entertaining appearance. He talked about bad winters and said he'd been studying the birds and other weather barometers for many years and had predicted he might have ended up short of fuel the winter of '47. He answered questions about going without seeing company for long periods of time. And he told stories. Outrageous tales of how he once went to remove the chimney from his kerosene lamp only to find it was so cold the flame had frozen to the glass, and many tales of his marksmanship.

"You know last winter a funny thing happened. I was scanning the landscape out the window one moonlit night, watching the large, feathery snowflakes sifting through the moonlit atmosphere when I spotted a lone deer standing within rifle range. Anyways, this was too good an opportunity to pass up, so I grabbed my gun, opened the Town Hall door so not to let it squeak and carefully drew a bead and blazed away. But the animal never fell. I fired again. Still nothing happened. Something was queer. Well, I took hold of my hunting knife and worked up close. I was looking forward to starting off on a breakfast of deer steak. Now you boys and girls probably aren't going to believe this, but I'll bet you a ten-dollar mink pelt it's true. I watched that deer and soon found out that what I'd been shooting at wasn't a deer at all. Rather, it was a deer's shadow! Seems the big buck must of come through laying down his trail, caught a whiff of human scent, sprang down the bank, crossed the frozen flow and began to hightail toward the cedars on the other side. But as he leaped so fast, his shadow got to lagging. It was so cold that night that his shadow froze right in his hoof tracks. It was so real you couldn't tell the difference until you got right up to it."

This was the sort of story that enchanted Sportsmen's Show attendees, who could only dream idly of living their lives in the woods. Just as the students at Saranac High became acquainted with the hermit of Cold River Flow, so did thousands of others through the show and the media. For a little while, Noah John Rondeau was a celebrity.

Courtesy E. A. Harmes

Dr. Latimer and Noah.
Courtesy C.V. Latimer, Jr, M.D.

FAME & $HEKELS

Chapter 10

Rondeau Relates His First Experience

By Wednesday evening, February 26, 1947, the day Noah returned to the state conservation commission's headquarters at Lake Clear following his high school program, he recorded, "I write my report of Sportsmen's Show to *Essex Co. Republican.*"

The experience of being lured from the mountains' subzero conditions into the limelight of attention had wholly changed his life focus.

The hermit's first of many future reports to the *Essex County Republican* newspaper follows:

> This is Noah John Rondeau, Adirondack Hermit, sending report of unusual "Hermit Hop" to New York City; and …
> 9 day's programme at Sportsmen's show; and Hop Back to Conservation Commission's headquarters at State Fish Hatchery at Lake Clear.
>
> And to go back to first knowledge to me, of the debut; it began on Jan. 10th when E. W. Petty of Conservation Department, cut aerial figures over my 6 foot Town Hall.
>
> The Plane was very white in part; and in part very rosy; and against the blue, winter sky—it looked as if a gold fish had escaped the aquatic and took to the airel [sic].
>
> Mr. Petty dropped a note, which, when rescued from a snow drift—dispatched: I was wanted by Conservation Commission, Feb. 15 to 23, At National Sportsmen's Show at Grand Central Palace, N.Y.C., So I gave Officer Petty, a "Yes" by tracking

large size letters in the snow.

As the time passed so I could not make it via snowshoes and get there on time—and—so—I would not be at the show.

Then, Feb. 11, the airel Gold Fish came back and dropped another note which said "Don't come out—we're coming to get you with Helicopter tomorrow."

And so,—Feb, 12 at 8 a.m. the Helicopter arrived and landed on Cold River Ice—150 feet from my Wig Wam—as the first landing ever made on Cold River with any kind of Plane.

And on said Feb. 12, the Helicopter made 9 trips, from Saranac Air Port to Cold River and return, and took 4 men to Cold River and then took them back one by one—to Saranac; and then, took the hermit out also. And it took over 7 hours to do the job. Feb. 13, I made quick trip to Black Brook.

And on Valentine Day at 3:30 P.M., I embarked on Colonial Plane and shortly after dark—landed at La Guardia Field, New York City.

Cameramen and reporters were lined up and as Miss Rene La Beau put kisses on my cheek—the photographers shot their flashes.

And then for 3 hours They kept me busy.

I made broadcast, posed for pictures & etc.

And I had a most busy, 9 days at the show, using Mike and amplifier and reached from 2000 to 3000 people each time. The speeches (talks) were from 10 to 30 minutes; and collectively reached nearly 1,000,000 people.

And I wrote over 2000 Autographs.

I was on five Radio broadcast including 1 tellevision.

I saw very little of the show or the city, except, what my routine took me into.

I put in long hours, then wrote post cards at hotel; I never could have stood it, if it had not been for the fact, that I loved it.

And my talks were brief to each group. But I'm sure I made thousands of friends.

FAME & $HEKELS

HERMIT KISSED BY STEWARDESS—Noah Rondeau, left, 63-year-old hermit from Cold River Flow, N. Y., is kissed by Colonial Airlines Stewardess Rene La Beau as he leaves plane at LaGuardia Field, New York city, Friday. Rondeau left his crude shelter home where he has lived for 33 years to appear at the New York State Conservation Department exhibit at the Sportsmen's Show in New York ciyt. (AP Wirephoto)

Rondeau Arrives in New York for Show

Courtesy Unknown 1947 newspaper

New York City has its faults,-No doubt; But I only saw two that I call "Smart Fools" and only saw two men in hot argument, and for the total number I saw—I could see worst in the country.

And I certainly met thousands of Ladies and Gentlemen, of education and refinement and with beautiful appreciative kind spirit.

And no matter what the joke is; New York City met me with kisses. They brought me ice cream; They gave me a Gold-Plated Fob, and a dancing Doll, photographs and artificial ducks.

Courtesy of Richard J. Smith from Noah's photo album

And no clergyman could command more real attention that I got,-with Natural History of Mountains and Vallies; even if He preached all day, on Jonah and the whale and got the Fish to demonstrate.

And another side worth-while to me, over 300 of my personal friends called on me.

A lady from Staten Island—whom I never saw, called and brought me a "Fruit Cake" wrapped in paper, tied with twine and under string a $5 bill; and all because, her beloved children had toasted themselves at Cold River open camp fire, as they watched parade of summer Moon over Santanoni Range.

And my friend—Attorney J. L. Gregory of Binghamton, N.Y.—an old man—69 years old and for 3 years—stricken with

Cold River near Doc Latimer's camp. Courtesy C.V. Latimer, Jr. M.D.

a "tired heart;" and only allowed 6 hours per day out of bed;- and, Feb. 19 He boarded an Air Line and with His Son—Dr. Wm. B. Gregory of Owego—came to Grand Central Palace.

And I'm sure that the Gregorys and many others came to the show just to see the "Mayor of Cold River."

Now, I'm resting at Lake Clear.

And March 1st to 9th, I will be at Albany Sportsmen's Show.

Thanks to my many "Good Friends."

—Noah John Rondeau

Albany Bound and Beyond

RONDEAU TELLS OF HIS EXPERIENCES AT ALBANY EXPOSITION

Noah John Rondeau, famous Cold River Flow hermit, has again written to The Record, this time on stationery of the Hotel Ten Eyck, Albany, dated March 3rd, and reads as follows:

"'As a Hermit Sees Albany Sportsmen's Show.' At noon February 28th, I left the Conservation Department's headquarters at Saranac Inn and headed for Albany. Forest Ranger Toomey of Keeseville was appointed to drive the car to Albany and then be my valet for the duration of the

Courtesy *Essex County Reporter*

According to Noah's diary, he did go to Albany and apparently enjoyed the ride:

Friday, February 28, 1947. Nice weather. Saranac Inn and Albany. Toomey drive Conservation car along High snow banks—decked conifer trees: Saranac Lake, Placid, Keene, Pottersville, Chestertown, Warrensburg, Lake George, Glens Falls… 5 P.M., Room at Hotel Teney. [In code Noah wrote: "Met enthusiastic Mrs. Perry."]

The next day the Cold River hermit was the master of ceremonies, cutting the ribbon for the opening of his second but by no means final Sportsmen's Show. Noah was on a roll, enjoying every moment.

In the following months Noah John Rondeau was whisked to photo sessions, interviewed by big and small newspaper reporters and sought out by writers with designs on extensive magazine coverage. He appeared in televised newscasts. Radio broadcasts scooped him up. He became a kind of celebrity. His image was captured on advertising posters and

Clarence Whiteman hunting camp. Whiteman met the hermit during Rondeau's first Sportsmen's Show. He accepted Noah's offer to visit and deer hunt in 1949 and 1951. Courtesy Whiteman photo

emerged on postcards. Crowds loved him and he loved the attention.

In the pleasant turmoil of finding himself an instant pop idol, he shook hands, signed autographs, and told stories of living in the wilderness. It was an astounding experience for a man who sought the silence and isolation of the forest in 1913.

That winter, Richard Smith recalled he saw Noah in two newsreel clips. "My old, dear, close, grand woodsman was standing on a platform by an airplane at LaGuardia Field in New York City. He had on a long navy wool overcoat. His favorite muskrat hat topped his head. He was standing beside Colonial Airlines Stewardess Renee LaBeau. She kissed him as he left the plane. The next time I caught a glimpse of him when he was touring Paramount Studios in New York City. The movie actress Arleen Whelan was planting a kiss on his cheek, above his bushy whiskers. The old boy was looking skyward with a silly, dreamy-like stare. He next turned, face out, gazed right at the camera and said he found life in the big city to his liking—especially when pretty ladies

March 1947. Rondeau at the microphone when senior Leslie Farmer interviewed him for a KSLU radio station at St. Lawrence University in Canton, N.Y. Courtesy Leslie G. Farmer

kiss him! What more could Noah do?"

Months later when the old friends were once again reunited in the silence of Cold River, Noah informed Richard that his February visit to New York City had been his first glimpse of the metropolis since 1920, when he traveled there as a guest of Dr. Charles Leonard Christiernin. The doctor had been taken with Noah's interest in astronomy, biology and geology. "I even visited the Hayden Planetarium while visiting the city," Noah said. The return had been "an enjoyable experience." He described his impressions of the first show and the helicopter that had taken him there. He also included an explanation about the bevy of blondes who descended on him to plant kisses on his chin tufts before flashing cameras. "Confidentially," he swore to Richard, "I didn't kiss them. They kissed me."

Richard shed his Army uniform that summer and returned to the Adirondacks. The men would spend twenty more years together before the former hermit's trail would come to an end.

The crowd would see the old hermit with his muskrat cap, leather jacket and long, gray beard sitting in front of his Town Hall stage. He would tell stories and motion to his seeded pack basket. He didn't want to hear the sound of any coins. He just wanted paper bills. Smith said he'd blow the money he received as fast as he got it.

A contented hermit puffs his favorite "goose-egg" pipe. Ca. 1930s. Courtesy Phil Wolff

Clever? Yes, but honesty and considerate treatment of his friends and fans was the core of Noah John's individuality. He was not just a huckster/showman, but a sincere huckster-showman whose candor instantly moved his listeners.

Noah had a love-indifference relationship with money—just as he did with his new-found celebrity. He liked the comfort money from appearances brought, but there was something about "riches" that he found off-putting.

Richard Smith illustrated nicely Noah's attitude about money and his growing personal recognition during the late 1940s and early '50s. He didn't feel Noah changed his views or disposition much throughout that period of exposure. Noah understood the cash payments for services made it easier for him to afford food, and he was known to pull out a wad of rolled-up bills and hand them to a cash-strapped family member as well as to tuck a five- or ten-dollar bill in a gift envelope for someone's birthday, wedding or some other occasion. "He was very generous," many remembered. He also understood there would be a limited window of opportunity for his exhibit and his appearances at shows. "It was all about audience appeal," thought Smith. Noah knew

An Outdoor Guide Goes Indoors

Noah J. Rondeau, in New York for the first time since 1920, working in front of cabin, brought here from up-State, at the Sportsmen's Show in Grand Central Palace.

The New York Times

fame was fleeting. "Noah said all this fuss was like a new type of fire cracker to be used on the Fourth of July. There is a lot of interest as long as it is on display but after it is exploded the interest dies out."

Chapter 12

Widespread Fame

Noah loved being back at the river, entertaining people who had met him at shows and now sought out his camp. He also loved being out there on the road with the valise of knick-knacks he held up and talked about when addressing groups. He had no thought of cutting back on his appearances after attending the initial wave of sportsmen's shows. He was finding himself in demand at various venues such as county fairs, business and civic groups, father and son dinners, women's groups, and the Boy Scouts—he was even an attraction at a hydroplane race on Lake Flower and was looking forward to being head of the "carnival," as he referred to the parade at Saranac Lake's winter carnival.

He recorded many journal bits, often in hermit cipher, about addresses he made. For example: "Had a Mountain Lunch and a Hundred minutes talk on The June Day, [I] need no Professor's Polish." "Gave 10 min. Key Note address." "I put on 15 min. speech." "6 PM speech. Big supper. Big crowd. Dance. Good time." "I write speech." "8 P.M. at men's club (social center). 9 P.M. speech." "I talked, wrote Autographs, sell Photographs and answered questions."

Once Noah realized that simply recounting his life's experiences—and telling a few tall tales and jokes—could pull in decent revenue, he discovered something about himself he had not known. His talent for entertaining small groups at Cold River was easily transferable to large crowds of total strangers. His wilderness world seemed interesting and valuable to thousands of people. Although most would not have even considered living as Noah did, they got a vicarious thrill from hearing him tell about his hardscrabble life in the mountains.

The hermitage. Courtesy Edward J Fox

By October 1947, Noah had been hanging out more and more outside of Cold River. He told his diary: "At Saranac Inn Locality." Much of his time was directed at busily building a homegrown enterprise. Noah received compensation for posing for four portraits painted by artist S. Y. Willick. He'd spent countless hours building a new and improved replica of his "city" set on a wheeled platform that would be trailered to events. The set included a sweeping hand-painted background on fabric to resemble the sky, mountains and trees "trimmed Cold River style." It could be knocked down and stored to await winter shows, and Noah was proud of his innovation and his months of labor. He drafted and mailed to the editor of *The Essex County Republican* a summary of his work on it. It was printed in the November 14, 1947, issue of the newspaper. A portion follows:

> Hear Ye—this is the Mayor of Cold River City—population 1.
>
> …I just came out from Cold River; And I brought out 400 pounds of my Cold River relics including Deer and Bear skins, old guns, paddles, fishing tackle, deer horns, bear skulls, home-made rocking chair, archery, tackle, violin, bear traps and many other home spun wonders.
>
> And now—my plan is to build an elevated platform—a replica of my Cold River Town Hall, plus a Wigwam, plus scenic oil painted back ground.
>
> And when these 4 major items are trimmed with old stumps and a Wilderness Floor of dry leaves and Crow Foot vines; and furnished with the original Cold River furniture—plus the tro-

phies of next hunting season and the furs of next trapping season, to January— it is intended that this enterprise will be the best of its kind ever put on exhibition, at any show, anywhere.

And it is clear to the mayor that the grandeur of this outfit will make Noah's Ark look like a toy that Robin Crusoe might have made to amuse Friday while the deluge went by as a mere sun shower.

And it is also clear to the mayor's vision that when he steps upon his platform in a large city next winter and starts to deliver an English speech in French, and as the audience beholds the dignified step over a rusty bear trap and sees the musk rat cap plus whiskers and red patches—no one in audience will need to be tickled—anywhere—with a feather to evolve a laugh.

Richard Smith said about all of this business activity, "Noah always knew he was not in the same class as an entertainer," but just the same he wasn't going to let a first-rate opportunity pass by. "As time went by, he felt expectations rising about what he might do. He wasn't going to try to be a star." But could he cut it on his own on the Outside?

The late November scene is "winter-like in the Big Mountains," Noah observed. "The Trees are beautifully loaded with snow. I look over the scenery and check the Beauty." December found him living at 4 Alpine Terrace—the home of friend Phil McCalvin.

There is no doubt that Noah's attitudes about stardom affected him. It's true that he decided by the end of 1947 that he would eventually have to leave Cold River. Just when, however, was the question. There had to have been that question in his mind: If he couldn't trust this new kind of lifestyle, what chance did he have?

As it turned out, he did take that chance.

From January 1948 through 1950, Noah was clearly on a roll, the toast throughout New York's North Country and points across America's Northeast. During those times Noah was out and about more. Cold River sportsmen got to see him only briefly, and not as often as they might have liked.

Phillip and Helen McCalvin's home became one of Noah's first Outside residences. He boarded at their 4 Alpine Terrace home, using one of the spare bedrooms off and on for several years. Noah knew Phil from Phil's Civilian Conservation Corps days when he served at the Cold River side camp. Phil and Helen not only opened their home to him, but treated Noah as a family member—even relying on Noah to care for baby Gary while they were away.

Helen recalled that one day while she was working, Phil wanted to do some target shooting. Noah said he was more than happy to babysit. "When I arrived home, I couldn't believe my eyes. Gary was sitting in the highchair and Noah was spooning him dog food from a can." When Helen exclaimed What are you doing? Noah, acting surprised, nonchalantly answered, "It was the only way I could keep him from crying—besides, he likes it."

In Utica's Sunday, March 28, 1948, *Observer-Dispatch*, reporter E. Clifton Moore was all over Utica's Sports and Boat Show. The headline read, "Hundreds Inspect Varied Exhibits."

> Rondeau was on hand as scheduled with his two huts and entertained extensively beside his own hut, a replica of his Cold River abode. He proved to be the big drawing card with the host of early visitors and was kept busy signing autographs and telling the fans his experiences in the North Woods....

Appearance after appearance, Rondeau was more prepared. Not only did he entertain the attending public with readings, but he also broadcast over radio station WGAT—"three and four minutes," according to his notes—discourses on subjects such as "A Bear Eat Me Up," "Hatchet Burnt Up," and "Fishing."

By 1948 Noah talked at length about preparing for the approaching winter (1948), but Ranger Betters had his own opinion: "I got a sneaking suspicion Noah isn't going to stick in there [at Cold River].... The old fellow's failing. ...Yep, appears to me as if Noah's hermit days are near finished."

Richard Smith said he had a similar hunch: "I'm willing to believe

Courtesy Edward J Fox

Noah had already made up his mind to reluctantly leave Cold River by 1946. It was his health. I think Noah had thought that he was not as fit to perform the more strenuous tasks at 'Chateau Dee Wigwam Poles'—cutting and hauling wood, for instance. After decades of hard work, dragging wood by hand and wood cutting, it was evident to me that as his source of wood had to be cut quite some distance from the teepee store houses, the work became harder. Green poles are heavy. And the driftwood brought down river and deposited there by high water wasn't all that easy to haul up the riverbank either."

Noah told friends and visitors, "I want to die right here in my woods. I can't see going outside to live now. I'm too old to make a living. I only hope I can stay here. I like it." Nevertheless, he was also a man who thought practically. He reasoned there could come a time when he might not be able to make it in the woods; thus, his mounting interest over the past year and a half in raising chickens on the outside.

City-dwellers found the hermit's range of knowledge and vocabulary extensive, although a well-read person might have found his spelling and library limited. His daily journal was open and on display at shows. It might have seemed like pretty dull reading—as most of the daily events Rondeau recorded were ordinary. Yet his days were full. Onlookers were

Noah liked all the seasons. Noah and Richard J. Smith, 1946. Courtesy of Richard J. Smith from Noah's photo album

free to read for themselves an excerpt of a letter written in a large, clear, flowing hand by Noah—sage and poet laureate of Cold River—or read an example from his diary.

> *Thursday, April 24, 1941.* Cool, breezy, part cloudy. At Big Dam. Plenty sparrows, Juncos at wigwam. First trout below dam (2) Big doe eat pansys 10 ft. from my bed last night. Seagull fly over Flo. 1 PM white throat sparrow in Town Hall. 9 fish [caught so far].

Noah liked all the seasons, but freely admitted: "I like Spring the best of all. It's the time of life, the most inspiring—the birds come back and get busy building their nests and preparing for their young.

"You know, all year long folks look forward to spending a few days here, or even a few weeks. Then they go back to the cities, talk about it all winter and plan for the next year when they can come back here again. They must find something they need in the mountains."

Noah would say, "No matter how late spring is, it's springtime when it comes, and thoughts of spring are good always, in our mental parade. The longer the winter, the more appreciable the spring. The arrival of birds, the song of frogs, the sun gaining in north latitude, the grass greening, the working of pollen, the colors, the trees putting on summer dress—and there are days in May when I can see the grass greening during the hours of sunshine."

From January through December, you might say Noah worked two jobs: Hosting the Cold River exhibit, lecturing, and off-and-on returning to the river to live a slightly hermit life. His situation certainly was not as devoid of people as it once had been.

Cold River Hill continued to be a sought out destination for the curious who had met him at shows. Whether he was at camp or away, backpacking tourists walked over his "streets," took in the views and snapped pictures. Some took the time to really see his world by photographing captivating Cold River landscapes: snow on the peaks with brilliant leaves below, reflected in a mirror pond; evening light in pines and hardwoods around a remote stream; the sculptured beauty of boulders in the river; the High Peaks looking like pewter with new snow under a low overcast sky—each a work of art by itself.

> *Wednesday, September 1, 1948.* Cool last night—To day Perfect Summer. I collect Flower's Seeds. I read *We Took to the Woods* [by Louise Dickinson Rich]. I collect Pearly Everlasting. I investigate View point from which to paint North Mountains of Seward Range.

"Ah, is this not happiness?" He wrote in code after seeing the first frost the morning of September 16th. Later that day he transplanted "a dozen cedars" and began to bring in his squash and potatoes, repeating "Ah, is this not happiness," having finished reading **The Art of Writing** by Lin Yutang. In September he began another of Yutang's books, *The Art of Reading.*

A favorite snapshot of Noah's. Courtesy of Richard J. Smith from Noah's photo album

FAME & $HEKELS

Chapter 13

Spoiled for Hermiting

Due to the handsome income received from tours of sportsmen's shows, fairs and other appearances, the Cold River hermit could now have every variety of food to satisfy his needs. "In a sense, Noah was 'spoiled' for hermiting," said C. R. Roseberry. "Besides, he was getting on in years. The monetary reward of his truce with civilization" melted away his identity with poverty and subsistence living.

Doctor C.V. Latimer Jr. remembered an August Rotary Club meeting of his father's in Deposit, N.Y., that might have even shown Noah's waning lack of interest in talking. Club members were always asking Doc Sr. to bring Noah along to a meeting whenever he came to town, and "Father

Courtesy Adolph G. Dittmar, Jr, D.D.S.

COLD RIVER CITY is what the

was eager to show Noah off. The members had heard so much about him and what he meant to Dad. Arrangements were made. Noah planned to tell a grand story, perhaps about Adirondack Air or Wildlife Welfare. The arrangement was to leave Noah at the family lodge while Father made his evening house calls. Once they were completed, he returned, dressed, and looked for Noah, only to find he was nowhere in sight. Not knowing what had happened to the guest speaker, Father headed off to the meeting, offering profuse apologies that the hermit wasn't able to attend. On his return, he learned Noah had lain down to take a nap. Later on, he finally did address the club."

Doc Latimer Sr. and Noah were both at a crossroads in their lives with Cold River country in 1949. When Noah stopped at Latimer's Camp Seward in the fall, the men's thoughts were of Jay, Bill and Ruth Gregory's passings. Jay and Doc had entered the valley in the teens together as young men. They had swapped tales during rain, sleet and snow storms. They had hunted and fished in changeable winds that altered their plans, and had dined like kings on C.V.'s famous feasts and eaten Noah's "best ever" fish fries. The entire Gregory family had arranged to have hundreds of pounds of tools and supplies brought into the valley for Noah, whose iron determination to live a quiet life in the mountains might not have lasted as long had it not been for their generosity in bolstering his stretched resources.

Doc Latimer said that throughout those years, Noah was willing to turn his hand to boost his well-being. Yet his schemes rarely worked out quite as he hoped. At sportsmen's shows he was a trophy, a curiosity, and he knew it. He immediately thought of how he could turn curiosity to commerce, making money by selling himself. He offered handmade leather crafts, little canvas money bags and red pillows filled with balsam and pearly everlasting, along with other items he deemed profitable. Along with his autographed photographs and post cards, he offered his services for a fee to speak at clubs and business functions. His robust speaking style, vigorous wit, and delight in exchanging strikes in the entertainment arena meant that he spent much of his late 1940s and early '50s life gyrating from one engagement to the next.

Noah had been living comfortably in McCalvin's house when he began to feel as if he might be on the brink of some sort of transitory fortune and fame. Whether it would be limited or widespread, he didn't know, but he could see success ahead. In code he penned "I order another 1,000 photographs."

The income and recognition that he had once perhaps thought of as a mere flash in the pan were becoming more of a reality with each passing gig. Noah seemed to be going places—not real stardom, but remarkable for a man who had lived for decades in a remote home in the wilderness. Noah John's story of retreating from civilization, bucking authority and "Jack Ass Democrats," choosing to live among "sun-washed High Mountains and Deep Vallies" attracted the public's fancy, and the self-educated and self-proclaimed Mayor of Cold River City was now inspired to share his world with props and tales with all who cared to listen.

Shirley Miller, with her parents' help, wrote Noah a long letter closing with "From Your 'Honey Bunch.'" Shirley's correspondence is among hundreds of letters Noah received from children once he became better connected with the outside world, as he sometimes referred to life beyond his "Little Brook."

If Noah had been keeping a scorecard of the number of children with whom he became friends and pen pals, the list would be long. With each little thing he did, Noah earned the respect of numerous families who took him in. He might not have realized it, but much of his popularity came from doting audiences that saw his caring side.

Erwin H. Miller, whose family lived in Burnt Hills, N.Y. shared,

> ...we requested the N.Y.S. Conservation department to make Noah available for our Boy Scout fundraiser. They did so and he stayed at my home for two nights. We had a great show with all the attractions ...My youngest daughter was about three years old at the time and she sat on Noah's lap in a rocking chair. His long beard fascinated her and he seemed to enjoy entertaining her. He was soft-spoken and very clean—not a rough and gruff backwoods creature. His language proved he had some education and it was evident from his conversations he enjoyed literature. My wife remembers our daughter believed that he was Santa Claus. He was a salesman and loved to push [the marketing] of his photographs, leather pouches, fake Cold River eyebrow pencils, balsam sachets, little ointment cans of bear grease and so forth. He enjoyed our continental breakfast.... He was an extremely gracious house guest. We Millers welcomed him back a number of times in subsequent years.

John L. Hasenjager remembers meeting Noah at Camp Borton on Cayuga Lake, near Ithaca, N.Y., where he spoke for almost an hour. "The one thing I recall about it was his telling about a big bear that died in 1920 and it had been dead ever since," Hasenjager said. Noah recalled it was "A happy long day at Scout Camp Ground" and there were "1,000,022 Grass Hoppers in the grassy field around the great campfire."

Often Noah's 1949 journal noted that Phil McCalvin drove him to various places, including to Bill Petty's Conservation Commission office and to Ampersand Park's entrance.

Bill Petty had helped Noah set up a savings and checking account and had volunteered to help him manage his money. Noah wisely accepted. While he might have rejoiced at having so much cash roll in, until Bill intervened the money was often squandered.

It's interesting that Noah noted in code: "...Gary McCalvin -27 mo. old wake up and have me put perfume on Him," then went on in detail about Gary's potty training, which he had been helping out with.

A number of times when Noah was left off at Ampersand Park, it was with the anticipation he needed to arrive at the river in order to receive packages of food that had been purchased at Bill Mullen's grocery and transported to the storeroom in Lake Placid airport until an air drop could be made.

Each time he returned to Cold River City, although most of the contents had been removed to the Outside, Noah still found the old place welcoming. He'd write: "music was in the air... I view Night Hawks, Robins, Northern Flickers, Juncos, Blue Jays, and Water Birds.... Chipmunks and Sparrows. No Gas Stations-To hell with them. No Dogs on every corner- To hell with them. No Church Bells in my Ears, To hell with them. No one spieling for God To hell

Forest Ranger Lucius and Noah. The Shattuck Clearing ranger gifted the bearskin to the hermit so he could make purses to sell at the trade shows. Courtesy Earle Russell

with the Myth. What freedom alone in natural primitiveness; and what unsatisfactory waste of living in civilization- serving Gods, Religions and industrial slavery."

Nowhere in his 1949 diary does Noah tell why he moved everything but the bare necessities out of his Cold River huts, only that he did. Those who knew him have a wide array of speculative thoughts: it had to do with his activities and appearances; he recognized his declining strength and health; he enjoyed the creature comforts at McCalvin's home; there was far more security living on the Outside.

Courtesy Phillip G. Wolff

Whatever the reasons, Noah was going to survive, and he was going to continue to delight in the knowledge that he could at least, in the short term, share the bond of love he had for the wilds with as many people as possible for as long as anyone wanted to engage him to remain in the spotlight.

It's obvious that his love of solitude was not truly over; the days he spent alone would be by choice from now on. One of the things he enjoyed the most in those days was taking river walks both upriver and downstream to check Camp Seward, to hook up with Ranger Russell at Shattuck's and to visit at Plumley's Point. Nature observations were standard entries: "Up early. Robins 'cheer up'"… "Deer at 1st. Brook above Dam…" "…5 Deer-Tails gallop east in Dead Flow…" "…Night Hawks screech. No Mice at Cold River Town Hall…"

Throughout the summer months when at camp, Noah entertained hermit-seekers, continued to ramble around his surroundings, and had hermit-type fun with the wild animals. The general theme had to do with setting out macaroni and salt and watching the deer; feeding raccoons canned corn and pork and beans mixed with rice, and then calling them cranky when they growled at him; catching mice in Victor traps with bits of potted meat; and chastising any animal that left droppings or cherry stones on his grave.

He also continued to add improvements to his Ash Ground ["Place of Hermit Dust" where he wanted his ashes to be buried]. Over time he lugged five very large flat stones, "2,000 pebbles" and, he estimated, a 200-pound stone out of the ground that marked "Deer Trot Path," moving it to his gravesite as a permanent marker. (Today's sightseers to Cold River Hill who are determined to push away brush in hopes of finding the site will be disappointed. Bulldozer activity to remove fallen timber during the 1950s displaced the hermit's "Pebble Tray," which he had arranged against the north end of the intended permanent boulder on his Ash Ground.)

Over the years Doctors Latimer Sr. and Jr. had been checking Noah's health when they came to camp. By 1949 Oscar Burguiere was no longer around to help transport supplies from Camp Seward to Big Dam and help drag the necessary poles and logs so Noah could stay warm during the long heating season, and Richard Smith was more occupied than ever as caretaker for five families' homes on Lake Placid.

Rondeau's many short notes about carrying camp possessions from Cold River Hill to a cache near Mountain Pond, where Ranger Bomyer would then load them into his truck and transport them out of the woods, was the handwriting on the wall. Noah apparently sensed that his time by his beloved river was about to come to an end. His long-held wish to die and be buried right there would probably not come true.

On November 25, 1949, Noah noted in code he took his first bath in thirty days in preparation for his train trip to New York City and was looking forward to another interview.

November 26: …9:53 P.M. leaving Saranac Lake on Sleeper for New York City…Up at dawn in my little apartment on Sleeper. As train moves along the Hudson River feeble dawn and flying gulls. Belmont Plaza Hotel is a splendid Satisfactory place to stay-anytime while in N.Y. City.

Friday, December 2, 1949. Cloudy, mild, noon- showers. At N.B.C. International Theatre – "We The People" Television Rehearsal at 3:15 and 6:15 P.M. Broadcast at 8:30 - 9:00 P.M. "Yipee-i-Yi, Yippee- i- Yay!"

Letter dated December 7, 1949:

Madison Avenue
New York, N.Y.

Dear Noah,

I want to thank you for the splendid performance and wonderful cooperation in making last Friday's WE THE PEOPLE such a successful one. I hope the strain of all the rehearsals required by the combination broadcast and telecast was not too great and that you left with a warm spot in your heart for WE THE PEOPLE. If we can ever be of assistance to you, please don't hesitate to call us and again many thanks.

James Sheldon, producer
WE THE PEOPLE

Noah first returned to the McCalvins' house, where he observed "Santa Claus is busy And so is Old Saint Nick." He wrapped and mailed seven Christmas packages and posted sixty Christmas cards. Before going to his sister's, he went with Phil "to [a] picture show." Far along in the month Phil drove him to celebrate Christmas with his sister Priscilla McCasland in AuSable Forks. Noah said he played the role of Santa by helping to trim the Christmas tree and fill his niece's and nephew's stockings.

Chapter 14

Slow Progress Away From the Wilds

Noah recorded:

Monday, January 16, 1950. Heavy Rain last night. Today: Sunshine, Bare Ground, Cold wind. At Saranac Lake, N.Y. I call on Photographer-14 Academy. Call at C.C. office. I shop at G.L. Gray's. (Decoded: Sadie Shumway come and telephone. Cutting pork.) Evening: Willets come and play cards. Agent callselling (Decoded: Jesus on a clock.) Philip McCalvin Helen Duprey Married 1946.

Tuesday, February 21, 1950. 29-39 degrees below zero last night. Today: Calm, Nice Sunshine. At Saranac Lake, N.Y. At 4 Alpine Terrace the water pipes froze. (In code: I paid $10 rent for March.) I talk with H.V. Holmes over the wire. (In code: about speaking engagement in Marathon. I get civilization distemper germs from Gary.)

At age 67, Noah was no longer poverty-stricken. Back at the river at this time of year, Noah would have reported, "As long as the roofs didn't leak, I just read or wrote or took cat naps and waited for improvement." The January deep dip in the thermometer was nothing out of the ordinary in the Adirondacks, and there is not a single complaint in Noah's diaries about extreme weather. But this season would be different.

In fact, Noah's movement from wilderness to city life was gradual. He had some minor heart spasms, according to Doc Latimer Sr., which made him realize he would have to leave the hermitage, but not completely abandon the digs. He planned to return to use the cabins as a short-term camp. "He wasn't going to totally give up the old ways," Richard Smith pointed out. "His knees and hip joints were strong. He wasn't lame and his eyes were half as keen as an eagle's so he could still pick out a standing deer and see antlers—he'd just needed to be closer to civilization. Living with the McCalvins was easier on his aging body. He was resigned to become, as he put it a 'bloody bugger city feller.'"

His diary does reveal a bit of fiery reaction to typical civilization advertising.

> *Tuesday, February 21, 1950.* 29-39 degrees below zero last night. Today: Calm, Nice Sunshine; At Saranac Lake, N.Y. At 4 Alpine Terrace: water Pipes froze. I talk with H.V. Holmes over the wire. (Decoded: Marathon day. I get distemper germs from Gary.)

Courtesy of Richard J. Smith from Noah's photo album

Wednesday, February 22, 1950. Cloudy, cold. At Saranac Lake. Again: I have to listen to an American Hateful Fool of a Radio; Never a Radio in my Home! 7 o'clock: Again, and yet, the Radio is still Advertising in my Ears. Ironized yeast, True Love Story by Walker. I'm sick of American weak minded Radio Whoop.

Courtesy of Richard J. Smith from Noah's photo album

On the 5th of March, William R. Burton from Bainbridge, N.Y., wrote Noah about speaking at a sportsmen's banquet on March 28. Noah was to receive $25 plus traveling expenses.

"…This will be a great occasion for us sportsmen in Bainbridge. There are quite a few men in this locality who are acquainted with you and are eager to visit with you again…" wrote Burton.

H. V. Holmes, who had informed Burton that Noah was free, was a Marathon, N.Y., business owner and a paying hunting and fishing client of Noah's for more than a decade. He lived in New York's southern tier, a hotspot that funneled great numbers of sportsmen into the Adirondacks.

As a warm-up for the event, Billy Burger picked up Noah on March 15, whisking him off to his home, The Pipemakers, in Westport on Lake Champlain for a few days. On one of these days Noah spoke for "60 minutes at Westport Hi-Wi Club" about spending his 55th birthday atop the summit of Seymour Mountain. The occasion landed him, he wrote in code, "3 kisses from 3 Belles" at the gathering. Noah seemed to enjoy being pampered at The Pipemakers. He later wrote in code, "5 P.M. Mrs. Lillian Burger spread blanket over me. There's Nothing like it for us Old People."

Bette O'Hern and Bob "C.R." Bates. 2007. CR gave Bette GPS instructions on how he travels through Ouluska Pass Gap. Courtesy Author photo

Noah watches the Conservation Department' helicopter land on Cold River Flow. Courtesy New York State museum

FAME & $HEKELS

Tuesday, March 28, 1950. Summer Like. Sunshine Nice Spring day. At marathon and Bainbridge. 8 o'clock: to School with Mrs. Lu Holmes. (Mrs. H.V.). 2 o'clock: To Bainbridge with H.V. Holmes, call at Several Stores with Holmes, Burton. Supper for 258 at 7:30 dessert for 30 more; Then, about 10 Brief Speakers. 9:50 to 11:05 I give 75 minutes, Lecture on Hermit Life and Hermit Debut. (In code: I sell about 68 autographed photographs.)

The tiny one-time Adirondack mining town of Tahawus knew how to sponsor a sportsmen's show, opening for the second year on April 1, 1950. Noah noted he "...met many people, Good Show, good crowd—good weather."

James R. Fazio penned of the three shows, "They may not have been the greatest shows on earth, but to the residents of Tahawus" they were a high point and "they also provided a surge of extra income and fame that was envied by every town in the mountains."

Charles R. Begor spoke about the mining town. "The idea for a show in Tahawus originated with the fact that our [very distant] neighbor was Noah Rondeau."

Florence Breitbeck was one of the estimated 10,000 visitors that poured into town for the shindig from every corner of New York State in 1950. For a population of about 750 to see an influx of that size, the show had to have been extraordinary. She said, "A girlfriend and I heard the notoriety of the first show and just had to attend the next year. It was a beautiful morning when we packed the makings of a Girl Scout Hunter's Stew and left Ballston Lake for the Adirondacks, where our hearts reside. We drove back roads all day and in late afternoon eventually arrived at the high school auditorium/gym. I remember Noah Rondeau and the replica of his teepee. They had fly-casting competitions in a big pool and a man who handled a large snake. There were homey exhibits, topnotch talent from among the leading outdoor sport heroes of the day, numerous rod and gun sponsored exhibits and crowd pleasing trained bears. "On the way down the mountain we came around a bend to find the road strewn with still frozen ice cream bars on sticks. We could not witness such waste without doing our part."

Tuesday, May 9, 1950. A Perfect Vernal Day. Saranac Lake – Corey's, Ekhund. Robin cheer-cheer up! I find dead Wood Thrush. It seems, killed by Telephone Wire. Car ride to Corey's Road. I work 7 hours cleaning camp ground. All day: Robins "cheer-up." Work: cutting brush, raking dead grass.

Friday, May 12, 1950. Vernal Sunshine. At Saranac Lake, N.Y. I order 2,000 business cards. Received 12 photos from Studio. Paste 8 photos in album. Bill Petty phone: "You are wanted to speak at Rotary Club in June at Oxford, N.Y." Geo. Delaire phone: "The American Legion want Exhibit at 2 days Sportsmen's Show at St. Regis Falls, N.Y. May 28 - 29."

In May, Noah was invited by his friend Karl Eklund to place his full-scale replica exhibit on the triangle of land between the two drives that leave Route 30 and turn onto the road to Coreys.

Sunday – Monday, May 14 -25, 1950. Perfect Vernal Sunshine. At Saranac Lake – Coreys. Ride to Coreys with Philip McCalvin. We set up the Wigwam. First: on camp ground. Dinner in Wigwam. I sleep in Replica of Town Hall. I set up Karl Eklund's tent. I cut Balsam and make Pillows. Build stone fireplace.

In late spring Noah planted a garden, listened to the birds, enjoyed nature and continued to add improvements to his movable replica. Living in full view of the main highway between Tupper Lake and Lake Placid gave him the opportunity to enjoy visitors who stopped by and to peddle his variety of hermit-made knickknacks. He sold 100 autographed used canoe paddles Mr. Holmes had given him, and tanned pieces of deer skin donated by Roy Lash.

Wednesday, June 14, 1950. A Nice June Day. Coreys Saranac On Train. I go to Saranac Lake, Board 9:10 pm. R.R. Train at Saranac: I call at Montgomery Ward- at E.L. Gray's. Troy Laundry. Confab with W.A. Jeffery in car near Saranac Supply. I write Dr. A.G. Dittmar.

Thursday, June 29, 1950. Clouds and Sun. Afternoon showers. At Coreys N.Y. 10 O'clock: I go to Saranac Lake with Norma Cardinal. I shop at Bill Mullen. 2 pounds Scrap Leather from Berman Co. Minn. (In code: 7 pm Miss Dwetel I make 2 tobacco bags Haircut, Beard Trim)

Wednesday, July 5, 1950. Sun and Clouds 6 P.M. Shower that flooded Town Hall at Coreys N.Y. Callers: Sutro's and 22 from Syracuse University. (In code: I put my arm around old lady.) Among the 22 men (young men) from Syracuse University. They got away with my good pliers. I will be 67 years old tomorrow.

Thursday, July 6, 1950. ...I am 67 years old—N.J.R. born 1883. Karl Eklund bring me a Bottle of Pepsi Cola. Acriolelis (In code: Bring me a slice of slam bang.) Callers: 2 Mrs. Hollenbeck—Carol and Daneimorra Party, and [a] Priest Bus tour from Tupper Lake. Mrs. Acriolelis make me a Birthday cake— we celebrate Evening at Snack Bar. Last Night a Deer within 50' of Cold River Town Hall. Noah John Rondeau born 1883. (In code: shoot arrows for 2 ladies.)

* * *

Bob Bates is one of those folks Noah talked about who waits all year for his June fishing days and for autumn colors to return to Noah's river. He been going into Cold River for twenty years—and still counting. Poor weather has not discouraged him. When my wife Bette and I met "CR" (for Cold River Bob, a nickname he acquired years ago for his devotion to the her-

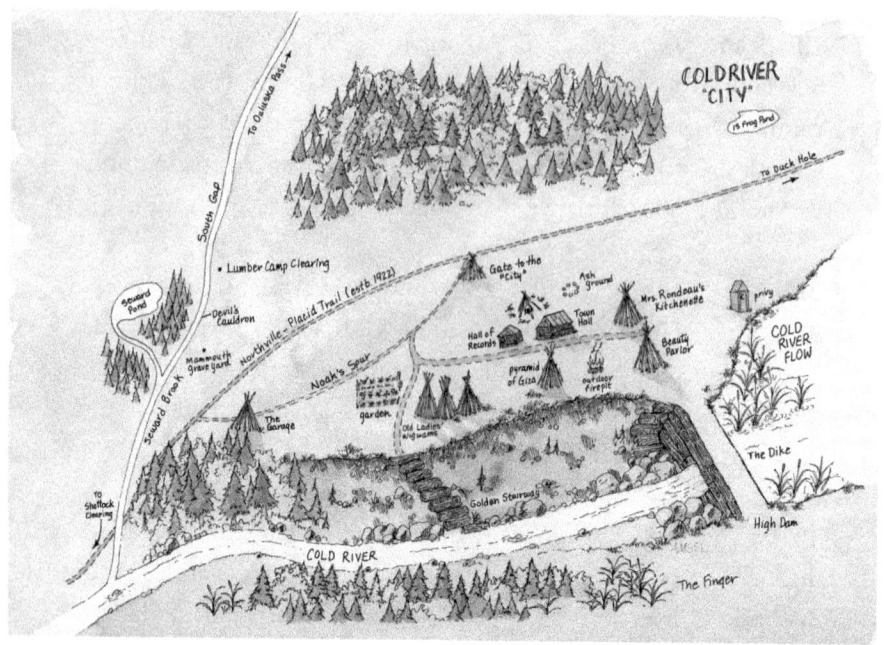

mit's backcountry) we camped with him in the fall of 2007 along the shore of Boiling Pond—an earlier term for Seward Pond. After several days of bushwhacking, Bette and I bid CR good-bye. We knew a storm would be approaching within twenty-four hours. A few weeks later we received an email from CR. The jest of it read: "I'm home. You vamoosed at a good time. I spent 5 days in HEAVY rain in the tent, but had a heck of a good two weeks. I'm already getting a Cold River itch. Can't wait for next June."

CR does find something—if only for a brief moment he and others "seek escape from the inescapable tensions, the persistently vexing problems, the frenzied, stepped-up living pace that is synonymous with our stage of civilization," reported Mary Malcolm Creighton. Creighton was inspired by Rondeau when she interviewed the hermit during the 1947 sportsmen's show in New York City. She called Noah John "a scientist, self-tutored and therefore limited, but with a keen mind. He has lived in the backwoods all his life. He has a passion for knowledge. To supply the necessities of life he once worked long hours for little money, with no time left for study."

I'll let Creighton speak for CR, Bette, me, and all the other people who have longed for a taste for Cold River. "There in the mountains they can momentarily revert to the very basic elements of life—God and nature. There they can experience not only recreation but a re-creation of body and spirit. Thereby they can return to the compounding complexities of their own personal worlds with renewed strength, with unclouded vision and a clearer sense of values and—above all—with the peace of God in their minds and hearts."

Rondeau's 1950 diary entries continue.

Tuesday, July 25, 1950. Clouds and Sun. 10 drops of Rain on Tent. At Coreys N.Y. I make 2 Best Blue, Balsam Pillows. Callers: Geo. From Schenectady we shoot arrows. (In code: Lady who saw me at Brainbridge called.) I make an awl 3 Indians from St. Regis call (In code: I send request to Flossie White. Sundown Yummy good feed of Slam Bang stains by anvil is venison. I wash my A_. Amen.)

Thursday, August 10, 1950. A nice Summer Day. At Coreys N.Y. I dig a pail of Potatoes. Callers: Dave and Edna Bushey. I take down Wigwam and Archery Target; and make ready to move to Santa Claus-City at North Pole. I call on Dan Emmett.

Friday, August 11, 1950. A Perfect Day. Coreys and North Pole. I call on Mrs. Eklund. (In code: I give her 5 dollars.) 2 Truckmen call and pick up my Replica and take it to North Pole N.Y. Caller: Dan Emmett Afternoon 5 Men set up for me. Mr. Lewis make a Yellow Birch Broom for me. I call on Grays. Bill Mullen, 4 Alpine Terrace and Reis Pharmacy.

Saturday, August 12, 1950. Perfect Weather-Perfect Business At Santa Claus City North Pole N.Y. I do the Roll of Santa Claus 8 ½ hours. (In code: I hug 50 young girls. 20 women) Florence A. Mennie, 110 Ayer St., Rochester 13, N.Y. She brought Daisies. A little Tot.

Monday, August 14, 1950. A perfect Day of Sunshine. In Santa Claus City at North Pole. I take the Roll of Santa Claus 8 ½ hours. Make me up cream, Rogue, Paste able and Powder. Callers: Peter Breen Party.

Tuesday, August 15, 1950. Perfect Sunrise on Parks Ground and the slope of White Face Mountain at Santa Claus City North Pole, N.Y. Callers: Madeline Dodge and about 50 young Boys and Girls from AuSable Forks. Mrs. C.J. Titcomb Pete of Niagara Falls. Napoleon Bonaparte, born 1769.

Thursday, August 17, 1950. Perfect Sunrise Day continues At Santa Claus City at North Pole N.Y. Callers: Eugene Freeman, Mrs. Brace Audrey. (In code: I hug a few ladies. I get 25 cents from holy dad.) 6 P.M. I call on Mr. and Mrs. Santa Claus. Clarke and Elizabeth Chaplayne, RD2, Worcester, N.Y.

Tuesday, September 5, 1950. Quite Cloudy, few glimpses of Sunshine at Santa Claus City North Pole N.Y. 8 ½ hours-Santa Claus Duty. I call at Workshops met Mrs. Westport.

Wednesday, September 6, 1950. Perfect Sunrise a Nice September Day. At Santa's North Pole. Callers: Mr. Norman Donald and Mrs. Donald and their Grandchild, Mrs. Jackson from Long Lake. (Mr. and Mrs. C. Moa. Mr. and Mrs. Ed Muffert)

Monday, September 25, 1950. Morning Roofs are white; Ice on water Pail in Wigwam put up Argument to not give up the Dippers. Slight Breeze Brilliant Sunrise. I'm Santa Claus 8½ hours at North Pole, N.Y. Clarke Chapalyne get pail of water and carry it to His Door for me while Elizabeth linger in Bed. 1:15 P.M. chat with Grace Hudowalski at North Pole. ...O'clock: I watch Penumbra of Earth's Shadow advance on the Moon; But Atmosphere is too hazy for Eclipse to be worth while.

FAME & $HEKELS

Tuesday, September 26, 1950. Cool-Smokey. Very hazy almost enough to blot out the Sun without real clouds of Aquatic Nebulosity. Last Night: Lunar Eclipse was a failure for show due to Smoke like Haze. I autograph Photographs and Leather Goods. (In code: 5 nuns, brown-white Black Vails 5 women. I sell 7 leather bags.)

Wednesday, October 25, 1950. Cool-cloudy. Early Morning Showers. Mid Day Sample of B.B. Snow at Santa's City North Pole N.Y. callers: Mr. and Mrs. John Miller of AuSable Forks, Bill Petty and Paul Delaire (In code: I put 600 dollars in Bill Petty's care.) Deer Hunting Season open.

Thursday, October 26, 1950. Like Stingy shake of salt, snow covers ground; and more generously on the Mountains. At North Pole, N.Y. Callers: Geo. Redman, John Koop.

Tuesday, October 31, 1950. Perfect Sunshine; Like summer day without Bugs. North Pole Saranac Lake. With plenty of help I take down Wigwam & Town Hall and move to Lake Clear and Saranac Lake. I Saw a Rough Grouse on White Face Mountain Highway. The Ride from North Pole to Lake Clear and back to Saranac Lake was most perfect; calm, warm and clear; AuSable River and Mountains are most beautiful. (In code: Santa Jim Duketts & all most kind.) At noon: I call on John Koope and Clarke Chapalyne at Santa's North Pole home.

Wednesday, November 1, 1950. A nice November Day. At Saranac Lake. I pack and store Hermit Riches (In code: call at laundry, P.O. and cleaners.) George Barnard Shaw dies at 11:59 P.M., at the age of 94. This afternoon: Two Puerto Ricans made desperate attempt to assassinate President Truman. I help Philip McCalvin to Linoleum the Bath Room. Lucius Russell kill a Bear (a very large Bear).

Thursday, November 9, 1950. Windy-Cloudy At Cold River Town Hall. Big Dam. I clean camp Make New Bed of Blue Joint. I drive out mice and set a Trap. I look over my city streets Cold River.

Wednesday, November 15, 1950. Very Cloudy. Mild Temperature at Town Hall Cold River. I skin a Deer's Head and Neck. I boil a can of Slam Bang. I prepare American Fool Tags to compare with American Fool Law. 9 P.M.: Alice Breen Nee Rondeau died.

Tuesday, November 21, 1950. ½" Snow fell last night. Today: Very cloudy – Snowed 2". Blustery-winter like at Cold River. 1 P.M.: Jack Smith and Raymond Dressel Jr. arrive Hunters from Watervliet. We 'Canvas Roofs' on the Town Hall and the Hall of Records. (In code: They occupy Hall of Records.) I cook a Slam Bang Gullion.

November 24, 1950. Letter from A.L. Belden, Fort Ann, N.Y. Mr. Noah Rondeau

Would it be possible for you to address the Fort Ann Rotary Club on Wed. evening Dec. 13th at 6:30 o'clock? We meet at Spauldings, formerly called the Busybee at 6:30 for dinner and have a half hour of speaking or entertainment and get finished at 8:00 sharp. Our president was talking with you during the summer at Santa's Workshop and you thought you might come in Dec. Your prompt reply will be very much appreciated. A.L. Belden Program Chairman

Sunday, November 26, 1950. Still Breezy, after 35 hours of worst Forest Destroying wind ever in Ampersand Valley. (In code: Morning ablution.) I make 3 canvas money bags. I bake a Pot of Beans and get supper for 3 men working to clear fallen trees from road. Happy Day at Ampersand Pond-Resting-after a Cold

River Hunt and Mastering a 12 Point Buck. (In code: 3 Brandy slings) Ferns and Moss from Walrus Rock, Ampersand Pond.

Monday, November 27, 1950. Quite cloudy, calm and mild. At Ampersand Pond. I make a Canvas Bag (In code: I go Mid Day and trim Blanchard McNeil doe. Cook some tag meat. Throw some in Lake Bullshit.) Happy Day at Ampersand Pond. (In code: cooking doe) Persisting Beech Leaf from Ampersand Garden.

Tuesday, December 5, 1950. Last Night: Snowed 7". Today:- Sunshine and slushy. At Saranac Lake. I call at Gray's and at Newberry's. (In code: I buy deerskins from Dale Bushey.) Chat with D.L. Bushey; and chat with E.S. Dyer; and with Bob Liddy. (In code: Invite to moose venison supper on 12.10.50.)

Sunday, December 10, 1950. Last Night: 26 above zero. Today: Calm and perfect sunshine. A nice day, late in Autumn. At Saranac Lake. I have civilization's Distemper. 8 P.M., I call at Reis' Pharmacy and Drutz's Grocery. Shirley Mason go to Schenectady.

Saturday, December 16, 1950. Quite cloudy, mild. At Saranac Lake. I receive 9 Xmas cards. I send out a Doz. I call at E.L. Gray's. I ship 2 Deer Hides. Confab with Bill Petty. (In code: I order 300 seeds from Bill Petty.)

Sunday, December 24, 1950. Cloudy and cool. At Saranac Lake. At 4 Alpine Terrace all day. I get agreement from Campbell-Fairbanks for New York Sportsmen's Show. I get 12 Xmas cards. Mrs. Bessie Moubar call. Santa is busy Trimming Xmas Tree. (In code: 1 Bath 25 days. Geo Bona borrow 2 dollars from Phillip. I receive Box from North Carolina. BH.)

Over time hundreds of people made a long hike to see Noah's Cold River home.

Chapter 15

Richard Smith Reviews Noah's Acceptance of a Santa Job

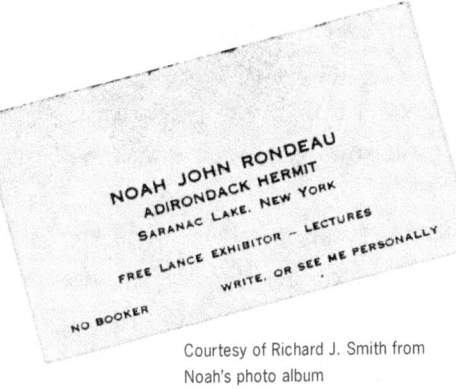

Courtesy of Richard J. Smith from
Noah's photo album

On August 10, Noah made preparations to move his replica exhibit from the highway at Eklund's Triangle. "I take down Wigwam and Archery Target, and make ready to move to Santa Claus City at North Pole," he recorded in his diary.

The following day he visited with Mrs. Eklund, paid her five dollars, and helped two men load his belongings onto a flatbed truck. That evening he noted: "…North Pole, N.Y. Caller Dan Emmett. 5 men set up for me. Mr. Lewis make a Yellow Birch Broom for me. I call at Grays, Bill Mullen, 4 Alpine Terrace and Reis Pharmacy."

Richard Smith filled in some 1950 gaps about Noah:

"During the late summer of 1950, Noah moved his cabin and wigwam exhibit from Coreys to a spot along the Whiteface Mountain highway in sight of the gateway to Santa's Workshop in Wilmington. It was a short drive from my River Road home."

With Noah's genuine beard, wire-rimmed glasses and pleasant manner, the old hermit was tapped to become a Santa Claus at the Adirondack theme park.

Courtesy of Richard J. Smith from Noah's photo album

"At Santa Claus City, North Pole, N.Y.," Noah wrote, "Perfect Weather - Perfect Business...I do the Roll of Santa Claus [for] 8 ½ hours. (In code: I hug a few ladies. I get 25 cents tip from Holy.)"

Smith recalled that Noah made a perfect St. Nick. "He liked the work and enjoyed the attention," and yet there was an ever-present Cold River tug. "He was always promising we would head back in. There were some steel traps he wanted to re-trieve that had been squirreled away for decades, but we never did find the time."

On August 21, while he was playing Santa, Noah jotted in his diary, "An American Thief took the Horns off my white deer skin today, and he got away with them; he wants a relic souvenir to hang on his wall to re-mind him that he is a Thief." And, the following day, "I discover some-one stole one of my canes.... An American Fool, about 35, peeled bark from a Silver Birch and give it to His young Son and Daughter. What a fine souvenir he got them!"

The North Pole was becoming old hat by September 6th. "...1 o'clock: An American Fool write his fool name on a Silver Birch Tree while 2 other fools watch with approval. And, at 3 o'clock another American Fool scribe His Fool Name on the same Birch and 3 Fools watch- smiling like a puck-ering string unpuckering."

Garda S. Babcok shared with me some details about Noah's employ-ment at the park.

Noah's position as Santa at the North Pole was a temporary assignment. Mr. Reiss, the financial backer behind Santa's Workshop, promised my Uncle Donald Finlayson the position of Santa Claus just as soon as his beautiful white beard filled in.

During the time Noah acted the role of Santa, Uncle Donald and my mother, Carmen Sourwine, were also employees of the very popular roadside attraction. Mother was head cashier. My mother and uncle dressed in gnome outfits. Mother was a beautiful lady. Noah called her "Sweetwine."

A troop Boy Scouts paid a surprise visit with the hermit. Courtesy of Richard J. Smith from Noah's photo album

One day, at closing time, Mother had just locked the admission booth, had the cash drawer under her arm and was swinging the entrance gate closed when a carload of rowdy Canadians drove into the parking lot. She politely told them the park was closed for the day. One man boldly walked up and stood looking her directly in the face, threatening he'd take the cash box if she didn't open up.

Noah was living in his Town Hall replica set up near the entrance. He overheard the commotion and knew Mother was in trouble. Suddenly the cabin door opened and out he came with a huge bow drawn back, an arrow pointing directly at the belligerent man. "If you touch that little lady, it'll be the last thing you do," he warned. His posturing caught an immediate response. Without another word the people piled into the car and careened down the road toward Wilmington.

Mother thanked Noah. She liked him very much. Noah comforted her, saying something about how he would always keep an eye out for her, then tipped his head far back letting out a robust "Ho, Ho, Ho." Mother said he often overdid the sound to the point she questioned if it ever scared some children.

Following Halloween, Noah packed up his furnishings, dismantled the Wigwam Town Hall exhibit and arranged to have it moved—lock, stock and trimmings of deer horns and bear skulls, pots and kettles, traps, bows and arrows and other "hermit riches" —to be stored at Lake Clear along with "$600 I put in Bill Petty's care" he wrote in code. Deer hunting season had opened.

Noah's journal recorded the move.

> *October 31 - November 1, 1950.* Perfect Sunshine, like summer day without bugs. From North Pole to Saranac Lake. With plenty of help I take down Wigwam Town Hall and move to Lake Clear and Saranac Lake. The ride from North Pole to Lake Clear was most perfect, calm, warm and clear. I pack and store Hermit Riches.

While staying in Saranac Lake, Noah shopped and packed supplies in preparation to return to Cold River for the deer hunting season. He flew to Plumley's Landing on Long Lake, then hiked into Shattuck Clearing, telling Ranger Russell, whom he rested with at Buck Horn Camp, that he expected an air drop of supplies over his hill-top city. His notes tell he hunted up to Cold River Flow. "At sundown saw a deer south of Dead Dog Slough."

Following deer hunting at the river, Noah returned to his rented room at the McCalvins' home at 4 Alpine Terrace in Saranac Lake. Throughout the following weeks he attended a Conservation Council Convention, shopped, visited friends, and complained in his diary, "I'm taking Bromo Quinine, I have civilization's Distemper. That's what people call 'a cold.'"

Following his recovery, Noah attended a moose and venison dinner party at the Fish and Game Club, wrote Christmas cards, visited with Bill

Petty at the Conservation Commission, and helped the Mc Calvin family set up their Christmas tree. Throughout Christmas week he arranged clippings and photographs in his album and scrapbook, "secured agreements from Campbell Fairbanks for New York Sportsmen Show," and celebrated Gary McCalvin's fourth birthday. He noted the event was an "elaborate anniversary." Before the end of 1950, Noah noted he had arranged dates in 1951 to lecture at The Pipemakers and the Tahawus Sportsmen's Show and to appear at other exhibits.

* * *

Rondeau's initial journey to the Outside agreed with his age and his practicality. The prospect of earning money became more important because it represented plenty of food and an ability to pay for comfy surroundings. Quite suddenly he was privy to electricity, indoor plumbing, central heat, railroad, air, bus and taxi transportation, hotel rooms, restaurants, and all the other accoutrements of a well-paid presenter. In Smith's words, "Noah was very horse-trader savvy."

For a man who had managed to pare his life down to Thoreauvian simplicity, his Spartan existence and experiences ironically became a rich source from which to draw.

His public recognition and small financial gains definitely brought about some changes in his attitude. His friends said that Noah never considered he miscalculated anything.

It's understandable why people who remove themselves from the social order are invariably drawn back to the civilization that they always wanted to leave behind. They return when they are worn out in body or spirit and in need of support and security. Of course, Noah was still young at heart—with a youthful conviction that Smith had always known him to have. That would never change.

Bill Petty helped Noah set up a bank account and helped the hermit manage the hundreds of dollars he earned for each Sportsmen's Show he attended. Courtesy of Richard J. Smith from Noah's photo album

Chapter 16

A Healthy Savings Account

Noah made a good financial haul playing Santa. When added to the previous year's savings, his bank account fattened considerably. He couldn't predict when the bubble of public interest might burst, but until it did, he acted as any businessman would—sending out letters of inquiry to capture the interest of promotional companies. *The Sporting Goods Dealer*, a trade magazine Noah read, reviewed Sportsmen's Shows sponsored coast-to-coast. Attracting the attention of a sportsmen's show sponsor on an international scale, such as the American and Canadian sportsmen's show, or finding a backer like the Boat Trades Association, could nail Noah a venue that would be advertised on a national scale among manufacturers, wholesalers, jobbers, sports, recreation seekers and vacationers. He knew the income would be substantial.

***

Despite his business plans, all through the late summer and autumn of 1950, Noah had anticipated his return home to Cold River. Deer hunting season opened October 25. The weather was beginning to show signs of winter as October drew to a close. "Like Stingy shake of salt, snow covers ground and more generously on the Mountains," he observed on October 26. November 1 found him helping Phil McCalvin linoleum the upstairs hallway and talking about old times they had along Seward Brook and their "Chowder Days" on Cold River Hill.

Deer hunting season was always a special time of year for Noah, but unlike Doc Latimer's crew, who had always arrived at Camp Seward with a kind of triumphant joy, Noah had not looked on whitetail season as a

Big Horn Camp at Shattuck Clearing, Cold River. Courtesy Ed Kornmeyer

special holiday until this year. Having enough meat to get him through the winter had always simply been an absolute necessity. This year, however, he did not plan to winter over at the river. At first, he wasn't even sure about returning to the river because of an injury he was still nursing on his arm, but the Cold River urge lured him back.

Thin wisps of smoke from the interior ranger station at Shattuck Clearing's Big Horn Camp smokestack filtered through the brisk air on Wednesday, November 8. "At dawn," Noah jotted later, "I go and skin a Bear's Head and salt the Hide. And then walk 7 miles up old River Trail. A Bob Cat hang on [a] Pine Limb at Rightmeyer. 2 Large Bucks hang [at] Camp Seward. I see a large Deer in Cold River at mouth of Seward Brook."

Harold Rightmeyer's and Clarence Whiteman's groups were two of the newest crews of deer hunters that had recently started coming to Cold River territory. Rightmeyer often hunted Sugar Bush Hill in the vicinity of the Calkins Brook jeep trail. Whiteman's party camped along the flats near the Big Eddy.

Noah skinned a deer's head and neck, then boiled it in preparation for a big kettle of Slam Bang. And to prove he was an honest hunter, he noted, "I prepare American Fool Tags to comply with American Fool Law."

FAME & $HEKELS

Tuesday, November 14, 1950. Mild and cloudy at Cold River...
9 a.m. I shoot from Town Hall Door and kill a 12 Point
Adirondack Buck. The last 3 years: I saw the Buck about 100
times near camp; and recorded him a score of times in my Diaries. And I knew 9 of his beds. Recordings: 8-31-48; 6-24-49;
10-16-49 and many other dates. I fed him Bread, Pan Cakes,
Salt, Sugar and Oat Meal. Today: 2 bullets took Him almost instantly at standard best. Deer hair blown on snow by 2 Bullets.

Both Camp Seward's log and Rondeau's diary took notice of higher
winds between November 18 and 24. "Blustery-winter like" Noah noted
on November 21. Throughout the six-day period it had been breezy, very
cloudy and growing colder by the day. Doc Jr. said his father was not a
bit worried. Even if it turned cold enough to snow, the packer would still
arrive with the wagon. Both camp owners anticipated what worsening
wind could do, however. Noah noted that he re-canvased his roofs with
help from Jack Smith and Raymond Dressel Jr.—two hunters who had arrived from Watervliet. Doc's group, taking a page from Noah's preparations, banked the base of their camp with soil, limbs and cobblestones,
and weighted the roof sheathing. Having taken these precautions, the
men enjoyed hearty feeds and passed some time drinking coffee and talking hunter's gossip, dry and cozy inside as they consumed Slam Bang
Gullion.

Being back at the river gave Noah a good deal of contentment. Now his
days were made of something besides adhering to requirements set down
by the Santa's Workshop administration, following a time clock, and an-
swering the same questions over and over. To be sure, he looked forward
to getting together with Lou Russell at Shattuck Clearing and the men at
Camp Seward, Clarence Whiteman and other hunters who had befriended
him when they came. He welcomed the freedom to enjoy life on his own
terms and with his old friends, and his diaries record no complaints as they
do during the times he worked as Santa.

The high winds that were recorded from November 18-24, however,
led to an event that left Noah no choice about where he would live the

rest of his life. Hyped as The Big Blow of November 25, 1950, the hurricane-force winds created unprecedented devastation throughout the Adirondacks. Conservation Department Commissioner Perry B. Duryea said, "The wind damage is way beyond anything ever experienced in this State and possibly anywhere in this country."

The Big Blow forced Noah to abandon any hope of ever returning to live on Cold River Hill. He got through the storm somehow, and the next day managed to work his way out to Ampersand Pond. Years of logging would follow to salvage timber and at the same time prevent a colossal forest fire.

Probably because Noah's letters were so interesting and descriptive, H. V. Holmes often submitted them to the local paper. The following was published in the *Marathon Independent* on Thursday, February 1, 1951. It describes Noah's experiences at Cold River the year of the Big Blow.

Last election day I started for Cold River city; I went by Tupper-Long Lake way. Left my supplies with Helms Brothers fliers to be taken by air to Cold River later. Now two deer hunters came along and they were going down the lake to Plumley's Camp so we chartered Helms's 4-passenger plane and in a few minutes made an aquatic landing at Plumley's dock. Coffee and cookies at Plumleys and a hug for the cook, and then I was on my way to Chatlock [sic: Shattuck] Clearing and before I reached Big Horn Camp I came on to Ranger Lucius Russell and a minister who were skinning a big bear; and later lodged with them at Big Horn Camp. After supper I bought the bear skin from Mr. Russell and I made arrangements to send the bear hide to Rochester with my specifications 'How to tan big bear.'

On November 8th I reached my own city hall. I have not been home in nearly a year. And the Mice have taken over; and there were deer tracks in the Wigwams. I Burn the Old Bough Bed and Washed all Dishes and I got Two Arms full of Blue Joint hay to make me a Cold River feather bed. It took nearly two days to make the Town Hall function in Cold River City style. But I was on my way and in due time my Finger Bowl and

Doc Latimer Jr, and Noah at Camp Seward located above "The Big Eddy" (also called "The Black Hole"). "I remember the morning this picture was taken shortly after I returned from WW2." Noah walked into camp. He greeted me, "good morning."
Courtesy C.V. Latimer. Jr., M.D.

paper Napkins arrived by air and were dumped in the briars. Now I was right at home and soon prevailed to make the mice recognize my authority. There were plenty of deer and I had a good time looking over the city. I found a quart glass jug full of sugar. It had been hid since 1934. It was getting late autumn and quite cold and at times snow but the Mountains and Vallies and Forest was beautiful; and it means so much to me because I know every tree like a flying Squirrel.

There was hunters six miles down the river and beyond and also in Ampersand valley and several called on me. I gave nearly all the venison to the hunters and took the horns and hide for my exhibit. November 25, I came out as far as Ampersand Park and the big wind storm began the last night I was at Town Hall. As I came 12 miles down there were very few trees down across the road but the wind storm was not half done and I found that though there were no trees across the road but west of the Park

A face lifter-NJR 1930's. Noah beautifies Mrs. Rodger Jones after 13 mile hike to Cold River City.
Courtesy Dr. Adolph G. Dittmar, Jr.

for four miles to Stone Creek bridge the beautiful forest was a slash of six feet deep. Three caretakers from the Park and a dozen hunters and about twenty men sent by Conservation Commission took two days to cut out four miles of road west of Ampersand Park. I cooked for part of the workmen at Ampersand Pond and I came to Saranac Lake Nov. 28 and west of the Park. I could not tell where I was, only when I came to a brook or special marks. It's a narrow road cut through a 6 foot slash and by standing in a car and looking over the slash I could see Ampersand brook 600 feet away. In any direction you can see a half dozen yellow birch per acre still standing braced by the slash, and their broken limbs are hanging.

There was no charm, Noah had to admit, that could right the destruction of the woodland. His cabin had been spared, but the windstorm claimed 10,000 acres just in the Cold River territory.

Knowing a careless hunter, angler, camper or mountain climber could start a forest fire of untold magnitude, the state closed the Adirondacks for three years.

"It was a reasonable decision," Richard Smith said. Noah agreed, "...But he had been silent for quite a while," as they talked about it. And when Smith was done talking, Noah asked Richard if he would help him go back when it was allowed to retrieve a few last items he'd left in his secret Mammoth Graveyard hiding place and in the buildings on Cold River Hill.

As December rolled to a close, Noah studied seed and poultry catalogs, received and sent Christmas cards, confabbed with folks and followed a routine typical of any resident in Saranac Lake. He enjoyed a dinner and get-together at the McCalvins' home with mutual out-of-town friends on Sunday, December 17.

December closed with a reminder of how normal his life was aside from his fame and all the venues where he managed to turn a tidy profit. There is no way to know how he felt about coming back to live in the "fool civilization" he had so often disparaged, for there are no diary entries about it. However, 1950 does close with a reference that shows he still thought of himself as somewhat of an Outsider. He repeated, "I'm taking Bromo Quinine, I have Civilization's Distemper that people call 'a cold'."

Chapter 17

Permanent Life on the Outside

Eight days into the new year, Noah was attending to business. In beautiful flowing script he penned a five-page letter to Mr. William Shilling in New York City. A portion follows:

January 8th 1951

Mr. Shilling: In July 1949...I made plain-that Your services as a Broker for me, were, discontinued. ...I'm not interested in your agency Please don't book me. ...Your Post Card of Jan. 2nd 1951 asked if I would accept New York Sportsmen Show-in Feb. 1951 if you arrange....

...I already have a contract for [several] ...Sportsmen's Show[s] in 1951. And I don't need any One to arrange for Me; and will not pay commission to any One, under the circumstances....

And as to the 'Photos' I have them 2"x6" and fairly well autographed @ 25 cents each you can get 12 photos by sending $3.00—and this is not a bribe to open the door for you to Book Me or come get a commission: I frankly warn again, "Please don't book me, I will not accept a contract thru your hands and will not pay you a commission."

It's evident to me, that, I'm still on Your List; and that you are persistent to involve yourself for a commission; and in the meantime, I'm sure that, You Understand… according to my letters to you: I'm off Your List, you are not to book me, I will not sign a contract by you or your agency and I will not pay you a commission because your services were unsatisfactory. Please understand Mr. Shilling and please don't write me; I have something to do beside writing to report what I have written before.

I prefer, not to be offensive but in cases like this, I have to make double sure that I'm understood. I know, it's too bad, it's unfortunate but, since you would not leave Good Enough alone; I had to take the stand that I took….

Please, leave Bad Enough alone and if You try to collect a commission from me Mr. Shilling-I'm quite sure that you will learn—A Hermit is not just Old Bark from the Sticks.

Noah John Rondeau

Newspaper reporters who covered the 1951 show in New York City continued to feature stories about Noah, still one of the most popular features at the Grand Central Palace. Fellow Cold River deer hunter Clarence Whiteman said his wife and he had visited Noah both in New York City and later that year when they attended the Tahawus show in April.

Clarence said Stacia was "tremendously impressed [by him] and what a name—Noah—Biblical in nature and certainly of visage. I still have the pictures of Noah pretending to ride atop of a huge buck pulled by me and members of my hunting party in 1949. Picture, if you will, Noah sitting astride a large buck. He was clad in tattered red-checked hunting pants and with his long gray and black beard, he resembled Santa on a hunt. We had tied branches to the horns. It made the antlers look enormous. We pretended to be Santa Rondeau's reindeer team as he pretended to crack a whip over our heads and hollered 'On Clarence. On Johnny. On Tom and Joe. To the top of Cold River Hill, now onward you go.'" A gleeful scene indeed.[1]

1. Clarence tells about his Cold River connection with Noah and the home movie he made in Adirondack Wilds: Exploring the Haunts of Noah John Rondeau (In the Adirondacks, 2013).

Cold River. For some people, an escape can last a lifetime. Photo by Author

* * *

Invitations to speak continued to arrive. By this time Noah had devised an organized filing system. Received letters were labeled "Lecture Inquiry." They were placed in the original envelope and filed in a shoebox by month. On the front of each envelope he marked:

W-4-12-1951 [date letter was written]
R-4-16-1951 [date Noah replied]
A-4-21-1951 [date Noah received an answer]

Edmund Gilligan was ecstatic that the Tahawus Sportsmen's Show was repeated. He deemed it one of the best in the land, and added, "…It is pleasant to learn, too, that Noah Rondeau, the hermit, will be hermiting at the show. As an amateur hermit, I sometimes feel a little doubt about Noah's status. He is supposed to live on the land, you know, but the last time I saw him he was striding through the Commodore lobby and I couldn't help wondering where he was going to knock off a legitimate diner. I hear that the National Association of Hermits would like to discipline Noah for gadding about so far from his hermitage on Cold River. The trouble is that the boys can't get together, it being against the rules...."

On Thursday, April 19, 1951, Noah responded to a news report that caught his attention. "I hear Gen. Douglas MacArthur speak from the Nation's capital. The speech, 42 minutes, was by a Man with 52 years military experience—a 5 Star General just recently fired by Harry S. Truman—President of the U.S.A. and an American Ass. The Speech was most appropriate and by far the best ever made by an irreproachable Military General."

Noah's success at an April Rotary Club meeting in the coffee shop of the American House in Au Sable Forks was reported to the community of readers of the *Adirondack Record-Elizabethtown Post*. Noah spoke of "the scenic beauty of his mountain retreat, the beautiful flowers, birds and animals that flourish there. He touched upon his appearance on TV at the exclusive Versailles Restaurant while he was attending the annual Sportsmen's Show... The hermit whose fame has spread to all parts of the United States impressed his listeners with his excellent discussion of subjects he knows so well...."

On May 2, Noah reported the "Grass is greening beautifully" in Lake Clear when he took a "Beauty walk with Marilyn Petty" following his offering a hand to Bill Petty, who was using a blow torch to "scrape old Paint off Petty's old Guide Boat." Prior to the stroll and being driven to Petty's home in a "Conservation Truck," he had talked with Bob Reed in Malone about addressing the Rotary Fair Club and setting up his "Replica Exhibit" at the Franklin Hotel, and with Leonard Safir at New York City's Rockefeller Plaza "over the wire."

Folks at the Malone event heard him speak twice. His addresses were orchestrated stories he called "A Bear Eat Me Up" and "Mick Swallowed the Blarney Stone." *The Adirondack Record-Elizabethtown Reporter* reported "...Noah put on a show, made several brief speeches, and was the cynosure of all eyes, the older people gazing in wonderment at him no less than the youngsters...."

For years after leaving Cold River, Noah lived the life of a vagabond. While his financial outlook was good, Noah must have taken someone's advice or been concerned that his fame would be fleeting. His writings do not tell the reason, but on May 11, 1951, Noah walked out of Essex

County Social Services with a Social Security card.

By June he moved his living quarters from McCalvin's in Saranac Lake to Wilmington—boarding with Madeline Dodge, who said, "I harbored a soft spot in my heart for Noah." A Cold River-style teepee went up in Madeline's large yard. He worked a few days a week on house repairs and yard work chores in exchange for his room and board.

Madeline humbly recalled that "Noah put great stock" in her honesty. She told me, "He left his entire collection of papers and personal writing, including his prized manuscript, with me." DeSormo used it to lead off his 1959 Rondeau biography, a collection of remembrances with snappy titles like "Caldron Flavor and Crying Cats," "Streamlined Snow," "Hank and Maggie Disappear Among the Clumps of Cats," "Radio Screech Owls," "Cow Bell Carols," "Gram's Quiz," "Pondering on a Wedding Cake," "Sleeping on a Wedding Cake" and dozens of other short stories of his early life before he began his hermit days.[2]

> *Friday, July 27, 1951.* Sun and Clouds. 6 P.M. Sprinkle. At Wilmington. I walk to Orrs' Bird S--- on Choke Cherry Road. An American smart liberty Dog in car, near Sidewalk almost jump in my face as I pass on Side walk. To Hell with the American Liberty…

Sandwiched between the diary pages for August 12 and 13, Noah affixed a two-page hand-written letter from a young girl. His own handwritten notes point to "Judy's Statements," "Judy's Envelope," and "Judy's Kisses" next to the eight X's with which she closed.

Judy's note reads:

> Dear Mr. Rondeau,
> I haven't had time to right. My two little cousins have been up here for two weeks. I am 9 years old. The picture of you I got,

---

2. Noah's self-composed "Recollections of Sixty Years" is part of the 1969 North Country Books, Inc. publication, *Noah John Rondeau, Adirondack Hermit* by Maitland De Sormo. "Recollections" includes detailed information about Rondeau's life, beginning when he was a young boy in 1889. While it was a true validation of his early life, Noah never finished the project. In fact he stopped in mid-sentence with no explanation.

I hung on the wall in my bedroom.

Judy was Leslie Farmer's daughter. Leslie said he became a fan of Noah's the day he interviewed Noah at the ranger station in Saranac Inn, March 1947: "I was attending St. Lawrence University. This was a project for the campus radio station KSLU. I interviewed him between trips to the New York Sportsmen's Show.... He told me he had a great time in New York and in fact 'Went a little Hollywood.' As I recall, on this interview recording Rondeau spent quite a little time reciting poetry he had composed, mostly about little babies...." Farmer hoped the recording had not been destroyed over the years. Inquiries in 1991 did not turn up anything regarding the broadcast.

On "A nice day when school began in Wilmington," Noah recorded in his diary for the 4th of September that following a three-hour talk with Nick O'Reilly, he and Lee Chadeayne left the village of Wilmington for a five-day backpack vacation at Indian Falls among the lofty high peaks. "Call at Lake Placid and Drive to Adirondack Loj; walk to Indian Falls by dusk. Supper, campfire, to bed—dream of bears..."

September 5th: ...I check up 34 kinds of Trees, Shrubs and Grasses within 50 ft. of Lean-To. I wash at Flume above Indian Falls. I go below the Falls + 1/8 M. + a long walk to see Lee swim. 3 o'clock: Beauty Sleep on Ledge near Flume. Sun Down: I get 1 Gal. Glass Jug N.W. of Indian Falls Ledge.

September 8th: Last Night: Ice on my Plates. Today: Perfect Sunshine. Calm, Beautiful in the Mountains. Indian Falls to Wilmington. Breakfast with Dr. and Mrs. Stone and Lee Chadeayne... We walk to Adirondack Loj (4 m.) with packs; then drive to Wilmington. Good Mountain Time; and brought home a gal. glass jug from Mt. Marcy.

Doc Latimer Sr., Oscar Burguiere and Noah had exchanged several letters by the end of 1951. Their correspondence kept one another up to date

Noah shares his experiences with Helen Colyer Menz and Mary Colyer Dittmar. During the first sportsmen's show the hermit of Cold River had received more than 1,000 letters from people asking how to become a hermit. He was also a guest of the "We the People" N.Y. City radio program. He was heard over Station WWNY, Watertown, and the Columbia Broadcasting System. Courtesy Dr. Adolph g. Dittmar, Jr.

with what they were doing. Doc's October 19 communication to Oscar said he had learned Noah was making plans to move to his sister Priscilla's Hill Top Ranch along Rolling Mill Hill Road in AuSable Forks.

Noah's letter confided he "was not working very hard anymore so I can get out in the woods…." more often. "They have not opened Cold River as yet…. I will never go up again as it is too strenuous for me now. I might go into Shattuck next year, if they open that section and if… [Ranger Lou] Russell has a Jeep so I would not need to walk in…."

Time was marching on for the old Cold River fellows. "While a new year only marks a passing of time, which goes on no matter what is done to turn it back," wrote Noah, "people should not regret passing years or fear death at the end. The fear of death stops us from living, not from dying…so make the most of each day…"

Richard Smith said that was one of many pages he borrowed from Noah's philosophy. "Each precious moment we live in health, and honestly enjoy our accomplishments and friendships made, makes our lives worth living," he said.

FAME & $HEKELS

Chapter 18

A Living Exhibit

Noah John Rondeau got paid to be himself. He made the rounds at speaking engagements describing life in the wilderness at thirty below in a hut that was often buried so deeply in snow it sometimes showed only as a mound from which a smoking chimney jutted up. He spun fantastic yarns; he entertained his audience with true life accounts, offering first-hand advice at ladies' teas and luncheons as how to properly trap a huge black bear should someone in the audience decide to take up trapping as a profession; and he described his wilderness flanked by seven major mountain peaks, all over 4,000 feet high. The hermit would graphically describe the beauty of mountains and forest, snow-buried and shining in the winter sun so that anyone listening might be easily persuaded take up backpack-

Courtesy of Richard J. Smith from Noah's photo album

ing where "summer comes so late in Cold River that the fourth of July doesn't arrive till the fifteenth of August."

Noah was born on July 6, 1883, of French-speaking parents in the Jackson Hill section of Upper Jay, in the northern Adirondacks, in the so-called high peaks region. Spectators learned he divested himself of the world's worries, its "Big Business" and what he termed the "slavery of industrialism" in favor a forest pine, of hackamatack, of fir and beech, in sober contemplation of the future of the world.

March 6, 1948 Mereda and Carol Barnes. Noah met these children at his first Albany, New York show. Courtesy Edward Miller

That Cold River bluff sanctuary is about a one-hour flight from his childhood home as an Adirondack crow flies.

By the early 1950s, the hermit had enjoyed the delightful taste of appearing at well-paying sports shows and basking in the limelight of publicity. One newspaper reported that Noah began his talk by pointing out his thirty years "alone in the woods had brought him a variety of experiences, but not in public speaking." He asked his listeners' indulgence because his "public speaking was largely done to chipmunks and stumps —and half my English is French anyhow, so I may stumble and break my vocabulary." The colorful hermit then proceeded to delight the audience with descriptions of his "little cluster of pole wigwams with tables rigged from an old flat-bottom boat and handmade furniture [which] are favorite camera subjects for the visitors."

Richard Smith remembers:

> Noah was a natural showman when addressing a crowd or back at Cold River. In spring, he became obsessed with thoughts of the meddlesome chipmunks and red squirrels. He'd imitate the

FAME & $HEKELS

1934 Ruins of bridge that spanned big dam. Gay Prue courtesy of Grace Hudowalski

animals, pretend to pick up a spruce cone and chatter. Then he'd make believe he was running up the poles on a wigwam, stand on the top, play the Jew's harp cone, all the while doing a jig as he kept time with his 'tail' wagging. The act didn't leave much doubt in our minds, as he was able to reproduce almost an exact rendition of the animals' antics. Noah said, 'Blame it all on the fact that remoteness brings out odd behavior in an old man…he just can't account for.' That's the way he performed at talks. Once he got into high gear, he could hold an audience spellbound for hours, seemingly with little preparation or notes of reference.

According to Smith, Noah was one of three invited guest speakers for the evening at a Lions Club banquet in AuSable Forks one winter. The other two were college professors.

The professors decided Noah would go on first as he, being a hermit, would not have a long-winded speech prepared, and would get it over quickly and leave the podium with plenty of time for the other two speakers.

Well, Noah spoke for two hours. Throughout the majority of that time, maybe half the time, the audience was rolling in the aisles, weak from laughing at Noah's humorous presentation. The MC told the two professors they could stop Noah's discourse, but they said they wouldn't hear of it, replying they never enjoyed any speech as much as Noah's, and besides— what they came to say would be so boring, the audience would leave. Noah's funny side and his sound wisdom could not be duplicated or improved upon even by two learned educators!

What follows is a shortened bear chase story Noah told based on penciled notes Smith said Noah made when preparing some of his tales. The lengthy article went on about accounts of hunting and trapping and an early bear hunt "on the north slope of Santanoni Mountain" that included a five-mile chase of a 350-pound bear "with a head as big as a basket" as the bruin roared downhill with the hermit's 22-pound trap dangling from its paw with "the sound of the clanking trap and some 40 pounds of huge log being dragged through the thick woods."

"The bear circled, apparently an attempt to shake them loose. Despite the handicap of four feet of snow, thick balsams and the drag of the trap, bruin kept his chains rattling until it sounded like a blacksmith shop in motion. Finally the hermit caught a glimmer of the bear coming up out of a little ravine, I knew I'd get him; he had the trap, but I had the gun." Shaking from weariness and the nervous strain of stalking the enraged beast, unseen but at close quarters, Rondeau failed to deliver a fatal shot.

The bear finally "stubborn'd and stopped." Rondeau explained that he didn't go right up and jump on him because he didn't like to scratch the pelt. Drawing a careful bead, he fired one of his last "catridge" between the bear's ribs. "He never even growled but just humped up his shoulders. I didn't know but what he was going to spit the slug out." The bear failed to fall over, "although I waited around five minutes to see if he'd change his mind," so Rondeau took off up the trail to camp. When he returned next day, the bear was gone. Following the bloody trail, he closed in on the bruin in a thicket, where they both got the same idea simultaneously. "He went the other way, and so did I." Finally, on a tote-road, he got a clear shot and put two bullets through the bear's neck. "They weren't more'n an inch apart. I didn't see why he stood up after one bullet and laid down after the other, but such was the case." Even then Noah waited five minutes before he went near the carcass, because "if a bear can hold his breath that long, he's not bluffing." Rondeau reported he "had to move half of him at a time." Climaxing his talk, the hermit exhibited snapshots of the big bear and other scenes around his lonely Cold River "diggings," and recited a poem he had written entitled "Sunrise on Lofty Peaks."

By the Tahawus Sportsmen's show in early spring 1951, Edmund Gilligan used the word "carnivalism" to describe the events. Gilligan said sportsmen's shows were "reaching a point of carnivalism which begins to rival the circus. The so-called sports on the programs were becoming odder as time draws on." He'd heard of one show where swimmers actually pretended to be fish and fought against rod and reel. There was another where wild animals were kept in an overheated carnival alley, with no fresh air to breathe, even if they wanted it. After a day or two some of the captives didn't care much about breathing any more. For those reasons, and others too numerous to mention, he went along with those men who were "not happy in such Coney Island atmosphere."

James R. Fazio took a more conciliatory view toward the shows in his "The Greatest Show in Tahawus" article in the March/April 1983 *Adirondack Life*. He wrote:

> They may not have been the greatest shows on earth, but to
> the residents of the tiny Adirondack mining town of Tahawus,
> an unusual succession of sportsmen's shows were the high
> point of the year back in the early 1950s. They also provided a
> surge of extra income and a fame that was envied by every
> town in the mountains.
> The [Tahawus] sportsmen's shows extraordinaire happened
> in the springtime of 1949, 1950 and 1951, swelling isolated

Noah told the models that posed with him that he was not interested in becoming a New Yorker.

Tahawus from its usual population of 750 to more than 18,000 as visitors poured in from all over New York. Then, at their zenith in 1951, the shows suddenly stopped. The crowds never returned, the star attractions slipped into oblivion, and all that remains is a dusty box of yellowing records, a crumbling building, and the happy memories of the thousands who witnessed the great events.

"Noah had been one of the most popular features of these shows," reported Ranger Hulbert Toomey, who was a friend of the hermit and who represented the Conservation Department at the Tahawus April 28-29 show in 1951.

Noah was among the outstanding performers at Tahawus. Toomey said he shared space with the hermit. Noah's "deerskin clothes and a bear skin coat captured the interest of all who attended. To be able to talk to a man who lives entirely on what he traps, snares or shoots with a bow and arrow was a real thrill. Noah was located in the Conservation building at the Tahawus show, where there was a large display of various exhibits including animals from the Department's Delmar Game Farm."

For a man who gave up on civilization because he said, "Big Business was getting too big…that a man can't swing a double-bitted axe anymore and grow vegetables on a patch of land and make a living," Noah certainly capitalized on his "discovery" in 1947 and found a narrow vein of shekels and fame in the goldmine of sportsmen's shows.

It was a fitting conclusion to this unique Essex County folk character's many public appearances.

Part III

Life beyond
Cold River

Chapter 19

Smith and Wilkins Help "Mr. Whiskers"

Bill Wilkins, Richard Smith's close boyhood friend, knew about the aging hermit's disposition. Stories about Noah's rough side were no more typical than those about other local characters. Wilkins had also known Noah's gentler side, and was happy to spot him meandering down the road in Wilmington for a visit, or to listen to him talk about plants or a book or magazine article he'd read.

Courtesy Dr. Adolph G. Dittmar, Jr.

Wilkins donated a wonderful picture he snapped of Richard standing guard over Noah as he "sawed on his 'Stradivarius'— that's what he called his fiddle. I used to go into the hermitage with Red [Richard Smith], his brother Bernard and Max Bickford. When we would get there Noah would sometimes dance a little jig and say, 'I'm glad you came.'"

Wilkins recalled Richard and Barnard Smith and Max Bickford all used to visit the hermit in the 1940s. "One time I remember, it was late in the hunting season. He'd been guiding for a doctor that had a camp downriver from his. Noah asked us to help him bring food supplies that had been left there. The four of us went downriver with empty pack baskets; on our return we had all we could do to carry it all back. Noah was so glad. He fixed

Inside Mrs. Rondeau's kitchenette wigwam.
Velma Hunt spoke about seeing Noah in 1946 at the Burnt Hills Sportsmen's Show. She said, "The hermit loved the crowds of people that visited his exhibit. He hammed it up like mad and responded to all the questions. The crowds just loved him. People threw money on the stage for him. He demonstrated some of his equipment. I wish I would have had the chance to invite him to my house for lunch."

us a good meal of potatoes, rice, and bean soup, but mostly we ate venison. When I went up there with Red and Bernard, Red would make us stuff our packs mostly with dry stuff—beans, rice, macaroni, tobacco and some canned stuff. We would really be loaded.

"Richard and I grew up almost next door; as adults we still lived in close proximity. One day when we both had time off from work, we decided to drop in on Noah when he lived in his exhibit on the side of Whiteface [Mountain Road]. A man from Lake Placid had a hot dog stand and some caged animals as an attraction. I remember a bobcat, an altered ex-perfumed skunk, and two raccoons. Being close by, Noah looked after them at night. At the end of the season, he offered to sell the raccoons to Noah."

Wilkins was also part of a four-man crew that helped cart out the final truckload of possessions from the Big Dam camp in the aftermath of the November 1950 storm. Noah asked the fellows if he could "hire" them to do some work for him, said Smith. "That was like asking a fox if he would like another piece of rabbit."

When the Ampersand Park and Ward Brook fire truck roads were cleared for travel and Noah was given permission, he hired a truck to go in as far as Mountain Pond. From there Noah's work crew walked the six miles to Big Dam. "While Noah sorted loads," said Wilkins, "we carried the things out to the truck. We felt sure Noah felt a little heart-broken as he left the hermitage." Richard said he was with him at the Gate to the City. "Noah turned and said, 'So long old friend; I'll be back.' I think he might have even had a tear or two in his eyes that very last time, but would have been too embarrassed to shed them."

Chapter 20

Life on the Outside

Hermit hop. Courtesy of Richard J. Smith from Noah John Rondeau photo album

The year 1951 found Noah living at 4 Alpine Terrace, Saranac Lake, N.Y. with Phil and Helen Mc-Calvin. Noah had made his last hike out from the hermitage to civilization at Coreys, N.Y. The devastation left by the hurricane and advancing age kept him from ever returning

Phil McCalvin recalled that when he and a few other fellows from the CCC side camp would hike downriver on their time-off to visit Noah, "The camp cook, mostly gave us loaves of bread to donate to his cause. Noah would spread slices out and dry the bread. In that way it allowed him to use it over time. Drying it kept mold from growing.

"Years later, when Helen and I learned the Conservation Department closed the woods, he had no choice but to find living quarters. We offered him our spare bedroom. Noah didn't take charity. A suitable arrangement was made where he helped with house chores and babysitting our infant son, Gary, in trade for room and board."

Selected daily recordings made by Noah follow—misspellings, strange capitalizations and all.

Chapter 21

The Hermit's Journals

It is assumed that soon after Noah arrived in Coreys, N.Y. in 1913, he began to keep a diary. In their earliest form, his diaries were small pocket-sized notebooks that held short notes and sketches. On any particular day there might be a brief note about the weather, his location, observations and daily events. Around 1919, Rondeau began to keep a more detailed day-to-day diary. Those records were destroyed.

According to Peggy Byrne, who talked to Noah about the fire that razed the Schoenheels' summer cottage where Noah had been given permission to live for the winter, Rondeau's tone indicated he was sorry his earliest diaries had been destroyed. Noah told Byrne, "My diaries are like my poems, poor scribble. Early in 1929 I lost diaries of 11 years and they were well-written in Cold River style."

Among the destroyed articles was a register that dealt with Noah's caretaking jobs and his occasional guiding business. The first-person account would have been a valuable record of Rondeau's pre-hermit activities.

Archie Petty, then a high school student in 1929, wrote this note in the Petty family's "Corey's News" home journal that provided evidence of the scope of the lost possessions.

> "A small cottage which was occupied by N.J. Rondeau was burned to the ground Monday afternoon about 4 o'clock. Sparks from a small stove caused the blaze. Rondeau lost all his belongings, among which were a valuable camera and typewriter."

From my research, I have endeavored to create a list of Rondeau's known diaries and their location. The lion's share is found at the Adirondack Experience's library at Blue Mountain Lake. The letters "RS" indicate the diaries Rondeau gave to Richard. J. Smith for safe keeping before Noah's passing. Smith said those years described the significant connection between the two fast friends. In 1993, before his own passing, Smith willed them and a lot of other Rondeau memorabilia to the Adirondack Museum, now known as the Adirondack Experience.

The diaries at the Adirondack Museum are for these years: 1930, 1932, 1937, 1939 (RS), 1940-1942, 1943 (RS), 1944 (RS), 1945-1948, 1949 (RS), 1950 (RS), 1951-1954, 1959, 1964 and 1966.

Eight other Rondeau diaries: 1953, 1955-1958, and 1960-1963 are in the possession of the Lake Placid - North Elba Historical Society (The History Museum) in Lake Placid, N.Y.

Rondeau's 1967 diary is owned by a private party who wants to remain anonymous.

Thumbing through the logs, one will see that by the 1930s Rondeau began to develop a cryptic code.

Over the years the code developed into elaborate-looking hermit hieroglyphics used to record whatever he chose to. While the code was an academic exercise that helped to dawdle away the idle hours, it did serve a useful function. He used the code to keep an accurate accounting of all his legal and illegal kills—the deer, bear and fish he caught. By the 1920s, Noah grew increasingly wary of game protectors. That motivated him to create the code. As far as I know, it was never used to conceal any dark secrets.

Portions of my two books *Life With Noah: Stories and Adventures of Richard Smith and Noah John Rondeau* (North Country Books, 1997) and *Noah John Rondeau's Adirondack Wilderness Days: A Year with the Hermit of Cold River* (The Forager Press, LLC, 2009) discuss in depth Rondeau's code-making process and how to read and write in his code.

Examples of the typeface used in the production of Rondeau's 1958 diary in this book was created and copyrighted by David Greene in 2009, and is officially known as "Noah's Code." Green's code is based on Rondeau's 1940s final version of code.

Rondeau's yearly journals helped to keep track of the day and date and significant events.

Up to the early 1940s he occasionally left Cold River, to spend the Christmas holiday with friends and family. Upon returning, he experienced months of total isolation before seeing another human. Having a visitor would be a red-letter day.

It was often thought long lines of code hid private information, however as you will see in the 1958 examples, the code represents considerable ingenuity, but those truncated entries dealt with everyday events.

What follows is a random sampling of Noah's life from 1950, the time he left his Cold River diggings, to 1966, the year before his death.

Noah boasted that not even expert cryptologists would ever crack his code. That claim held true until the early 1990s. It's also a good guess Rondeau never dreamed readers would find his diary entries curiously interesting—enough so to appear in print. But as his popularity at sportsmen's shows and other appearances has proven, his diaries before and after the shows have provided, as Maitland C. DeSormo wrote, "an excellent index to his thoughts, moods, impressions and experiences."

In my personal study I have found, as might be predicted with all his references to the use and care of his "Cold River replica," that Noah, like other aging people, lived mostly in the past, yet still made the most of each day.

When I asked Richard Smith if he thought Noah might have considered publishing his thoughts an invasion of his privacy, Smith replied immutably, "Heck no." On the contrary, "Rondeau was aware of his regional rising stardom during the sportsmen's shows era." The one-time hermit might never have predicted he'd become part of Adirondack folklore. Smith did say, however, that Rondeau would have wanted "a fair and honest rendering of his life." And that is a truth I have always followed when writing about this remarkable person.

While reading Rondeau's entries, keep in mind that he wrote for himself. There are many spelling, punctuation and grammatical errors. His use of capitalized nouns is immediately obvious.

A sample of his handwriting shows a script in a beautiful, flowing, Spencerian style. Over time, his writing shows an ever-increasing shakiness that indicates growing infirmity.

Smith, who was taken by his friend's artistic and musical interests, would add, "Noah's refined handwriting could have graced the United States Constitution. And he was articulate. His voice had a distinct timbre. I vividly recall how soft spoken he was as he responded to my questions. The only time his voice became shrill was when he talked about the game protectors, 'the all-American son-of-a-bitches' whom he identified as the main source of all his trouble with the Conservation Department. I was also impressed by his living as comfortably as he did, in spite of the lack of creature comforts back at the river."

DeSormo added, "Moreover, since those bygone years contained such a mixture of the pleasant and the unpleasant, it is not difficult to figure out why a hurt and sensitive man would show occasional outbursts of lingering bitterness and vindictiveness."

What follows is a starter sampling of Rondeau's final sixteen years from what he most often referred to as his "riches." As you read, imagine Rondeau as the "maker of fancy diaries," as he referred to them, complete with "Wigwam smoke and Fly Specks a Specialty."

Chapter 22

Throughout the 1950s

New Year's Day, 1951
Belated Monkies

In Evolution there were men and monkies without God's for
millions of years before Bible, myths, liars. God
presumptuously made the first man from a handful of dust
that was not a week old. Let fools be fools and liars
be liars even the kind of monkies that go to church with Bibles.

Lest We Forget

The days went one by one, 1950 is done.
And now it's a random scoot around the sun
1951 has just begun.
We have a diary with us yet
Lest we forget dear Roosevelt...

February 2-3, 1951. Down to zero last night, today 20 above and nice
Sunshine at Saranac Lake. I fletch 30 arrows. I autograph 25 photographs.
I call at commercial printing, Reis Pharmacy and Troy Laundry. I put target heads and broadheads on 12 arrows. I assemble and pack many items
to take to New York Sportsmen's Show.

February 10-11, 1951. Last night 35 below. Today 20 above. Nice Sunshine at Saranac Lake. I buy a cake at food sale. I take down Remington
Rifle and pack for launching for N.Y.C. I mend and wash socks. I sew very

December 29, 1939. Noah with the Pipemakers in Westport, N.Y. Courtesy Jean Burger
Cushman

cute stitches of Red Yarn on my Hermit Vest. 10:30 at Carnival Parade:
Tom Fink and Natalie Bombard crowned King and Queen by Mayor Alton
Anderson. I autograph a few photographs. Later I do fancy stitches of Red
Yarn on my Exhibit Pantaloons. 9 P.M. Walter Winchell "political windbags
a mule telling a donkey he's an ass." I assemble Exhibit property.

February 22, 1951. Calm, mild, beautiful sunshine in New York City.
Breakfast in Pine Room, Belmont Plaza Hotel. 11 a.m. at Blood Bank.
12:30 on T.V. I call on Grace Hudowalski at her Exhibit. I made a record
for Italy (Vocal record). 6 p.m. Made five minute Record for Rod and
Gun Club.

February 23, 1951. Long Island Exhibitor bring me four oysters. Got
cheque for $800.00 from Campbell-Fairbanks. With two men dismantle
and pack in 3 hours.

FAME & $HEKELS

February 27, 1951. Morning Sunshine, then clouds, rain and snow as we go from New York City to Saranac Lake I check out from Hotel Belmont Plaza. I meet Russell Marshall at Grand Central Palace. They load my Replica. We wheel out. 10:30 p.m. Saranac Lake.

March 22, 1951. Very cloudy and cold. Snowflakes in the air at Saranac Lake I paint my Fisherman Hat green.

March 28, 1951. First Robin. Nice Vernal Day. Saranac Lake to AuSable Forks. Call on Dr. A.G. Dittmar. 6 o'clock to Jay with Doctor. 7 o'clock supper with Brotherhood. 9-10 o'clock I speak to about 40 people. Subjects: Cold River, Hermit, Red Patches, Natural history, Old Maids and finally (tale) "Mitchell Micke" Mick Swallowed the Blarney Stone. Midnight to bed at Dittmar's. Good time all day and half the night.

April 4, 1951. "In flowing handwriting," said Eddie Vogt, the columnist of "Our Town" that appears in the Adirondack Daily Enterprise, "come a letter from my good friend, Noah Rondeau." Vogt said he had "been wondering where John was."

Dear Ed,
I observe that you observe that someone observes that perhaps N.J.R. is out of town. Well, to make that we are all talking about the same fellow will say… The Noah Rondeau I know is a queer fellow. Sometimes he's a Dude in New York City Grand Central district; sometimes he's a hermit in the sticks. Sometimes he smells of pretty perfume and sometimes it's just the odor of a woods animal. And he has whiskers not long enough for a primitive Moses but too long for a modern Airedale. Now the mayor of the above measurements boarded the Greyhound Bus and went to Au Sable Forks on Mar. 28th. And at 6 P.M. he went to Jay with Dr. Dittmar. At 7 o'clock he had supper with the Brotherhood Assn. of Jay and Wilmington. At 8 o'clock he listened keenly to the business meeting; from 9 to 10 he spoke to the association as clever as Mitchell Micks that swallowed the Blarney Stone. Mar. 29th at mid-day he dined with the Rotary Club

at Ausable Forks and he spoke 35 minutes in a half an hour. Mar. 31 he returned to Saranac Lake on the night bus and at the moment of scribbling he's at 4 Alpine Terrace.
Noah John Rondeau

April 10. 1951. Calm, Very mild, quite cloudy at Saranac Lake. Received card from David Dittmar and letter from Dr. Ditt. Billy Burger call on me From Pipe Makers; near Westport on west Lake Champlain. We had a Splendid Visit.

April 11, 1951. Cloudy and showers at Saranac Lake. I stay in all day not feeling too good with slight indigestion. Harry S. Truman is not fit for filling a Rat Hole in a pile of stable dung.

April 13, 1951. Cloudy Morning—Then a splendid day with plenty of Sunshine. 8 O clock: I join Sears and Green Leaf Chase. Motor to Lake Clear—pick up Don Bousquet and Motor thru Tupper Lake, Long Lake, Newcomb to Tahawus at 11 O clock. Conference with Mr. Chas. Begor and others. A splendid Dinner at Tahawus' serene hospitality. Returning watched a Grouse 10 ft. from car for 5 minutes. The ride (150 miles) was beautiful.

May 3, 1951. Perfect sunshine and cool air at Lake Clear – Malone. I move with part of my replica from Lake Clear to Malone. Beautiful Mountains, Vallies and Waterways, Grass Greening, Robins Singing. Malone: Noon- I have dinner with Rotary Club and Vaudeville Entertainers. I speak a brief 5 minutes at Franklin Hotel then set up Replica Exhibit. Next day 8-12 at Show I addressed audience twice "A Bear Eat Me Up" and "Micke swallowed the Blarney Stone." I autograph and sell photos.

May 12, 1951. Scattered clouds and a lot of sunshine. On the Train and in New York City. At dawn and on I watch the gulls along the Hudson River. The banks and trees that were winter dead have vernal dress of vernal green and white flowers and purple spikes decked their heads. I call on

FAME & $HEKELS

N.B.C. 2 p.m. On television at 30 Rockefeller Plaza. 8 p.m. I check out. Standard Time on sleeper.

May 13, 1951. Calm and perfect sun at Saranac Lake I watch sunrise from New York Central train. I arrive on sleeper at Saranac Lake at 7 o'clock. 3 o'clock I walk to Peck's Corners. I write 4 letters.

May 14, 1951. A perfect vernal day Saranac Lakes – AuSable Forks. Talk to Madeline Dodge. 10 o'clock on Greyhound bus. 11:15 at AuSable Forks. I call on Dr. A.G. Dittmar. Dinner at Dr. Dittmar's. 3:30 at Dr. Dittmar's office, one tooth extracted. I confab with Madeline Dodge. I walk to McCasland's Hill Top farm. Supper and lodge for the night.

June 26, 1951. Sunshine morning then cloudy at Saranac Lake. I engage a truck to move to Wilmington, N.Y. I pack Hermit Riches.

June 28, 1951. Breakfast at Gateway. I dance at Gateway with Alice.

June 30, 1951. Cold, damp, cloudy morning at Wilmington, N.Y. First customer from Rochester buy photos. I shop at hobby house. Thanks June for thirty June days. Come again June in 1952 after May.

July 7, 1951. Nice Sunshine at Jay Wilmington. Up at Sunrise, I dismantle and pack Replica to move to Wilmington. Breakfast at Gateway Restaurant. Order of Archery and Tackle from L. E. Stemmler Co. P.M. Halsey Payro Family call.

July 22, 1951. Very breezy, a nice Summer day at Wilmington, N.Y. Archers call to show their American f(p)oxophilite [sic] skill by jumping on the bow- bending it, pulling the string then expanding the Fool chest American liberty.

September 4, 1951. A nice September day Wilmington - Indian Falls. I talk 3 hours with Nick O'Reilly. 2 o'clock launch out with Lee Chadeayne.

Call at Lake Placid. Drive to Lodge. Walk to Indian Falls by dusk. Supper, campfire to bed. Dream of bears at Indian Falls.

September 29, 1951. Last night colder than Hell. Today freezing morning at Wilmington, N.Y. I put on Winter underwear, wool sock, Bean boots. I paint my strong boxes varied colors.

October 11, 1951. Morning overcast. Day continues overcast at Wilmington, N.Y. One hot water, cold air, adulation "Holy Bath," beard trim Cold River style. Enthusiastic couple from Saratoga call and see my photo album. 7 o'clock. To Keene Valley with Dittmar's for ADK gathering at Air Port. Mr. Burt led Song Fest and at 8 I speak 50 minutes to over 100 people. Refreshments and home to Wilmington.

November 9, 1951. Breezy last night. Today sunshine, cool air at Wilmington, N.Y. I take down and store Replica platform. I bank the house. Two American Fools scream on the road; next day they enter an old vacant house, then they thumb for a ride. They show in general they are Americans tough, weak-minded and as foolish as Fool Liberty can produce anywhere.

November 14, 1951. Mild, cloudy. 2 P.M. shower at Wilmington. I buy a chicken from Melvin Peck. 10 o'clock I go hunting. I hunt south of Morgan Mountain. I saw a dozen grey squirrel nests, 1 Canadian woodpecker and 1 piliated woodpecker. Nice ground, beautiful woods. Not much game. Predominantly trees, forest is especially scented with wild cinnamon-like odor in new carpet of leaves. Throughout December at Wilmington. Kids call and get Xmas trees. I play violin. Pecks bring me a big supper.

Chapter 23

1952

January 1, 1952. Very mild, breezy, thawing. Snow about gone. Brooks roaring at Wilmington, N.Y. Hear Ye, Hear Ye. I pick up knocked down Replica of Cold River Town Hall and store under cover. Village children call.

> "Lest We Forget"
> The days went by
> One by one.
> 1951: Now, it's a random scoot
> Around the sun
> And 1952 has just begun.
> And we have a diary with us yet
> Least we forget "Dear Roosevelt."
> Roosevelt, President-elect, everlasting ex
> And running yet was Roosevelt till he was dead.
> And now that he's dead and gone to Hell
> Riddance is hard to get. The Democrats are with us yet
> Firing Mc Arthur, Lest we forget Democrat as wind that
> follows Roosevelt.

***

Noah John Rondeau had put in five prosperous years of appearances by the time he penned his customary "Lest We Forget" opening act. Within the first five days of the new year, he had checked the trap line set around the Dodge home a dozen times. Madeline Dodge said when remembering her boarder-friend, "Noah had a humorous way of saying things. He'd

1946. Lt. to Rt. Harold McCasland, Noah, and Clarence Whiteman posing with a trophy buck. The story of "Noah's Lickety-Split Ride on Clarence Whiteman's buck" is told in Life with Noah. Courtesy Clarence Whiteman

set mouse traps with a bit of cheese as he whispered, 'Come to my traps for a vacation and avoid butchery by the neighbor's cat.' Each time he inspected the Victor spring-loaded setups he'd gleefully announce, 'Last night a mouse tried my trap to see if it would work, and it did,'" and each time Madeline congratulated him for a job well done.

Richard Smith retained a fair number of the accounts he and Noah shared as inhabitants on Cold River Hill. "Over the years I began to make notes whenever a particular topic, tiny as it might be, triggered a mental process which revived a memory of a long-forgotten story. Noah told many stories about mice. He said his Cold River Mouse tale "was a science fiction thriller" with an astonishing display of cryogenics.

Smith asked Noah once why he didn't have a pet back at the river. Noah's reply reflected a practical decision for someone who knew the limitations of living where winter's deep snow sealed one's isolation: "A cat is too stuck up. It never kills every mouse or rat and always saves a few for a rainy day and besides, cats tire of mice and would soon be after my birds." Noah would much rather hear a bird sing than hear a cat's yowling. "If one of my birds were killed," he'd say, "I'd have to condemn the cat to death. A dog, on the other hand, has to have something to chase and if not chipmunks and squirrels it would be the deer that come to my garden and walk through my camp yard as friendly as can be with no jumping on me with muddy paws or unnecessary barking at 3 o'clock in the morning." Noah had enough wild pets to enjoy, and he didn't have to feed them when there was often just enough food around in the winter for him.

It was interesting to learn about a few more of the books and maga-

Gary McCalvin and Noah. Courtesy Helen McCalvin Sawatzki

zines in Noah's repertoire of reading matter. Madeline named *Grit* as a newspaper to which he subscribed. "Invisible Government Seen In Busy Washington" was a headline he cut from that paper and pasted into his diary on January 28, 1952. Under the headline he wrote "Must be a Visionary Democrat seeing the 'Invisible'." He said of the *Grit* paper, "It isn't hell."

"Winter could be bitterly cold, but Noah never thought much about it," Madeline went on. One of Noah's daily chores was to chop wood and split kindling for the kitchen range.

"Oh my, but did he know his weather," Madeline continued. "'Well,' he would say, 'we're going to have showers but they won't last so long. You can go out in them and you won't even get too wet.' It might have been clear and sunny when he predicted an oncoming storm but sure as anything, later in the day it would pour.

"Noah wore long underwear year-round," as it was the fashion in the days when he grew up, when a bath once a week or less was held sufficient. I always thought he preferred animals to humans. He respected black bears. And, underneath all his guffaw he was a religious person.

A view of Cold River From below Noah's Hermitage. Photo by author

"After Noah moved in '63, when he went into Smith's hunting camp, he still continued to visit."

Monday, February 23, 1952. Noah did a short "beauty walk" and enjoyed a "Beer at 4 Alpine Terrace" as he inspected Phil McCalvin's new .270 caliber rifle "with Telescopic Sight" before he boarded a Trailways bus, bound for his sixth appearance at New York City's Sportsmen's Show. Upon arriving in Manhattan and checking into room 900 at the Hotel Belmont Plaza, he commented in his journal: "Many of the Hotel remember me of old."

On March 11 he was traveling again, but by Greyhound this time to AuSable Forks. "Call on Dr. Dittmar. 4 Teeth extracted. Ride with Dr. Dittmar to Halsey Payro." Eighteen days later he was back at the dentist's office: "Dr. Dittmar 5 fillings for my Teeth." After he walked to Payro Hill, Halsey Payro drove him back to Wilmington.

His board payment for the month? "I pay March Milk Bill."

The majority of his entries throughout the second half of 1952 cover his activities after moving to his sister Priscilla's farm at her invitation. He

FAME & $HEKELS

Courtesy of Richard J. Smith from Noah's photo album

went about his new enterprise cheerfully.

"I prepare Striped Grass and Lilac Shrubs (Shoots) and High Bush cranberry for transplanting," Noah noted on May 13. There was a flurry of phone calls and activity that day as he readied to "take load of Lumber to Priscilla McCasland's Farm." On May 14 he mailed a payment to the Murray McMurray Hatchery for an order of 236 chicks. Noah's dream of raising chickens had finally become a reality.

Due to his good fortune and the fair amount he received for his appearances, he had put away some savings and could count on paying his board, buying warm clothing and boots for the winter and having money enough to feel some financial security. This gave him the confidence to invest in what he thought would be a money-making scheme. It's speculation, but those who knew him said because of his often desperate struggle to survive, there was a seething unrest to find a way to "keep the wolf away from his door" now that he could not rely on the deserted shacks on Cold River Hill as a refuge.

Chester Rock doesn't remember his Uncle Noah well from when

Chester was a child in the 1940s, but he has young adulthood memories from get-togethers in the mid to late 1950s with Uncle Noah at his parents' Cadyville home and at his Aunt Priscilla and Uncle Sherm's home. Chester also served as family taxi driver, taking his uncle to Au Sable Forks,

July 3, 1952. A hot summer day at Hill Top ranch. I do a lot of hard work: Mowing Hay, weeding garden, building Poultry Ranch Feeding 200 chicks, 2 Pigs, one calf. Feed is high priced and there is so much work attached that success is impossible-very much due to the thief, robber and murderous American goat. St. Patrick (Halsey Payro) bring Ice Cream and Butter Milk. Sumac is a show of light-colored perpendicular spikes. The thief, robber, and murderer, the American government.

July 4, 1952. Clouds and sun. A nice summer day at Hill Top Ranch, Au Sable Forks, N.Y. I do a lot of work, garden and hay. Sister Persilla has gone to Jay to see Mr. Fourth of July to hallow the American Independence anything American government ever done has not been worth a pinch of Hitler's dung to me. Noah John Rondeau

July 11, 1952. A hot summer day after rain at Hill Top. I work on Poultry yard. Hoe beans. An American hawk got one of my prize white leghorns. Give Potato Bugs drink of Paris Green. My first spinach from garden. Evening I go to Cadyville with Payro Family and Sister Priscilla. The Trip was spoiled by 3 fool kids raising Hell in the back seat.

July 13, 1952. A hot summer day at Hill Top ranch, AuSable Forks, N.Y. I chop up big weeds for winter flowers. Set Wigwam Frame in Chick Yard.

October 21, 1952. Ice last night. Today cold morning. Ground partly white and sunshine on Colorful Scenes at Hill Top Ranch. I harvest a bag of cattle beets, beet tops and a pail of potatoes. 90% Sumac Leaves are shed. Climax of autumn is passed.

October 31, 1952. Mild, feeble sun through hazy atmosphere at Hill Top

Peggy McCasland and Mary Louise Coolridge called all made up in Halloween fashion. Radio announcer in Plattsburg says: "Vote next Tuesday. And for car service see Mason's Garage."

November 13, 1952. Ice last night. Today calm and perfect sun perfect autumn day at Hill Top I dig a pail of potatoes. A PLATTSBURG PRESS REPUBLICAN clipping Thurs, Nov.13, 1952: "President elect Eisenhower will sit down with President Truman at 2 P.M. E.S.T. next Tuesday to discuss plans for an orderly exchange of administrations." An orderly! Is Truman afraid that Eisenhower is in danger to become a worse American insult to the American people-, than the weak minded Ass that fired "Douglas MacArthur."

December 16, 1952. Sunshine and few clouds at Hill Top. I kill 4 chickens. Receive 2 Christmas cards. Joe Smith's home burn.

December 20, 1952. Perfect sunshine. Clear and calm at Hill Top. Priscilla Mc Casland go to Plattsburg to see Mr. Santa Claus. I cut up Pig's Head. I put hair remover on calf skin. I fry out Pig Fat. I selvage a can of Booth (Boot) Grease. Lord God! How the money rolls in.

December 25, 1952. A Christmas letter from L. H. Gillies in North Carolina appears on the date. The writer was an early purchaser of Rondeau's guiding services.

Dear Noah:
A gem to me you are in my vision. A friend ever faithful and true.
Whatever your task or your mission you were there at the yoke to do.
I found you to be kind and discerning of others who travel the road
and helped those who were deserving and toted your share of the load.
Now that we have reached the crest and descending the vale below
Let's keep our spirits at best and fires of friendships aglow. When we take
up our trail of our fathers and on to somewhere we pass. I pray we be
like brothers that we be good friends to the last.

Noah's pup tent. Noah claimed he'd lived in a pup tent before staying any longer at Hill Top Ranch. "I recall Uncle Noah boarded with Madeline Dodge while Melvin Peck was finishing up an old camp making it livable for him. Uncle Noah moved his belongings into a teepee beside the camp"- Shelby Richardson. Courtesy Richard J. Smith from Noah's photo album

FAME & $HEKELS

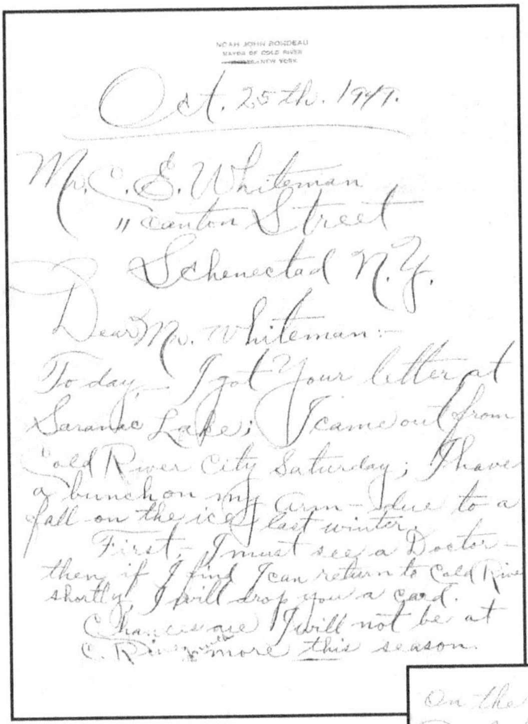

NOAH JOHN RONDEAU
MAYOR OF COLD RIVER
COLD RIVER, NEW YORK

Oct. 25th. 1947.

Mr. C. E. Whiteman
11 Canton Street
Schenectad N.Y.

Dear Mr. Whiteman:—

Today I got Your letter at
Saranac Lake; I came out from
Cold River City Saturday; I have
a bunch on my arm—due to a
fall on the ice last winter.

First; I must see a Doctor—
then; if I find I can return to Cold River
shortly, I will drop you a card.

Chances are I will not be at
C. River any more this season.

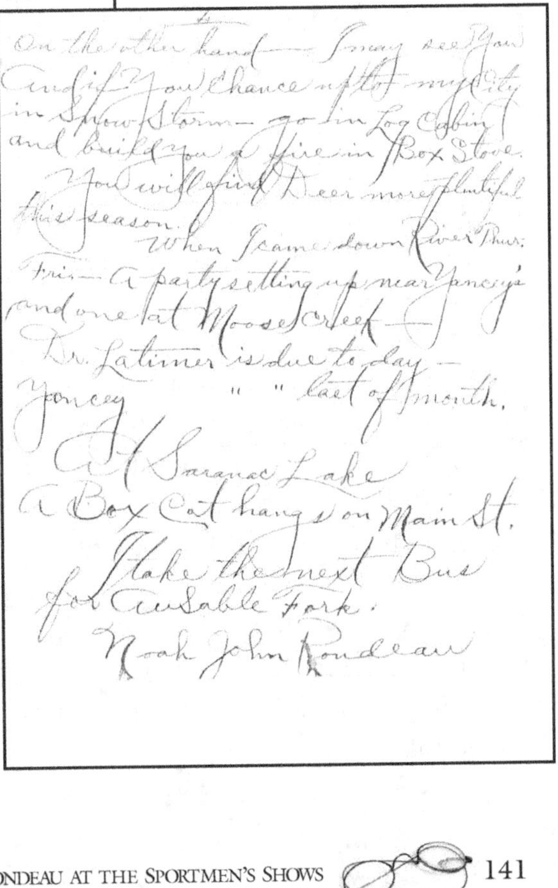

On the other hand — I may see You
and if You chance up to my City
in Snow Storm — go in Log Cabin
and build you a fire in Box Stove.

You will find deer more plentiful
this season.

When I came down River Thur.
Fri.— a party setting up near Yancys
and one at Moose Creek —

Dr. Latimer is due today —
Yancey   "   " last of month.

At Saranac Lake
a Box Cat hangs on Main St.

I take the next Bus
for Ausable Fork.

Noah John Rondeau

Chapter 24

1953

January 1, 1953 New Year's Day

"Lest We Forget"
The days went by one-by-one 1952 is over now it's a random scoot around the sun and 1953 is just begun. We have a diary with us yet least we forget the American ass that followed Roosevelt and in so of the Klu Kluxer the weak minded fired Mac Arthur to Jan. 20th he's with us yet then to Missouri he must get. Billions in the hole by Roosevelt is reminder we can't forget and by Truman, billions more plus insults never before.

It was the first week in 1953 when Noah penned a reply to the Essex County Department of Public Welfare's request that he contact the Social Security Administration. It would not be the last time he was required to provide information.

The paper trail to explain his business with Social Security is cold at this point. Richard Smith and Noah's nephew, Burton Rondeau, agreed it might have had to do with some follow-up regarding his income and what he'd earned during his time at the North Pole.

Prior to being employed as a substitute Santa, Noah bought a new rifle. That purchase got him in trouble with the Essex County Department of Social Services. Smith inherited that long gun. "It was a Remington Automatic .30-.06 rifle he bought early in 1951," said Smith. "Some people thought he had made a small fortune from his [sportsmen's] show days and lectures." There's no clear explanation at this point, but sometime around the end of 1949 or '50 he applied for and received welfare assistance. He was getting on in years at that time. Someone must have helped Noah to get it—maybe spoke up about what he needed to survive in Essex County. Somebody must have understood he'd come out of the woods, felt he was unemployable regardless of his fleeting fame and put him on the dole."

The welfare department seemed indifferent to his plight. "When he took the job as a substitute Santa Claus at the North Pole in Wilmington," Burton and Richard said, "they made him pay back

Courtesy of Ruth King

the value of the rifle." In the division's mind, if Rondeau had enough money to buy a new rifle, then he had been awarded too much welfare. "Noah was put out. He claimed they made him 'pay double for the rifle.'"

Burton said, "Uncle Noah could be a cranky character—the old-style independent stump-kicker kind when it came to accepting a decision made by a white shirt and tie county government man. "Noah found that in many ways living on the outside in the 1950s was shaping up to be very different from his 1940s poor but independent backwoods days.

***

January 3, 1953. Very Cloudy. Snowed 6" at Hill Top. I write Social Security Baltimore, Md. Pauline Collins called to buy $10.00 worth of

Plumbley dock Long Lake.
Courtesy of Jim Plumbley.

money (change). The Milk Man call, in snow storm. Late at night Snow Plow go by in the hill country.

January 19, 1953. I send Cold River Town Hall key to Paul Van Dyke, Forman, N.Y.

January 21, 1953. Calm, Mild Cloudy at AuSable Forks, N.Y. T Day Roman Catholic priest call on me for 30 min. confab; Subjects-Evolution, God, Communism. Lewis XVI beheaded 1793. [Next to a DAILY NEWS clipping and photo a beautiful French actress with the title "Denise Favors Grassy Knoll" Rondeau wrote:] I met Miss Denise Darrel in New York at Rockefeller Plaza Studio 3 Dec. 1, 1949. N.J.R.

Jan. 22, 1953. Eisenhower is best we ever had as President and he choose best cabinet ever called together but too late, we had FDR, Truman 20 years too long every wage earner must pay over $5,000 dollar tax to balance out of hole. I'm not interested in Fool American gods. To Hell with them.

January 24 1953. Mild, Overcast, Light Shower at AuSable Forks, N.Y. I read and Write. Priscilla go to town. I want President Eisenhower to consider coming out of League of Nations. Then confer with Cabinet-Then American People of US. Then, if a majority are in favor, I want Him to announce to the world at once, that We are out…and I want Him to call the Amer. Soldiers home at once. And I want Him to send appropriate apology where we have been traitors and murders.

February 1, 1953. A flock of snow birds call and again in my pigweeds.

February 6, 1953. Ausable Forks -Mild Spring like on Top of Hill. I watch the Wind gather Snow in its arms and whirl it up two feet high and scatter it like vanishing smoke. I call on Dr. Dittmar impressions for teeth. Clayton Burnah, an American French Catholic contributed head menial monstrosity has another brainless spasm.

February 21, 1953. I have civilizations distemper. That's what people call a cold.

February 20, 1953. I call on Dr. I ride to town with Halsey Payro. I call on Dr. Dittmar. Dr. Ditt put plastic dentures in my mouth then he make me bite on them and then he make me say "Mississippi." I'm pretty mad about Ditt. (Then he follows with some code.)

February 25, 1953. At Top of Hill. Clouds and much sunshine Nice winter weather. Mid day I take three hours at beauty sleep. The sleep worked; the beauty was a failure.

March 23, 1953. I look over my rusty nails and saws and conclude I'm nearly as rich as I was a year ago. I hear first chipmunk. I also autographed 28 photographs. [Several days later Noah recorded following "Crows have morning JUBILE. Priscilla McCasland have another Brain Storm to tell me, about, Chipmunks of a year ago; and a Puppy that pissed in the porch—and a cat I tossed on Jackson Hill in 1891.

April 21, 1953. Very cloudy. Snow is going. AuSable Forks. I read "TRUE" magazine. I write lines. Dr. A.G. Dittmar move Dentist Equipment to Plattsburg.

April 25, 1953. Cloudy and little showers. AuSable Forks, N.Y. Robins whisper and laugh and song sparrows jingle their small change.

April 28, 1953. I watched the grass greening and listened to vernal song birds and spent some time on my books.

May 1, 1953. Rain L.N. Today very cloudy at AuSable Forks. Welcome May Days. Rise Plants that were dead dress them up and put flowers on their heads

May 9, 1953. Since USA government is not worth a pinch of dung why? don't a dozen, sober-minded men of Fla. take Russel Long and kick him until he's bruised all over and positively rupture his internal then without surgery, medicine or clergy put him in a stall and if he's not dead in 24 hours repeat kicking, when dead cremate so his dust will not hurt a little child. (Rondeau's comment is in reference to a newspaper clipping he had glued to this diary page.)

May 11, 1953. Clouds and Sun, a perfect Day at Hill Top. I make several Random Scoots in pasture. Leaves are generally half-size. Early Flowers are blooming. [Noah's favorite flower was the bloom of the partridge berry, a small blossom with a slight fragrance, a little tiny plant "but the sweetest thing in the woods," is how he described it.]

May 13, 1953. (A newspaper clipping Noah saved read, "As to Russia General Eisenhower said flatly that if we're forced into a shooting war with the Soviet, we'll win and he thinks the Kremlin know it..."). Rondeau wrote: "Now, the Russians will be SCART so they will put a chapel with Roman Catholic collar on every street corner in the communist empire. Every Russian will go to confession three times per day until scapegoats of Israel scream in the wilderness like scared cats."

May 14, 1953. Very Cloudy fog and showers at AuSable Forks, N.Y. I watch the weather so it don't run away. Starlings line in a row on insulated

Electric wire at Alice's Shanty. A Northern Flicker steps proudly in garden near my window.

June 6, 1953. At Wilmington. Lightning Shower L.N. Breakfast - Restaurant. I call on Joe Rondeau. A hell of a fall at Strawberry Roan.

June 7, 1953. Wilmington to AuSable Forks. Shower L.N. Cloudy Morning. 10 O'clock shower on Wilmington Bridge. Call at Melvin Peck. Call at North Pole. Long walk-Tired. Rest at Joe Rondeau's. Chicken (Old Rooster) dinner. Ride to AuSable with Orville Rondeau. Spring Hens re set; Old Roosters make Sunday Dinners.

Big Horn camp, Shattuck Clearing and Forest Ranger Lucias Russell. Courtesy of Earl F. Russell

June 24, 1953. Extra, no matter what the Rosenberg's were according to peoples mind or scream now that they are electrocuted anyone with intelligence would conclude Julius and Ethel are harmless on way to dust but it's clear to any who read a N.Y. paper that had it not been for police patrol, mounted police and other guards there would have been at the funeral home the riot that Brooklyn never had before. [Several days later Noah penned a second opinion. Extra. Now, that Julius and Ethel have been murdered by the American Govt of the U.S.A. I hope the glamorous fool public is satisfied! But They are not! Satisfied!!

June 30, 1953. Sunshine and breeze, a hot day at Top of Hill. Thanks June for sun and rain blooming flowers and growing hay, lightning bugs and whippoorwills, ozone nights and thirty days. Thanks June for baby chicks. Visit Saranac Lake. Lake Clear, then Bill Petty, Tom Peckham at fish hatchery. Thanks for 30 days in June and commensute in schools. Thanks I saw advancing youth in best of life and best of June. Even in Winter on snowshoes precious are thoughts of June. Lilac's scent, apple blossoms under June moon and June grass in June perfume in June breeze in June.

July 1, 1953. Warm Sunshine, Overcast, Scattered Clouds, some breeze. 10 P.M. Evening: 2 little shows. Good morning at Hill Top. July: Take 31 days before August. Excuse our Black Flies. Mr. Raymond Greenier call from Mass.

July 6, 1953. At dawn: Robins cheer up. To Day: Overcast. I read and write. 3 P.M. Shower Then More Showers. And More Showers. I'm 70 years old today; and now, I'll be doing 71 before I do 72—Madame Curie died 1934, Noah John Rondeau born 1883.

July 22, 1953. On Top of Hill. I watched the hill and vallies, so they don't run away. Hollyhocks are blooming atop of spike.

August 2, 1953. I take insulation, paper and outer boards off from Town Hall replica.

August 11, 1953. Nice Day: Overcast. Nice fiery sunset. At Hill Top. I take roof off from Cold River Town Hall Replica. Peggy gathers apples for chickens. Blackberry Pickers get good results. Peggy Mc Casland leave Her Doll and crib out in the Pig Weeds.

August 29, 1953. The fields appear overripe, wooded hillsides have hidden brown only seen by people of maturing years. It's different tender vernal green it's approaching poly colors that we'll value in September.

August 31, 1953. Hot dry weather At Hill Top. I look over my new books. Thanks, August for 31 days—Growing corn and squeaking crickets, Ripening Fields and Happy Summer Days.

The empty hermitage was often used as a backdrop scene for photographs.
Courtesy of Bob Bates

September 1, 1953. September you're between August and October. You make the earth and sun change node. You paint the each and forest in poly colors and you bring the deer a brand new coat.

September 9, 1953. A nice summer day. Sun and Clouds and Breeze At Hill Top. I take beauty walk in woods beyond Stone Gap: Pine, Poplar and Birch-Golden Rod, Juniper and Asters (Code).

September 10, 1953. Hot Sunshine. A nice summer day. On Hill Top (code). Six Payros call. An Aerial Plane come within a mile and make a sharp hair pin and go back parell to first line leaving two white lines in the sky—each 1 degree wide hat persist for nearly an hour.

October 15, 1953. Perfect autumn day on top of hill. Hair cut, beard trim Cold River fashion.

October 21, 1953. Nice autumn day at Top of Hill. Peggy Mc Casland, 3 years old drop a toy metal dog and break his tail off. Peggy is the best girl I ever saw to break off dog's tail.

October 25, 1953. Nice autumn continues in Ausable Valley. Most of the leaves are gone and left the trees nude. I walk to oak grove. Acorns gone.

Left to right Dr. Latimer Jr, Noah, Dr. Latimer Sr. camp Seward Cold River.

(Code) Legally: deer Hunting season open; and Woods are closed because of dry weather."

November 3, 1953. Nice sunshine. No thanks politic. This is Fool Election Day to Hell with it.

November 5, 1953. A sample of 1st snow on the ground. A nice day at Hill Top. Ike and Mamie hide in shelter at Capitol at make believe "Balm Rade." I wish Amer. U.S. would put on a law to make people register and vote; So I could continue not voting and defy the American fool law. Noah John Rondeau

November 26, 1953. Among the hills Thanksgiving. Glad I'm an atheist but no thanks to God for that. Glad I found God a myth and "myth" is not anything. Thanks evolution, science, knowledge. I'm not jumping pearly gate to slide on sea of glass and no thanks to fool God for that. AuSable Forks I call at AuSable Forks, Priscilla Mc Casland swept in my bedroom, make my bed, and for first time in over a year she wash window and mirror and she put clean cloth on dresser and no brain storm.

December 7, 1953. Priscilla Mc Casland sweeps my bedroom and makes my bed. First time in over three months and she has another brainstorm again. I keep her in offensive and follow her up so she don't make a point.

December 11, 1953. Generous clouds and stingy Sunshine at Hill Top. I call at AuSable Forks. Priscilla Mc Casland sweep my Bed Room, and make my Bed; and First time in over a year she wash Window and Mirror and she put clean cloth on Dresser and no Brain Storm. What in hell is the matter with Her? [Noah apparently forgot that his sister performed the same tasks less than a month before.]

December 15, 1953. Yesterday the forest was decked in style. Last night: Thaw caught cold. Today Breeze, clouds, Sun. 2" frozen snow, bit of ice—spots of bare ground among the Hills. I write Christmas cards.

December. 23, 1953. Snowflakes frolic in the air and sun clouds and breeze frolic too. Peggy Mc Casland born in 1949.

December 28, 1953. Cloudy and cool at Lewis, N.Y. Mrs. Lidie Benedict call. Jack and Mrs. Goff and 2 Boys call. We kill soman big Deer and Bear in living room that I have to walk on Livers. Woodrow Wilson born 1856.

December 31, 1953. ½" Snow last night. To Day snow blanches ground, roofs and dead grass. Lidie and Violet make Home Made Bread. Lidie laundry my fancy Blue Denim overalls. Kath and Scotty come for the night.

Memoriam on the 12 signs of the Zodiac: If you wish to appear wise astrologically let down your pants and show off your guts.

(Next a quote from a newspaper clipping appears.) "The man of the signs first began appearing in almanacs in the 15th century and he is regarded highly only by astrologers and the foolish."

(Noah says to this): "Then what's the difference between wisdom of fools and foolishness fraudulent astrologers?"

Chapter 25

1954

In 1954, the same year Noah took his first and only cross-country trip to Birmingham, Alabama his Hill Top life had gone from pleasant to uncomfortable—but only in his view. By now some distance had come between all the public appearances and media attention he'd been receiving and his life at his sister Priscilla McCasland's on Rolling Mill Hill Road in Au Sable Forks. While he enjoyed the quiet and solitude of his private bedroom, Priscilla's place did not have the conveniences found at the McCalvin and Dodge homes. Drinking water was dipped from a well across the road and carried home in buckets. The old homestead lacked things of material value, but did provide comfortable basics. It was high on the hill, and Noah would say on some days it seemed to him he could almost reach up and touch the fleecy clouds. And, as he stood in the pasture on a quiet summer day, he was flooded with childhood memories.

Initially, Noah enjoyed setting up his poultry scheme. His daily jottings reveal the work and his contributions. He did much in managing the vegetable patch, but also joked how he walked "around and estimate[d the] value of my Pig Weeds."

Then, over time, an occasional blast of pure independent stubbornness surfaced. He did become prickly when things got to be too much for him. He resented directives from anyone, including sister Priscilla. Hubbub created by the two foster boys was also like a festering wound. The boys were boys. The more they heard Noah tell them to stay out of his room, *nobody go in, don't touch anything, keep your hands off my things*, the more they enjoyed pestering him. It was more of a game for them than their intentionally being malicious. "He didn't need them in his life," Shelby Payro, Noah's niece, pointed out about the boys. Noah preferred to be alone—it wasn't any different from the way he

felt after a long exhibition event or when he was back on Cold River Hill. One minute he could be showered with attention—and the next, he was perfectly happy to go about his business without anyone around. Priscilla understood his independent streak. Her brothers William and Alex had similar characteristics.

Richard Smith's bear trap cabin, near Duck Hole.

Priscilla understood Noah's balkiness. She also knew when she invited him to move in that he would need to adapt his once solitary style to a home life that included Priscilla, the comings and goings of her children Sadie, Jeannette and Jesse, their families, and two foster children. In reality it wasn't bad when all the plusses were considered, even though Noah would say he "liked crowds best when they were going the other way."

***

February 18, 1954. 30–42 above. Very calm and perfect sun at AuSable Forks. Planes hang white lines on invisible sky hooks. I put ladder against camp as precaution against fire.

Mary Dittmar and Noah. Courtesy Dr. Adolph G. Dittmar, Jr.

March 6, 1954. 20 to 30 above zero. Clouds wind bits of snow. On the Hill, AuSable Forks. P.M. Snow and wind make blusters as starting to jump over the Moon. In weeks robins will come from South; and fray the snow out of the bluster; and demand sunshine in which to sing and whisper. 11 P.M. Adlai Stevenson speak. Just like a Democrat - Damn good liar.

April 5, 1954. 32 above zero. Nice sunshine On the Hill. 8:30 - 9:00 P.M. President Eisenhower speak from the Capitol. I make batch of Eternity Tea.

April 10, 1954. 54 above zero. Very cloudy at AuSable Forks. First Blue Bird appears on Clothes Line Post. I get large Bear Skin, and Beaver Mittens from my store.

April 19, 1954. I saw Earl A. Vosburgh steal a muskrat from my trap in 1920. (Noah wrote in response to a newspaper clipping entitled "It Sure Hurt Pop." The article was about a father who forewarned his son before he commenced paddling that "this is going to hurt me more than it will hurt you." Shortly afterwards the father was taken to the hospital for treatment for a dislocated shoulder. Noah wrote:) "Yes, Leslie Orr, 30 seconds after paddling the boy if a stranger walked in and saw the boy staggering on the floor blind with tears with his little face turning blue because he can't get his breath and the little tongue crippling back in his little throat...Yes, Leslie Orr, you are a wise man to thrash your little boy until you dislocated your shoulder. Wish it were your Fool neck."

April 29–30, 1954. Perfect Vernal Sunshine at AuSable Hills. I take beauty walk in pasture and grove. The walk was lovely but my beauty failed to cope with the Sunshine. Thanks for 30 April Vernal days, that lengthen sunshine days, that liquidize snow that runs down hills, and rise the River that foams and sings. Thanks for swelling buds that break to bloom flowers to make honey and thanks for greening grass to fill the barn full of hay. Thanks for changes from March to May so many things set to make summer days. Come again April after March and stay to May in 1955.

May 24, 1954. A perfect Vernal day at Hill Top Farm in AuSable Valley. Under apple trees the ground is speckled with blossom petals. I plant beets, carrots, turnips seeds, squash, pumpkin, New Zealand spinach, pansies and nastialrums.

May 25, 1954. Breezy A Handful of Sunshine a Bushel of Clouds in Au Sable Valley. I fit second row of Logs on New Cabin. I add spinach to my collection.

June 7, 1954. Rain last night. Today very cloudy. Breeze, shower two hours – sun in AuSable Valley. Robins that left nest 5 days ago are good flyers. I overhaul cases and boxes getting ready to move to Wilmington, Adirondack Sportsmen's Show.

June 13, 1954. Rain last night. Today a Bushel of Clouds a Handful of Sunshine I finish log cabin. Ready to move. I paint eyebrow pencils. Priscilla Mc Casland return from L.I.

June 28, 1954. Sun Shine in the window. 4 P.M. wet with thunder. (A letter Noah received from Rudolph G. Wiezel appears.)

My Dear Reverend Rondeau,

Your exuberant message from the North Woods after a judicious spell of silence was most welcome. You are, it seems, as vigorous and active as an enterprising showman should be. I am sure that behind all of the circus you are still able to convey authentic Adirondackana to a few deserving and appreciative tourists. Our mutual friend, Dutch Heil wrote me that after the Fourth of July he accessioned Whiteface (Mt.) the hard way, cooped up in a car seated behind a steering wheel. He regretted not finding the hermit about the exhibition grounds.

By the way it is ten years ago -about this time, the last part of July, that we had the last Pow Woo in the inner sanctum of the lodge before the Great Medicine Man's own Wigwam facing the rising moon that sailed high over Santanoni and Kuchakrhea (sic). For some reason or another we failed to take minutes of that meeting or give an interview to the press with the fatal result that the profound thoughts and opinions borne of that somber session are now irretrievably lost to posterity. All kidding aside, I realize ten years with devastation of storm, fire in the woods and aging bodies have made a repetition of that meeting impossible. It only serves to sharpen the memory of that, and other moments in the more elusive retreats of the Cold River country.

I read about the drought and heat in the Adirondacks and fear that especially the blow down tracts are again in danger. What about that reported fire in the Cold River this Spring? Was there very much to it?

September 3, 1954. Last night lightning, thunder. Today cloudy, cool at Wilmington Sport Show. Show closed at 4 P.M. No crowd. State troopers call P.M. "How many deer do you kill each year? What's in the kettle?"

September 18, 1954. Very cloudy 2-4 P.M. then sunshine at Wilmington Grove. I go to North Pole with N.J. party (3 men, 4 little boys). And on to gate. Confab with John Morehead. I have Santa order to bring me an old maid for Christmas.

September 29, 1954. Perfect September Sun at Wilmington Grove. After dark American Fools of American liberties shoot several shots in parking lot then they draw near to my cabin and shoot a few more shots. When I step out of camp they turn a light on me and I start toward them. They run like guilty American dogs. To hell with that American blood and American flesh.

November 10, 1954. Sun and clouds at Wilmington. I finish fancy wash. Call on Grant Smith. I do final packing to follow the robins to Birmingham, Alabama.

November 11, 1954. A nice November day. From Wilmington to Saranac Lake. I ride to Saranac Lake with Mr. and Mrs. Grant Smith. I put up for the night at 4 Alpine Terrace. I call on W. E. Petty.

November 12, 1954. Nice November day at Saranac Lake. I meet with W. Petty and I call at the bank. 4:45 I board greyhound bus on way to New York City.

November 15, 1954. Quite cloudy, evening rain at Birmingham, Alabama. Splendid rest after 48 hours on greyhound bus. 7 o'clock Blue Jay called. P.M. beauty sleep. Mr. Willett called for news from the Hermit. We all go for supper at Mr. and Mrs. L.H. Gillies.

(Clipping from newspaper.) Troy, N.Y. Upstate New York has 600,000 more voters than New York City. Ives will be elected by a majority of 450,000. Signed: A Successful Predictor.

Noah comments: "The above printed voice is from an American prophet who has a weak mind. If wrong he'll hide and be silent. If okay he believes he can. The public will know he's a looser."

November 22, 1954. Cloudy and calm at Birmingham, Alabama. I write letters and cards. P.M. I have two hours of beauty sleep. With L.H. Gillies, I look at pictures, arrowheads and read poems. We spin local yarns and catch Musk Rats, make wild meat pie.

November 28, 1954. A clipping from a Birmingham News titled: "Thought You Were Dying?" Noah wrote: "When you think your dead or going to die, it's a sure sign that you're not dead. People who are dead don't so."

December 19, 1954. Very cloudy, speck of snow in air. Birmingham, Alabama. Visit with L. H. Gillies. Tracking big buck. We shoot at deer. Shake tree deer ran. Hunting bear. Hit bear in foot with hatchet. Drag bear out of woods. That Bear don't know to this day that is he is dead.

December 31, 1954. New Year's Eve. Cloudy and mild. 3 P.M. shower. The year 1954 was good for me. Many good experiences so that the last half was more satisfactory than the first.

Chapter 26

1955

The end of April 1955 found Noah living in his Town Hall replica in Wilmington, N.Y.'s Pine Grove. The Warren Terry family lived within easy walking distance based on the number of "calls" he mentioned, visiting with young Bonnie Terry.

Throughout the end of May Noah busied himself in his usual spring way, planting flowers and vegetables. Raising honeybees and building "cylindrical beehives" continued to be a project for Noah throughout the 1950s.

Noah John was seventy-two when Bill Benware helped him set up his exhibit at Keeseville on the 21st of August.

This once rugged and determined character had never expected to find himself publicizing the wilderness character of the Adirondacks, or spending an afternoon drinking Manhattans with thirty-two New York State Senators during a Sportsmen's Show in Albany. Now he was content to kick back wherever he could find a place to settle around Wilmington to garden and raise bees.

Courtesy Richard J. Smith from Noah's photo album

Left to right Bill Barzler, Fred Studder, Phil Rumbolt, and Bill White 1946. Noah had gained a new audience following his appearances at the Sportsmen's Shows.
Courtesy Fred Studer

Courtesy Bill Frenette

Courtesy Charles E. Thomas

***

January 6, 1955. Nice Sunshine and just breeze enough to make Pines wave their Hands. At 8507-7th. Ave. N. Birmingham Alabama. I brand Underwear, and Tie "Ala." Happy Day in Dixie

January 7, 1955. Cool last night. To Day: Calm and perfect Sunshine at Birmingham 8 a.m. I go to Town with L.H. Gillies ride to 73rd St. With Mrs. Houston. Confab Dr. Scott and His Mother and then we go to 20th. St. on Bus. Shop on 1st Ave and 20th St. – Back Home by Bus and Taxi. 7 P.M. Mr. Gillies and I go to Scout Meeting with Mr. Walker, Scouts have business meeting; Then Gillies and I speak; Then Scouts practice their training take photo Two Ladies come in and serve coffee and cake sell Autographed Photographs.

March 6. 1955. A newspaper clipping glued in the hermit's diary on this date says: "It is a crime to attempt to commit suicide in the U.S." Noah pens: "Anyone attempting suicide should make it a success, then U.S. Big Business can't do anything about it but, in case of failure it's occasion for arrest before judge, listen to grant, pose for photo, controlled writer fool newspaper, pay fine and go to jail, get lice, bed bugs and coffee not fit to drink. To hell with a country not fit to live in where suicide in not allowed."

April 18, 1955. Nice Sunshine on Trailway-Virginia to N.Y. City. 7:00 a.m. in Pa. from South I get soil for cup. At N.Y. City 11:30 am to 11:45 P.M. shift: Trailway to Greyhound. 1:15 a.m. Einstein died.

April 19, 1955. Cloudy and showers. Albany to Wilmington N.Y. on Greyhound. I store baggage in Cold River Town Hall. 9 a.m. Keeseville Met Dr. Bull. 1 P.M at Wilmington on Greyhound. Dead and green-grass from Pattersville, N.Y.

April 20, 1955. Cool, Cloudy. I call at my Town Hall. Build first fire in Drum Stove in 5 months. Call on Bonnie Terry before breakfast. Again:

Call on Bonnie after dinner; we tell big love stories.

April 21, 1955. Cloudy and Cool All day At Wilmington N.Y. Letter from – Mitchell. Covert. Evening: Frank Sprague and family call.

April 29, 1955. Sunshine at Cold River replica at Wilmington, N.Y.

May 25, 1955. At Wilmington I make pozy bed and plant sunflower, morning glory, phlox, marigolds, panzies and nasturtums.

May 28, 1955. I sow beet seeds, radish, carrots, swiss chard and morning Glory.

May 30, 1955. A nice day, full of clouds and sunshine at Wilmington, N.Y. I plant 15 Hills of cucumber seeds, some onion sets and Sun Flowers. Shirley Peck in Her 12 year done a wash, big enough, and good enough, to be a Credit to any woman. Evening: I go with Terry's and plant 5 Lilac Trees, on Terry's Building Lot.

June 30, 1955. Sun and clouds at Wilmington. N.Y. Thanks June for 30 days for vernal

Bette O'Hern on Cold River hill. Author and his wife Bette. Author's photo.

green and growing hay and Robins nest in cedar tree. Thanks for blooming flowers and Whippoorwills among trees, bridal wreaths and buttercups and working honey bees. Thanks for ozone in fair evenings on lilac scent in fresh breeze and narrow valleys among high peaks at Wilmington, Jay and Keene. Come again June after next May won't be too soon regardless of politics in 1956.

July 1, 1955. Hi July where in hell have you been since just before last Aug.?

July 2, 1955. I work on Spruce Cylindric Bee Hive at Wilmington. Quite cloudy 3 pm rain.

July 3, 1955. A hot Summer Day that wilt Squash Leaves on green vines. At Wilmington N.Y. Song Sparrows are singing and jangling their small change.

July 4, 1955. A very hot day-Wilmington-Jay. I go with Terry's, to celebration at Jay. Saw: Grant Joy, Boz Smith, Bill Hathaway, (of Lewis;) and Gib Manley, Mrs. Bruce, Rodric Rogers, Payros, Margret Madden, Crane, Charles Osgood, James Mickelson; Howard Moody, Asa King, Peter Breen, Bill Patterson, Ben Dodge, Carl Dodge.

July 25, 1955. (Title of newspaper clipping glued on this date read "Georgia Preacher Victim of Faith was bitten yesterday afternoon by a rattle snake that he had picked up in his

Bette O'Hern by the plaque that marked Knolls heritage.
Author's photo.

arms during a revival meeting to demonstrate that because of his faith in God he was immune to the snake's venom."

Noah wrote: "It's careless and rude of God to let his rattle snake bite his fool preacher and worse of God to let the fool die after the snake bit the fool."

August 21, 1955. A hot summer day and breezy at Wilmington. 11 o'clock I go to Keenseville. Dinner at Bill Benwar. I set up exhibit on duty attending exhibit until 10:30. Midnight. Home at Wil.

August 22, 1955. Hot sun a.m. P.M. Showers, Thunder and hail. At Wilmington. My pumpkins are putting on gold. "Pumpkin gold" is my choice color for floor paint. Even in cloudy gloom it hints sunshine.

September 3, 1955. Perfect September Sunshine. At Wilmington. I beauty walk among Gardens, Bee Hives and ripening Pumpkins.

September 9, 1955. Last Night: Killing Frost. Today: Nice Sunshine at Wilmington a.m.: I gather 2 kinds of Squash, 2 Pumpkins and a bushel of cucumbers. P.M. – I call at my Replica in Covert's Grove: And I gather 2 pecks of White Pine Cones; And some Juniper Berries. Morning: Coldest yet; Not a Honey Bee in sight; Lighting Board wet and froze. Perkin's Dog make savage race at me.

September 10, 1955. Last Night: Just enough rain drops on the roof to play Yankee Doodle. To Day: Very Windy; Sun and Clouds at Wilmington, N.Y. Mrs. Anna Lewis, bring me a generous box of ripe Tomatoes fresh from Her Garden.

September 12, 1955. Sunshine and cool atmosphere. At Wilmington. I knock down a handmade old desk and salvae nails and boards preparing to building a Bee Hive. I gather 60 Pistils of May Gold Seeds.

September 20, 1955. Windy and warm sun at Wilmington, N.Y. (Code) I wash more quilt blocks. I gather Lilac Seed. To Day: Back to my long handles, underwear.

FAME & $HEKELS

September 25, 1955. Clouds and Sun. Cool atmosphere at Wilmington, N.Y. I call at my Town Hall Replica. I gather a bushel of Pine Cones. Yom Kippur begin at Sunset.

September 26, 1955. Clouds and Sun, and Cool Atmosphere, early in Autumn at Wilmington, N.Y. I look my fabric over to make quilt blocks and I count my riches. Autumn Colors are climaxing on Morgan Mountain.

October 1, 1955. Nice cool more clouds than sun at Wilmington. I adjust 8 cleat in Bee Hive. Melvin Peck, 2 yrs old call on me and we go to Peek a Boo Harvest Bee.

October 2, 1955. Last night's frost blanched grass that had been green in crisp foliage on bordering trees that at sunrise poured a shower of leaves at Wilmington N.Y. I call at my Town Hall Mrs. Ernest La Pine says, "Autumn Colors are at Climax Best."

October 12, 1952. Sunshine continues. I put in a good day sorting sunflower seeds, counting my riches and taking beauty sleep. This Oct. 12 is like Oct. 12 in 1492 in which Columbus did not see America and before Columbus was born Scandinavians built a tower of stone at Newport and established "mooring" rocks miles west of Hudson Bay.

I count my riches, holes and patches. Honeybees are busy carting syrup in sunshine. I eradicate grass out of garden. Fool American time set back one hour today and how much am I offered for the daylight I saved the last four months.

2 AM Fool American clock set back one "fool hour." Cold, some clouds some sunshine and breeze with a snowflake frolic 4 PM a little flock of tree sparrows fed on ragweed weeds.

October 23, 1955. Hard freeze last night; Sunrise beautiful on West Mts. At Wilmington. Elms, Apple Tree and Maples are bare And Lilacs are green and Poplars are yellow. 7 P.M. Howard Moody and family call on me.

October 24, 1955. Cool, Clouds and breezy. 4:30 P.M. shower-lightning and thunder. At Wilmington. I'm very busy doing nothing; And going no where.

November 4, 1955. Quite Cloudy and a bit cool at Wilmington, N.Y. I bank Grover Cartwright's Bee Hive. I cut boards to make crib Box to hold Hay around Bee Hives for winter protection for Honey Bees.

November 5, 1955. Very Cloudy-Snow on Mountains and foot hills. Within a mile of 'Blow Street' and Snow Flakes in air in Valley. At Wilmington I nail board together and make a Bee Hive Crib. The Parrakeet got in a Pan of Kerosene.

December 18, 1955. Cloudy and mild. At Wilmington I overstitch 6 buttonholes and darn I put on winter wool underwear (arctic). Warren Terry busy putting up Christmas Tree

December 19, 1955. Cloudy and moderate temp. At Wilmington, N.Y. Mel and Benji Peck butcher Warren's Pig.

December 24, 1955. Quite cloudy and mild at Wilmington, N.Y. I call at my Town Hall. I receive 11 Xmas. Cards.

December 25, 1955. Breezy last night. To Day: Breezy, cool and cloudy at Wilmington, N.Y. 8 a.m. I am Santa Claus at Terrys Christmas Tree. I got a wool Sweater. Bonnie and Gary are busy. Evening: I call at Joe Rondeau's.

Dec. 31, 1955. Radio is an American son-of-a-bitch wreck to the mind. (Beside a newspaper clipping of Harry Truman smiling, Noah wrote:) "The one showing his teeth is the traitor, he kept Dexter White in government office after the 'red herring' knew that White was a spy and later he promoted White and sent him out alone internationally to represent people of the USA. To hell with American traitor Harry S. Truman.

Chapter 27

1956

"The Day after beginning the year," Noah dashed off across the first page of his new journal. It was January 2, 1956, and Rondeau was apparently still boarding at Warren Terry's home in Wilmington, a village with a population of 574. The first of the month was a time to sew "fancy stitches on Blue Denim Patches" and calculate the distance of the earth from the sun, taking into consideration "minus 4,212,000 miles for aphelion," as Noah wrote next to his figures.

What was Noah doing and thinking and enjoying all this time throughout his boarding house years in Wilmington?

For one thing, he noted he sold some of the possessions that had served him at Big Dam.

Noah enjoyed living in Wilmington. Morgan Mountain is a small peak directly north of the grove where he parked his replica, and behind Santa's Workshop. The entire range was called the Morgan Range, now changed to Stephenson Range, both area family names. He frequently hunted south of Morgan Mountain and often commented on its beautiful woods— "nice grounds... Not much game. Predominantly trees." He often noted that during autumn the "forest is especially scented with wild-cinnamon-like odor in new carpet of leaves."

Richard Smith said Noah had few thoughts of ever going back to visit Cold River, except when Smith talked about a homecoming. Richard said, "I gently tried to twist his arm."

Noah's life was as he wished it: Cold River remained a far-off love. He'd write, "I was watching a red squirrel select a spruce cone, take it up a tree to an overhanging dead limb where he prepared to do a jig on the limb and

Courtesy C.V. Latimer, Jr. M.D.

play a tune on his spruce-cone Jew's Harp, all the while keeping time with his tail tapping the back of his head."

Noah joked that "the happiest part of my day was opening the mailbox" and working around his replica in the grove. His garden plots and boarding house were a short walk away.

***

January 2, 1956. (Noah's calculations.) Earth in perihelion. 8 a.m. 90,215,000 m. from Sun. Minus 4,212,000 m. for Aphelion. See July 4th. Morning Sun-Cloudy day at Wilmington N.Y. The Day after beginning the year 1956.

January 3, 1956. Tuesday. Cloudy and mild at Wilmington I do fancy stitches on Blue Denim Patches.

February 4, 1956. Low 20 Below. To Day: Perfect Clouds, Calm, 6" snow on topo graph at Wilmington. I overhaul Fishing tackle. I build Trowling Outlits. Should white Emigrant Mongrels, of U.S.A. I find, that, Their God is Colored; Will They segregate Him; And, if He go with Mary Magdalene will they lynch Him?

February 19, 1956. Folded and placed on this page is *The Post Standard* newspaper story titled "Hermit Quits Woods Home." The multi-column Sunday features two photographs of Noah by his "replica of a cabin he lived in. The replica is part of a commercial tourist attraction at the village of Wilmington where Rondeau lives." The author stated Rondeau made it "clear he didn't intend to come out [from Cold River] nearly 40 years later as a walking

Looking at Boiling Pond. Author's photo

novelty." The article reported "Rondeau was suffering from a touch of virus last week but was up and around, eager to talk about his years of solitude and of national politics."

February 29, 1956. Sunshine Morning. P.M., Cloud at Wilmington N.Y. 10:30 a.m. – President, D. D. Eisenhower; announce "Readiness to run for second term, if G.O.P. wish to nominate Me."

10 P.M. – President Eisenhower at Washington, appear on TV and speak for 30 m. The Speech was beautiful, honest, clear; No Total show off, not High Kick-Just Honest Talk.

March 20, 1956. Tue. Today perfect sunshine, cold last night when calendar says Spring among major Adirondack Peaks nights below zero still feel like winter. Hard packed snow is four feet deep.

April 27, 1956. Sunshine, a.m. –overcast P.M. 3 O'clock Shower at Wilmington. Melvin Peck Jr. Make me sit in C.R. Rocking Chair and get Him a nail and He fix the Porch Floor; and then He take me to apiary, and He show me Honey Bees. Last Snow Ice vanish from northside of Town Sheds.

May 29, 1956. Perfect Sunshine at Wilmington. I do some work in garden. Mr. Roy Lash and Mrs. Lash call on me. Cherry trees are in bloom.

May 30, 1956. Showers, last night; To Day: Cloudy, 2 little showers at Wilmington. I work in garden and Flower beds and at Apery. Evening: I go with Terry's to cemetery; Wilmington and Mark Ville.

July 6, 1956. Rabbit Foot Clover. Cool. Overcast. Trying to rain at Wilmington, N.Y. I arrange Morning Glory Poles. I water garden. I scribble lines to Alabama. 10 p.m. Eating Cake Ice Cream. Happy Birthday. Noah John Rondeau, born 1883

July 7, 1956. A very hot day at Wilmington. I thin rows of carrots. I water all garden including Potatoes-Corn. I run 2 foot races with Bonnie Terry and Virginia Peck; I got beat every time, Bonnie is 7, Virginia is 6. I gather Flowers and Leaves for a memory pillow.

July 23, 1956. Breeze and Sun; of rain per sq. ft. at Wilmington. I tend Garden. Flower and Honey Bees.

August 17, 1956. Democratic convention comes to a close and they are ahead on two points. They have the best liars and the only living ex-president traitor in the USA.

Aug. 29, 1956. Morning glory flowers stay open all day in somber atmosphere.

September 2, 1956. Sunday. Sun and Clouds, 2 p.m. Shower at Grafton, N.Y. 10 a.m. Chas. Miller, start fire and a Clam Steam - Clams, Chicken, Sausage, Corn, sweet Potatoes and potatoes (20 baskets plus small baskets for Children. 2 O'clock: at least 20 people sit at long tables under apple trees to 20 baskets before we were all through a shower came. Hustle into camp. Until mid-night: We eat and drink beer. Sing all old songs; And I dance with Mrs. Chas. Miller. A splendid crowd and wonderful spirit.

September 3, 1956. A nice summer day at Grafton. I go to Long Pond with Jim Denaker and Ronald Doubert. Ronald, stung by Bee. Supper under

Apple Tree-Relax after yesterday's clam Steam. Very good. Debbie Miller, born-1952.

September 9, 1956. First frost last night. Today Perfect day At Howard Moody's. We drive to Lake Placid. P.M. We drive over Mountain to Lewis; Park a John Hathaway's: and We go east of Hathaway Farm and we have picnic lunch near Brook; and then We hunt for Ginseng. 5 P.M. Back to ca—Back over Mountain. Confab Harry Burpee on Hight of Land near Line of ChesterField Township. Wonderful Mountain View. Back o Moody Home.

September 13, 1956. Sun and clouds at Wilmington. I read "Beekeeping" by O. J. Dyce. I paint Oil Drum for Warren Terry. I gather 50 Pods of ripe bush Beans. 6 O'clock To Saranac Lake with Terrys Back at 8:30. 9:30 Adlai Stevenson speak from Harrisburg. The "New Nerve," is asking public to send contributions for Campaign.

September 28, 1956. White Frost L. N. To Day: Perfect Sun at Wilmington-Nolan Mt. Mrs. Warren Terry; take Me and Gary Terry 14 miles to Davern's Gate And then We take Back Packs and walk 3 miles to Foot of Nolan Mt. We set up camp, Cook Fancy Meal, Make Fancy Bed and set out Bee Boxes. During Night: Quill Pig gnaw on our Hotel Dee Tar-Paper. I saw and heard John Bull's Call, when He aborted "Boycott on $64,000 Program."

October 13, 1956. Perfect Sunshine. Calm and good colors. Wilmington-Keene. To Keene with Gary via Terry's car. Blanche Peck come for ride. I call at library and (Code) and walk to IGA. To Gardens with Mrs. Jones. Walk to salt lick (Code) and to Mt. Views. Lunch at Lean-To. Supper at Central School. Greenleaf Chase: Slides. Dance.

October 24, 1956. Big Frost L.N. Sunshine, Cool Air. Lilac Leaves gone at Wilmington. Sweet is the song of Honey Bees.

October 25, 1956. Cool Air. Perfect Sunshine to day at Wilmington, N.Y. I saw a few boards; and apply them on a new Bee Hive. Big Game hunting season open to day.

October 30, 1956. Frost last night. Froze my House Plant on back porch. To Day: Perfect Sunshine at Wilmington, N.Y. I crib and bank Cornwright Bee Hive for winter. Since the days of Wm. J. Bryan and F.D.R. Adlai Stevenson, is the best runner up to date. Over 4 years ago He was running; And He got up such speed, He did not stop in Nov. 52 So, He's running yet.

October 1, 1956. Rain on roof last night. To Day: Clouds and Sun at Wilmington. I feed last of 65# of Sugar and Honey to Bees. I pick last bouquet of Cornflowers (Batchelor Buttons) Ike speak 20 min. from his office Wash. D.C.

November 6, 1956. This is American Fool Election Day. To Hell (curse in code). To Hell with American Big Fool Business. All I got in America is my privilege to jump on the moon. Democrat or Republican I've been framed, arrested in several jails, got American lice and bed bugs but there was never an American son-of-a-bitch that ever convicted me.

November 9, 1956. Cloudy, cool. First Snow 8 a.m. Granules of snow 1 P.M. A handful of snow 4 P.M. 1" snow at Wilmington, N.Y. I cover and bank Bee Hives. I go to my Wool Underwear.

December 25, 1956. Snow gone and it's generally cloudy. 3 P.M. feeble Sun at Wilmington. A big day. Christmas Tree and Gary and Bonnie. Bonnie's New Doll is learning to walk.

December 30, 1956. Cold and very windy last night and today at Wilmington. Mrs. Melvin Peck to Lake Placid Hospital. Windows frozen all day. Water bottle froze. Warren Terry put tape around Doors and windows. I keep house with Bonnie Terry; we wash Dishes and tell Love Stories.

Chapter 28

1957

Noah's 1957 diary notes are voluminous, but hold no surprising details other than to acknowledge to the curious what he was involved in and perhaps the outcome. Newsworthy tidbits of the events that occurred in Cold River country: "I just saw Santa Claus pass by going toward Panther Peak;" "You'll find spruce [trees] like a woman of the gay 1890s—wearing its skirts to the ground just because Deer don't eat Spruce," and the more mundane but somewhat whimsical entries like this one at the base of Whiteface Mountain.

> *February 4, 1957.* 30° above. Cloudy and mild at Wilmington.
> I pick Frog Feathers and watch the weather go by.

Peck's Corner was Noah's term for the intersection of Route 86, the Whiteface Memorial Highway and Bonnieview Road. Melvin and Blanche Peck's family lived at the base juncture. The Terrys' house stood nearby, and it was there that Noah was still living. By 1960 Warren Terry moved and rented the neigh-
boring house. Guy
Stephenson said in an
interview in the mid-
1990s, "Noah used
to stay there. When it
was rented to Jennie
Pelkey, Noah just
came along with the
house!"

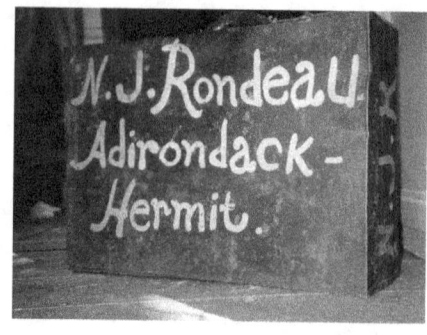

Noah's traveling case used for lectures. Made by Richard Smith. Author's photo

Noah John Rondeau Adirondack Hermit

* * *

January 1, 1957. Nice Sunshine, And Very mild. Wilmington. I call at Saranac Lake with 3 Pecks and 2 Terrys. I call at Stationery Store at Berkely Shoe Shop. Call at Memorial Hospital Lake Placid Confab Mr. Valentine. Evening: I sleek leaves in New Diary Book. I receive 13 Xmas Cards

January 2, 1957. Last night Colder than hell. Windows frost decked. Today: Sunshine, Calm and Cold temperature At Wilmington I bring in wash, 40 pieces – frozen. Mrs. Melvin Peck return from Hospital.

January 3, 1957. Calm and sunshine, cold Atmosphere. Wilmington N.Y. I count my riches

January 6, 1957. L.N.: 20 below 0. Spills of sunshine and spreads of clouds. At Wilmington Rough winter weather

January 7, 1957. Calm and sunshine; A nice winter day at Wilmington N.Y. I take walk about the apiary. I fill Cross Work Puzzle for $11,000.

February 3, 1957. 38 above. Cloudy and mild; Slightly thawing at Wilmington. Bonnie Terry go skating with Debbie Lewis.

February 26, 1957. 8 a.m. Sprinkes on roof Today: Clouds and Sun; Very mild. At Wilmington, N.Y. Honey Bees, first come out; and agitate in mild atmosphere. I send suit of clothes to Plattsburg cleaners. Nancy Peck, send me a piece of Birthday cake. Crows are cawing in south Wilmington. Nancy Peck, born – 1942

March 11, 1957. Bits of sun, a lot cloudy at Wilmington. Mrs. Terry bake Home Made Bread. Bonnie, all evening, play on my bed with her Play House. I receive letter from Lord (Oscar) Burguiere.

March 12, 1957. Mild and cloudy, and breezy. Wilmington, N.Y. I shovel out trail under Cloths Line. Warren Terry, refloor porch. Pope Pius Coronation 1939

May 30, 1957. Overcast Mid Day: 2 hour's Sun at Wilmington. I water Flower Beds. I plant 14 Sun Flower Seeds; And Bachelor-Button Seeds in 50' of drill. I confab Howard Peck through all the shades of dusk.

May 31, 1957. Sun and Overcast (Mixture) Nice warm May Day at Wilmington. I plant 5 Beets, for Seeds I ride with Cohen's Truck to Joe Rondeaus, walk to Gift Shop. Temperature is perfect; and Vernal Green. A 10 year old Boy, going up the walk with a Fish Pole on His Shoulder; and a chippin' Sparrow hops on the Cement 10' ahead of me.

September 1, 1957. Perfect Sunshine at Grafton: Big Clam Steam 27 People Song Feast and beer. Dance, jimmy and hop To midnight. Good Crowd, good spirit, good time.

September 2, 1957. Overcast 3 P.M. Shower Grafton and Troy. I spin yarn with Millers under Apple Trees. I gather Apples, with Donna Dobert. A Dozen of us, repeat the Clam Steam. Weeping Willow Leaf From Grafton. Denaker's front yard.

September 13, 1957. Breezy and overcast at Wilmington. Adirondack Hills are wonderful; And promise to be more wonderful.

September 14, 1957. Perfect sunshine, in late summer. At Wilmington, I feed Honey Bees, and watch Adirondack Hills putting on color to greet Autumn. 7 P.M. A TV Picture of the Adirondacks; and explained by Dick Young is good. This encircled belong to Sept. 13th.

October 5, 1957. Wood Sorrel-Rainbow Falls. Cool night, cloudy morning, perfect day of sunshine and Autumn Colors. At Wilmington. 8 O'clock: At Keene Valley. Register with Gary and Bonnie, Terry-At Keene Library. Call at J.G.A. Store. We ride to AuSable Lake with Mr. McDonald 10-11 Across the outlet for a Random Scoot; And at Boat House of Coffee at 12:30 then, (Rainbow Falls) 6:30 at Central School Keene Valley Big Dinner over 400 People, put a lot of food in Their Faces and out of sight.

October 6, 1957. A nice Autumn Day at Wilmington N.Y. I call at Gift Shop. Call at Joe Rondeau, call at Melvin Peck and at Warren Terry. Confab, Chipper and Pie.

October 13, 1957. A.M. Sunshine; And P.M. – Sun and Clouds. Wilmington N.Y. I watch for Sputnik 8:40 to 9:05 S.T: At 9:05 I saw a glimpse that may be Sputnik chances are, it was a plane or Balloon in Sunshine a long way off, and only a glimpse. Time reveal, I saw Sputnik; But just a brief 2 glimpses.

October 14, 1957. Overcast and mild Wilmington N.Y. 2:30 I see Bride and Groom TV 3 O'clock: Queen Elizabeth open 23rd parliament in Ottawa Canada. Yes, "Sputnik" may pass away: But Sputnik has been [word not clear] outside of Earth's Atmosphere eleven days; It made about 75 revolutions; It's first Ball (Big or small) ever kicked from Earth, through Atmosphere swift enough to go make Orbit. Thanks to Russians. D. D. Eisenhauer, born-1890.

December 22, 1957. A nice day of Sunshine at Wilmington NY. I call at Lake Placid Memorial Hospital –see Chappy Preston and Gary Terry. Beautiful is Panaram off Mountain as seen from Hospital; and Lake Placid to Wilmington.

December 26, 1957. Last Night: Snowed ¼". To Day: Very Cloudy, 1 P.M. ½" rain fell ¼" snow gone to Hell. 4 P.M Another shower 8 P.M. Another shower at Wilmington N.Y. I stay at home all day.

December 27, 1957. Very Cloudy—Quite Cool. At Wilmington I stay at home all day. I look over my Christmas Cards 8 P.M. Mrs. Lewis call me to Her Telephone I confab Mr. at Albany Times Union.

FAME & $HEKELS

Chapter 29

1958

"I reck [my] model of checkered Shirt—with Buttons, Patches and Thread," Noah John complained in his journal. It was January 12, 1958, and he was in laundry mode. Days earlier he'd noted a "23-three piece" clothes wash rolled through a hand-powered clothes wringer followed by sewing of patches "on fancy underwear" and shirts and trousers. The week was also a time to work a darning needle through threadbare sections of worn socks.

The washing was far easier than carrying water pails from Cold River up the Golden Stairway to Cold River Hill to the top of the bank, where he would scrub soiled garments against a corrugated zinc washboard set inside a galvanized wash tub. After much carrying of water, and rinsing and wringing, the clothes were hung to dry on a line stretched between trees in the clearing. In summer, the sun and wind dried the clothes rapidly, but in winter, the clothes froze stiff and needed to be carried inside to thaw to limpness. Drying at the Pecks' was far easier using the clotheslines in the cellar.

When snow was blowing outside the Pecks' house, the thick canvas-covered cardboard scrapbook Noah kept in his bedroom provided him with a pastime for both daytime and evening. Noah needed only to draw his favorite rocker over to where a floor lamp could throw its light upon the pages, and he would glue in the most recently received Albany newspaper clipping to the next page. It was a continually growing record of interviews and articles that supplied Noah with a register of reporters he'd spoken to and a history of his whereabouts throughout the years.

He added to his photo albums in a similar manner, adding notes and captions here and there. Snapshots taken by Ditt Dittmar, Jay Gregory, Doc Latimer, Grace Hudowalski, John Harmes and Richard Smith dom-

Courtesy of Richard J. Smith from Noah's photo album

inate the black-paper pages. There are pictures of Noah holding the arms of little girls as they did some high-step dancing moves, images of him signing autographs at sportsmen's shows, pictures of his Cold River diggings, funny ones of a hermit in baggy deer skin trousers, holding two huge wine bottles as he smiles at the camera. A number of pictures captured Noah beside people and holding ladies' hands as they walked or posed side by side against a storefront. In one curious picture, Noah is holding the arm of a lady decked out in a beautiful fur coat as they look each other in the eye. Noah drew conversation bubbles and an owl perched above the woman's left shoulder. She tells Noah: "The Owl is watching us." Noah's conversation capsule replies: "To Hell with Him."

More than in previous years, he chose to add details of the day's events in code.

Winter locked in around the Town Hall replica. Rondeau commented it was "set up in Winkleman's Grove." No entries indicated that it was moved from Covert's Grove, but native Douglas A. Wolfe clarifies the location:

"Covert's Grove and Winkleman's Grove is in fact the same place.

Covert owned a motel at the corner of Route 86 and Memorial Highway. It was later purchased by Herman Winkleman. Behind the motel up Memorial Highway was an Indian Village tourist site, but prior to that Covert apparently had exhibited some mounted animals at the location…and possibly also sold food [to tourists taking in the North Pole amusement park and those driving to the summit of Whiteface Mountain]. Winkleman built a second motel on Route 86 that bordered on 'Peckville,' but with no space for a tourist trap. Arto Monaco built a restaurant and gift shop at the corner and a small train for kids was put in."

Noah had nothing but time on his hands. A day's activity would include dismantling and reassembling his trolling rig and "One Hair cut Cold River Style" and "One Bath" followed by a long line of code.

* * *

January 8, 1958. Temperature, drag to and fro. Breezy cloudy and snow squall. Wilmington, N.Y. I laundry 23 pieces. ⵔⵅⵅ ⵏⵔ ⵀⵟⵅⵝⵉ ⵀⵡⵔⵟⵅ Ϙⵜⵏⵅⵟ Qⵝⵁⵝ ⵄⵟⵓⵓⵔ ⵏⵓⵝⵡⵝⵟⵉⵝ ⵔⵝ ⵀⵟⵅⵀ ⵄⵡⵡ ⵅⵡⵔ ⵙⵝⵅⵟ ⵖⵝⵝⵝⵝ ⵟⵀⵔ Qⵝⵅⵔⵟⵙ ⵗⵔ ⵗⵡ Ϙⵔⵔ

Decoded: All at Peck's. (Undecipherable….), Russel, Hickuk, Bessie Terry. Argument at Peck's. Too much Sneaky Pete for Melvin Jr. (Sr.?)

January 11, 1958. Zero to 20 (degrees) above To Day:-Sun, lots of clouds and windy at Wilmington P.M. Bonnie Terry, bring me News Papers. Chipper Peck Jr. and His Mother have supper with us. I patch underwear.

January 12, 1958. To Day: Nice sunshine, after a cold night. At Wilmington N.Y. Read from John Blackburn, Hugh Flick's note to John; And a clipping from Knickerbocker Press. I reck model of checkered Shirt-With Buttons, Patches and Thread.

January 25, 1958. Distant Clouds—Cool winter day, Snowed ½" at Wilmington. I prepare Sweet Pickle. Ϙⵏⵝⵝⵟ ⵔⵏⵟ ⵏⵔ ⵔⵏⵝⵝⵝⵄ ⵄⵝⵝⵝⵝⵟⵝ

Decoded: Happy Day at Warren Terry.

January 29, 1958. Snowed 12" last night and to day. Very cloudy and mild at Wilmington. I read some of my Poems. Mountains are beautiful in new snow. Evening: Gary and Bonnie go to hop, at Francis Peck.

February 3, 1958. A nice Winter day. At Wilmington, N.Y. I mount one trolling rig. One Hair Cut Cold River Style. One Bath.

February 7, 1958. Cold and Sun and Clouds at Wilmington, N.Y. We are out of Kerosene from 8 to 12—Then the Oil flood the stove—No fire until mid-night.

February 12, 1958. Sun and Clouds; Cold atmosphere at Wilmington, N.Y. I call at my stored items at Francis Peck's Rooms. I make a Medical Food Chowder. Abraham Lincoln, born 1809.

February 20, 1958. I cook supper of baked beans, warmed over baked potatoes and fried liver, coffee. I wash dishes.

March 5, 1958. Cloudy Mild Thawing at Wilmington N.Y. Mrs. Terry do laundry for me. United States launch another Moon, nearly as big as a pumpkin; And it's not known whether the "Pumpkin" is in orbit above atmosphere, or; a mystery in the Ocean.

March 5, 1958. United States launched another moon, nearly as big as a pumpkin and it's not known whether the "pumpkin" is in orbit above atmosphere or a mystery in the ocean. (Followed by a long line of code.)

April 6, 1958. Blessed are the liars for they have a majority that was never done before. Wonderful to be poor by Big Business after they are dead with more hunger in superstition of mind after dead in the dust. Heaven is rewarded for many things after death.

April 13, 1958. Nice sunshine Wilmington N.Y. Q⊖∥⊢⊖ ⌐⸌⫪ ⌀⸌∘⟍× ⫪⸜⟍ ⫪⸜⟍∘⟍ ⟍⸌⊢∣⸜⸍⫪⊢∣⸍□ Q⊖∥⊢⊖ ×⸜⫪⸍⊢⊖∘ ⟍⊢∣⊖⟍ ⸌⸜ ⌀⸌× ∣□ Ø⸌⸌∣⸜ ∣⸍⸍⸍∣⸜⸜ ⌀⸌∘⟍×

⟨cipher⟩ Decoded: Bessie say Carl found you painting. Bessie mother dined at Carl's. Last night Carl found you painting.

April 25, 1958. Sunshine-and Cold wind. At Wilmington N.Y. I confab Melvin Peck Sr.-⟨cipher⟩ Decoded: At Peck's Pig yard.

April 26, 1958. Sun and cold wind at Wilmington N.Y. I call on Francis Peck. I have beauty sleep at home. Evening: Francis Peck take me to Apiary; And We close Bee Hives so Bees can't come out; And, later I call at Melvin Peck's, Carl and Ruth are there; And Ruth laugh me in the face. ⟨cipher⟩ Decoded: Because Carl found the painting and she think I don't know it he found it over 3 months after it disappeared.

April 27, 1958. Nice Sunshine-Nice greening grass-Nice budding Lilacs. At Wilmington N.Y. Warren Terry, get Francis Peck to haul Bees from to Melvin Peck's. Two loads of Bee Hives: Lewis Help. I settle Bee Hives. How much am I offered for the "DayLight" I save by American Fools pushin American Fool Clocks to and fro. N.J.R. ⟨cipher⟩ Decoded: 13 days bath. ⟨cipher⟩ Decoded: 1 Hummingbird. ⟨cipher⟩ Decoded: June bug. ⟨cipher⟩ Decoded: 1 Big soft.

May 5, 1958. Nice day of vernal sunshine, grass is greening, birds are singing. Young leaves growing. Wil, NY. I get my Replica Town Hall and Wigwam from Winkelman Grove and move it to Melvin Peck's. I make a trip to Public Dump. ⟨cipher⟩ Decoded: I put shit in flower bed. June bug. Harold Peck work for me.

May 8, 1958. Very Cloudy and showers. Wilmington, N.Y. I plant Morning Glory seeds. I transplant Pansys. (In response to a newspaper clipping stating "The 8th of May is Harry's Day" Noah wrote:) "Harry: Where in Hell is Dexter White? Harry Truman, born 1884." ⟨cipher⟩

Richard Smith spoke at length with the author about his life with Noah as we ate lunch on top of this beaver lodge. Author's photo

Qₓ○─┤₊│₊ ₊✗◌─╤ │θθ─⟍□ ⊘◐│θ ⟍◐₊□ ┼⊙ ─○✗⌐○ ⊘─○◦✗θ⌐ ┼◦○ ⤰₊┼✗⟍θ○─│□ ◐○─◑│✗θ┤ ┼◦◦✗ ⟍○₊┤│₊ ⊙⌐○◦◦θ┤ ┼◦✗θ ⟍─◑│✗□ Qθ╟₊θ ○─⌐◦ ┼◦○ ⑨ ┼◦◦○─⌐ ↗⟍ ◐┤θ┤ ○─⌐◦ ⊙⌐○◦◦θ┤ ⟍─◑│✗ ┼◦○ │◦◦┼θ○─ ⑨⑨ ✗₊─┤◦◦θ⌐□ Decoded: I plant over 100 Morning glory seeds. June Bug. I plant 5 poles for climbers. Drunken fool bring Warren Home drunk. Bessie rant for 3 hours and then rant Warren drunk 63 [more] minutes.

May 9, 1958 Friday. Sun and Clouds-Cool air Wilmington N.Y. Midday I go to Plattsburg with Melvin Blanchard, Chipper Peck and Mrs. Terry. We shop at Fisherman's. Dandelion blossoms are good from Keensville to Plattsburg. Grass is beautiful, vernal green. 6 P.M at AuSable Forks Mrs. W. Terry discover, She lost Her Wallet. ⊘│⟍ ◦◦θ○─ ⊛⑤⊛ ⟍✗◦╟◦✗│□ ⊘┼θ╤ ₊◦ ⟍◌✗ ◦◦ ⊙○⟍◦○─┼□ Decoded: and over 100 blossoms. They go back to Pburg.

May 23, 1958. Clouds and Sun. Cadyville Black Brook. Herb Rock and Delia take me to Black Brook. At Wm. Rondeau: Several people call—

FAME & $HEKELS

Confab, Chester, Burton Orville. Mrs. Savage, Mrs. Clo. We spin big yarns.

May 26, 1958. Monday. Nice Sunshine-Cool air. Wilmington N.Y. I water garden (Flower) I plant Top Onions. I assemble two Trolling Spoons. ⊘⊷ ⊶+⟋θ⟍◌ ℺⫪ ♀☉ ⟋++⟋⤬◻ ☉☉⊘℺◌◻ ◌⟍θ ℺⟍◌+◻ Decoded: 11 AM. Arrived. My 31 chicks. June bug.

June 3, 1958. Cool morning after rain; wet grass-Perfect Sunshine at Wilmington N.Y. A variety of small Birds are confabing in several languages in the Elm Trees. I apply red paint to about 40 Trolling Rigs. Aging Dandelions, put on fuzzy white heads. Two Mosquitoes call in my room. ⊘++⟋⤬ θ⟋⤬⤬ ◌⎮ ⟋◌⊶⟋θ⊶◻ ♀☉ ⟋++⟋⤬ ⟍⎮+⎮+ +⟍◻θ◻ ◌⟍◌+◻ Decoded: Chicks walk on starter. 31 chicks doing fine. June bug.

June 4, 1958. Wednesday. Sunshine, Perfect June Morning; at Wilmington, N.Y. 6:45 P.M. Gary Terry and Edna Gay Auford? On TV in Plattsburg. θ+⊶+⎮⟍ ⟍⟍⤬⤬ ⎮θ◻ ♀++⟍◻ ℺θ⎮ ☉θ◻θ⟋⤬ ⊶+⟋⤬ ⊘ ⊶⟍⊶⊶⊶+θ⎮◻ ◌⟍◌ ⟍⟍◌+◻ ⊘+⊶⊶⤬θ ⟋++⟋⤬ ⟋⊶θ ⤬⎮⊷θ⟋⟍⤬θ◻ Decoded: Grind bull stone. Shit. Ben Peck pick 5 puppies. June bug. Little chixs are loveable.

June 17, 1958. Fourth Day: Cold, Windy cloudy and some rain at Wilmington, N.Y. I put 3 Glass Panes in south window of Pecks chicken coop. Melvin Peck, build a Rabbit Pen. I pull down Old Beaver Quiver made over 20 years ago at Cold River. I write order to Hurley-Madd for Warren Terry. I fished Cold River with Dr. Wm. B. Gregory; 20 Trout for our effort—1939.

June 23, 1958. Monday. Overcast-Distance clouds; calm and mild temperature at Wilmington, N.Y. Little Black Hen peck. Evening: I attend Commencement at AuSable Forks High School. ♀☉☉θ℺θθ⊶⤬⎮⤬ ⟍ ⟋++⟋⤬ ⤬⎮⎮θ◻ ⊘⟍+θ ⎮⎮ ⟋⎮⎮⊶◻ ⊘+⊶⊶⤬θ ⤬⤬⟍⟋⤬ +θ⎮⊶θ⟋⤬ ⟍⟍+θ⎮◻ ◌⟍◌ ⟍⊶+◻ ⊘ ♀θ⊘⤬⤬⎮◻ ⊘ ⤬⎮⟍◻ ♀ ☉⊶℺ +☉ ⊶⟍⊶⊶ ♀☉ ⟋++⟋⤬ ⟍⟋⤬ +⎮ ⟋⟋+θ◻ Decoded: 31 4 week old chicks loose. Cage to coop. Little black hen peck babies. June bug. Many flights take place. A hello, A job. 3 PM I put 31 chicks back in cage.

June 26, 1958. Lots of rain last night; To Day Overcast at Wilmington, N.Y. I fit 2 Boards, patching south side Town Hall Replica; Melvin Peck Jr. work with me.

July 6, 1958. Sunday. A bushel of Clouds and a handful of Sunshine; a Hot Day. At Wilmington, N.Y. Noah John Rondeau born 1883 75 yrs. today. Chas. Miller and Clera Mealy Married 1921 [Rondeau's code on this date is a lengthy tally of the date he ⦵⊢✗✗θ⟍ Q✗⟋⼂✗ Qθ⟍∘⊣ (killed black bears.) Only the decoded dates appear.] 05.03.1924; 10.27.1927; 12.12.1931; 11.07.1932; 10.28.1934; 10.29.1934; 06.08.1935; 11.09.1937; 12.05.1937; 11.11.1940; 05.25.1941; 04.29.1942; 10.23.1943. and 10.25.1943. [On Tuesday July 6, 1965 Rondeau wrote in code another extensive list of bears killed.]

July 12, 1958. Morning overcast, Then a nice summer day Wilmington N.Y. I wash 34 pieces of clothing. The usual Robin hop by chicken coop.

July 13, 1958. Last Night: Cool—Today: Sunshine and gentle breeze. Wilmington I clean out Chick coop, and put in fresh Hay and Gravel.

July 24, 1958. Calm and perfect sun. A Hot day. At Wilmington, N.Y. A white Minorca, crow seven times this morning. ⚲ ♂ ⟋∘⊣⼂ ∘⊖⼂⟍⼂ ∘⊖⼂θ✗ ⦵⦵⦂⦵⼂ ⦵⊢⊣⊣ Q⊢⼂⼂⼂ Decoded: C.H. Across Road. Russell KKOK. Dig Bit.

August 14, 1958. Clouds and Sun-Hot day. At Wilmington, N.Y. Mountain Ash Berries are Orange color. ♂⊢⼂⼂∘⼂∘⼂ ⊢⊖ ⊢⊢⼂⼂ ⊛⊛⦵ ⼂θ⼂⼂∘ ⊢⊖ ⟋✗✗ ⟋⼂ ∘⊖⦵∘⊖ ⼂⼂∘⼂θ⼂⼂ Q⼂✗✗ ⼂⊢⊢⼂ Decoded: Liquor. I find 100 cents. I call at ROR store. At M.E.C. Bull Shit.

September 4, 1958. Morning: Overcast, cool and slightly breezy. Mid day sprinkle. At Wilmington, N.Y. I water Sun Flowers and trim off yellow Leaves. Mrs. Delbert Warren, died-1955. ⊢⊖ ∘⼂⟍⼂ ⊛⦵⦵ ⼂θ⼂⼂ ⼂⼂ ⼂✗⼂⼂✗⼂ ⊖∘θ⼂✗⼂ ⦵θ⼂ ⼂⼂ ⊖ ✗⼂∘⊖ ⊖ ⊖⼂⼂θ∘⼂⊤⼂ Decoded: I pay 600 cents to old man Peck. Yes and 2 more 2 eatery.

FAME & $HEKELS

September 7, 1958. Much rain last night. Morning: Overcast. P.M. Bits of Sun and bushels of clouds. Wilmington, N.Y. 4 P.M. I call at Winkelman's grove. One rat and a chipmunk tried my trap today and it sprung.

September 8, 1958. Morning: Overcast. To Day—Out Brakes of Sunshine-Nice cool breeze. At Wilmington, N.Y. I put 4 Pails of Pebbles, as top filling on floor of my Cold River Town Hall Replica. Big American Business, turn off electric power at Warren Terry's Home; To hell with the American Son of a Bitch of a crooked organization—It's not fit to live with.

September 11, 1958. Morning: Overcast and Cold at Wilmington, N.Y. I go to Heavy Wool Shirt. 11:15 P.M. I see President Eisenhauer And I listen to His voice on TV, for nearly 30 minutes—As He tell of the danger to the U.S. and all the free world, according to the disposition of communism regarding Formosa and at least two more Islands near Formosa. Plattsburg celebrate—Battle of Plattsburg-1814.

September 25, 1958. Rain last night. Quite breezy, and Sunshine today. Wilmington, N.Y. MidDay: [coded symbols] Decoded: My god. Soft and farts. Ike H. Rogers, John Breen, Bessy Delbert, Warren, Tom, Alice, D. Cassovey, Molly, J. Bowe, old Lewis. Bent poppy, MO Ike Fioz.

October 7, 1958. Perfect sunshine at Wilmington, N.Y. Chipper Peck Jr. call. Sunflower Leaves are crisp, after freezing 3 nights ago. Mountains are beautiful with Autumn Colors. The Pope, sick: Then revived some-Then set back again; Not expected to live through the night. Francis Peck, 34 yrs. old today.

October 8, 1958. Perfect sunshine a.m. – P.M. Overcast at Wilmington N.Y. Pope Pius XII, died at 6:20 P.M. [coded symbols] Decoded: 1 soft. My god. From Mr. Welfare. 1 soft. My god.

October 12, 1958. Next Eclipse 3-24-1959. Froze ice last night. To Day: Very cloudy and breezy at Wilmington, N.Y. I wash 4 garments. 466 yrs. ago today, was just another Oct. 12th. in Columbus never saw America; and, when He (Columbus) came to West Indies, He did not know where He was going; And when He landed He didn't know where He was; And when He got back home, He never found out where He'd been.

November 3, 1958. Frost last night. To Day: Perfect sunshine. At Wilmington, N.Y. Gordon bring Kerosene. I wash 8 Handkerchief. Election is edging up.

November 4, 1958. Perfect Sunshine at Wilmington, N.Y. Breakfast I work 3 Hours. This is U.S. Fool Election Day; To Hell with it From 9 P.M. to 1 passed midnight I get Election Returns; then for 30 m. I get projection of New Pope Coronation. ⊖∘⊖⁻⟋× ⟁⁊⁊∘⁻₈ ♂⁊ ♀⊖××⁻ ⊖⊢⁻⟋⊢ ⊢⟋ ⊖×⊖⟋ ⟋⊢⁻⁊⎮ ⊖×⊖⟋⟋⁊∘⁻⎮ ⌃⟍ ⊖×⊖⟋⟋⁊⊖⁻⟍◻ Decoded: Peck. Coor. To Hell with it— Election Electors and Elected.

November 7, 1958. Lots of Clouds, specks of snow bits of Sun at Wilmington, N.Y. I insulate 16 sq. ft. ⟁⊖⁻⎮ ⟋⟁ ⟁⁊⁊∘⁻◻ ⊖∘⟁ ⁺⊖ ⎮⊖×× ⊕∘ ∘⊖⊖⟋× ⊖⊕ ⟋⁺⁺⟋×⎮₈ ♀ ⊖⟋⟋⊖∘⁻₈ ♂ ⁺⊖⊖⟍⊖∘⁻⎮◻ ⊛⊕⊕ ⁺∘⁻⟍⁺⎮∘ ♀ ⟋⎮∘ ⊛⊕⊕⊛ ⟋⊖⎮⟋⎮◻ ⟁∘×⟋⁺⊢⟋◻ Decoded: Ben J Coor PM I sell F Peck 20 chicks, 3 waters, 5 feeders. 100 grain. 3 cans. 1000 cents. Bullshit.

November 15, 1958. Very cloudy at Wilmington, N.Y. I do a lot of sleeping while the weather goes by.

November 17, 1958. Clouds and Sun at Wilmington, N.Y. I wash 8 Handkerchief. Melvin Peck Sr. and Peck's Pig died. ⟁⊛⊕⊛ ⟋⊖⎮⟋ ⁺∘⁻⁊× ⊕⁊∘⁻⟋⁺ ⊖∘⁊×⊖∘⊖⁺ ⊖⟋ ⁺⁺∘∘⎮⟋ ⊖⁺⁺⁺◻ Decoded: 600 cents from North Pole. Get first egg.

November 22, 1958. Cool, clouds and Sun Wilmington N.Y. Bits of snow on dry leaves. I patch checkered Shirt. ⊖ ∘×◻ ♀⁊⁺⟋◻ ⟁⊖⎮⎮⊢⊖ ⎮⊢⟋ ⎮⌃⊢ ⁊

FAME & $HEKELS

⊙∘θ ᴫθ□ Q̣ᵀ□ ⊙′∘∘θ⌐ |ᵪθθ∘ ⊣⌐∘ᴵᵪ⊣⌐⊣ ᴊᵗᵗ∘∘□ Decoded: 2 PM Soft, Bessie sit sang to Pete my- Warren sleep in rocking chair.

December 5. 1958. (In response to a *Daily News* article showing a hunter displaying a 60 pound dead bear cub, Noah wrote:) "To hell with law officers, big business all for $$$ to hell with American Big wonder."

December 14, 1958. A spell of cold weather and sunshine. Wilmington, N.Y. I cut clippings from almanacs; and prepare my Diary for 1959. George Washington, died-1799.

December 24, 1958. Sunshine and Cold temperatures. Wilmington, N.Y. I receive 6 Xmas Cards. Mrs. Warren Terry go to Plattsburg. 10 P.M. We have Christmas Tree—Pictures, gifts, young and old are very busy. Five year old Melvin Peck Jr. is busiest of all.

December 26, 1958. Last Night: 14 degrees below, Today, 19 degrees above. Clouds and Sun at Wilmington, N.Y. Long day in door; But would seem longer out in the Cold.

December 28, 1958. Cloudy all day-Not very cold at Wilmington N.Y. I paste Photos and clippings in Photo Album. ⊙ᵗᵗ ᴊᵗ⊣θᐟ ᴊᵗ ᴊᵗ ᴊᵪᵪθ ᵪθ⊣□ Q̣⊣ᵗᴊ ᐱ ∘⊣∥ ᵗᵗ ᵗᵪᵗᵗ∘□ Decoded: Dog tied to tackle keg. Shit and piss on floor. Bonnie Terry look over my Photograph Albums.

December 31, 1958. Cold atmosphere, and sunshine Wilmington, N.Y. I sew Pie's Shoe Q̣θ∥⊣θ ᐱ ⊙∘θ ᴊθ ⊣ᵗ ᴊᵗ ⊙᷄ᵪθ∘⊣□ ⊘ ᵪᵗᴊᴊᵪθ ᵗᵗ Q̣θθ ᵗᵗᵪ Q̣′∘ᵗᵪᐟ ⊙∘θ ᴊᵪ□ Decoded: Bessie and Pete go to Pbrg. A bottle of Bee from Harold Pcck. A foot of snow cover the ground. 🔒

Loggers Harvey Carr and Paul Crofut are preparing to load Noah's cabin onto their log truck. The director for the Adirondak Museum at Blue Mountain Lake has made arrangements to move the Hermit's abandoned cabin at Cold River to a new site on the grounds of the museum where the public will have a chance to view the home of the Recluse.
Courtesy Harver Carr

Harver Carr was one of the Walkers who worked on the project. Courtesy Harver Carr

First exhibit was set up outside on the grounds of Blue Mountain Lake museum. Courtesy Harver Carr

FAME & $HEKELS

Chapter 30

1959

After leaving Cold River, Noah never stayed anywhere that offered him the complete freedom he'd experienced in the woods. He had numerous beginnings and endings at various places from Saranac Lake to Au Sable Forks, to Black Brook to Wilmington. At all, he found comfort and security, companionship and conveniences, but no place ever felt just right.

By 1959, Noah had seasoned into a tough and determined man with many skills and crafts at his fingertips, all of which he had used to help him survive. He held on to his wooden shack, always referred to as the Town Hall replica, possibly because he knew he would never again experience wilderness life as he had known it. Besides, he now had the best of two worlds. Where could he find and afford another isolated spot and yet be close to village amenities?

Walt Whitman said at a far earlier age (70—Noah was 76 in 1959): "The old ship is not in a state to make many voyages, but the flag is still at the mast and I am still at the wheel." I believe it can be said that Noah generated his share of daily work both during the time he spent without seeing a human being and during the time he lived outside his mountain home. Judging from the number of funeral services he attended at the Whiteface Methodist Church and the notices of deaths clipped from newspapers attached throughout the diaries (Mrs. William Olney was the final datum on December 31, 1958), he undoubtedly had been thinking he had already outlived many of the people he knew. A pet saying of his was "Father Time is picking at my pocket." Was he averse to leaving when his time came? Apparently, nobody put the question to him as directly as I might have.

Edward A Harmes and Noah resting and talking during a hike to Couchsachraga peak 1946. Courtesy John M Harmes

Miller's Falls also called Natural Dam, Cold River. Noah called it the Nymph's bath tub. Authors photo

Noah and Richard Smith 1939. Courtesy of Richard J. Smith from Noah's photo album

Cold River City was like a forerunner of the late 1950s and '60s *Mother Earth News* sub-culture. Noah's former lifestyle might have looked like an idea that arrived before its time. It was probably one of the reasons newspaper writers found receptive audiences when they wrote about his inner resources and the ways he managed to live without material wealth.

It seems fitting here to repeat what naturalist John Burroughs said: "A man who retires into solitude must have a capital of thought and experience to live upon, or his soul will perish of want." Noah did have goals and purposes in mind, and he certainly was rich in experience. What he lacked at this point was money in a bank account. Had he had money enough, he might have purchased acreage.

Throughout the month of January 1959, the subzero temperatures and wind made the daily weather, according to Noah's diary, a mixture of "pinches of morning sunshine" and "snowflakes later in the day." His activity centered around Melvin Peck's chickens and spending hours of indoor time pasting newspaper and magazine clippings in his diary, followed by writing tirades such as political commentary: "Number 14 tongue twister: Tell-tale tongue, tell-tale trader twisted Truman." January ended with this entry:

January 31, 1959. Cold atmosphere and breezy at Wilmington, N.Y. Melvin Peck moved Bantams from Town Hall replica to hen coop. Mr. Enoch Squires [WGY radio reporter] call on me most of afternoon. We make three tape recordings. Big visit about Hermit Life, Adirondack Mountains, Vallies, Flora, Fauna, Fishing, Hunting, Trapping and Wig Wams and Cabins; And Astronomy overhead (Cold River Style).

***

February 7, 1959. Snowflakes in air at Wilmington, N.Y. A rough old winter. Earl Vosburg [sic] -you was a thief in Mexico, at Corey's, Tupper Lake, Saranac Lake, on Raquette River. A kleptomaniac, a thief. [Editor's Note: Rondeau's harsh comments were directed toward a newspaper article he pasted into his diary entitled: "Earle Vosburgh Age 65 Dies in Crash at State Road Bridge on Tupper Road," with the subhead, "The former game protector was employed at the time of his death as a gate watchman at Whitney Park."

March 27, 1959. Snowed 4 inches, very cloudy. A lingering winter at Wilmington, N.Y. 9 P.M. starting for Ice Cream and Cake at Gary Terry's anniversity. I hook my big feet in a Dog Leash and fall.

April 5, 1959. Sunshine and chill in the air. Wilmington, N.Y. First song sparrow jingle jang in the air. Confab with John Rondeau across bridge and meet Korean Rat at Strawberry Roan.

April 15, 1959. Perfect Sunshine at Wilmington, N.Y. Jet planes put white line in sky and hang fleeces of white wool on the lines.

April 26, 1959. Breezy, cloudy morning; P.M. perfect sunshine at Wilmington, N.Y. Three yellow violet blossoms picked by Mrs. Webb near St. Hubert's. I go with Webb's and Carr's to St. Hubert's Inn. Picnic, nice mountains and sunshine. We went as far as Chapel Pond then back to Wilmington. Happy outing.

April 30, 1959. Quite cloudy and cool. Wilmington, N.Y. I am sick due to too much pork fat. I stay in living room covered with electric blanket.

May 5, 1959. Perfect Sunshine at Wilmington, N.Y. Jet planes blow smoke roads in the sky. Robins sing in Elms. Song sparrows jingle their small change. I water the garden.

May 13-14, 1959. Nice days at Wilmington, N.Y. I walk to post office observing green lawns trimmed with dandelions blossoms and tender green Vernal foliage on deciduous trees. I plant morning glory seeds. The trees are greening. Leaves peek out tender vernal green is greening. Birds are gleefully singing. Dandelions are blooming.

June 2, 1959. Overcast all day at Wilmington N.Y. Call on post office and sport shop.

AT FIRST LIGHT
Night is done, the morning's come
Daylight's just begun, light refracts from sun
And it spoils the dark, of a long night
With increment light, before sun's gold arrive.

June 14, 1959. Overcast and a sprinkle of rain at Wilmington, N.Y. We have the oil heater going. I shorten pant legs and sew on 6 suspender buttons and remove zipper and put on 4 buttons and four button holes.

June 25, 1959. I'm sorting out Cold River Relics.

June 27, 1959. Morning overcast; At Wilmington, N.Y. Song Sparrow jingle his small change and Robins laugh out loud. A string of horn blowing cars went by a wedding. I have Chipper Peck get two of my cedar fishing poles. I'm packing up to go to Long Lake and Blue Mountain Lake.

June 30, 1959. A warm day at Wilmington, N.Y. I add a few items to my Museum collection. When I was a child in new mown hay I caught odor of sweet grass that often returns in memory. And after Autumn's frost Odors of frozen ferns Bring memories of the child In the new mown hay. Now in my old age I thank you June for thirty days. Thanks June for your precious ways That receive thoughts of odor of sweet grass In childhood's new mown hay. Come again June next year After May.

[Beside a newspaper clipping he glued with the title "Noah Might Have Been the First Albino on Record" Noah wrote:] "Blessed are the liars for they have a majority."

July 7, 1959. Morning overcast, P.M. clouds and much sun. Long Lake to Wilmington. 10 A.M. leave Long Lake. 11 o'clock reach Tupper Lake. Mid-

Day at Wilmington. I move my riches from Francis Peck's to my Town Hall.

[This note from Grace K. Martin is glued into the diary with this day's entry:]

> Dear Noah,
>
> Hope you are well and will have many more B days. I am taking care of an old man who is 91 years old but is fast slipping. Have been with him over a year. I did not go east last year or this but hope to in '60. My son is in Europe. It is hot out here and dry as punk. No rain this season. Grass is straw colored. Drop me a line when you have time. Best of everything to you Noah.

September 9, 1959. Morning overcast. Wilmington to Saranac Lake. 12:46 on Greyhound at Wilmington; 1:40 at Saranac Lake. Lodge at Alpine Terrace. Evening call on John's Spinach Farm. Beer, slide projection and hunting and trapping yarns.

September 15, 1959. Mrs. Putnam do ironing and she cook and wait on me. In evening: I have a hot sling for a night cap.

September 24, 1959. Morning overcast, hot day at Wilmington, N.Y. I make a hermit's soup.

October 6, 1959. Very cloudy at Wilmington, N.Y. I do sewing on winter underwear.

October 19, 1959. Biggest frost yet at Wilmington, N.Y. Last night cold, snowed like a generous sprinkling of salt. Brrr. It's cold.

October 24, 1959. All day cloudy and showers. Wilmington, N.Y. I do much sewing while the weather goes by. [Beside a clipping titled "Daylight Time to End," Noah wrote:] And now eternal rest. How wonderful that American Big Business tells us 'Officially' when to set hands of clock back and when to set them ahead. Those American sons-of-bitches have made a monkey of the clock and standard time. To hell with foreign name 'America' and Catholic. Vespucci on top of that now how much am I offered for the daylight I have saved.

Sportsmen shows were not all work. Courtesy of Richard J. Smith from Noah's photo album

Chapter 31

Throughout the 1960s

From 1950 to 1960, Noah had been searching for his niche in the Outside—a place he could feel he belonged permanently. By 1960 he had chosen the community of Wilmington and its way of life. The cost of living was low, the people were friendly, the small-town setting was encircled by mountains and the nearby forest setting felt homelike.

Noah's 1960 diary shows the seventy-seven-year-old still did physical work. His standard warm-weather uniform for work was typical for older men—baggy overalls with a button drop seat, shoulder straps that held up a bib front, no belt around the middle and big deep hip pockets that held a variety of articles including a kerchief—a bandana to folks today. His winter attire was favorite woolen articles, including a heavy, long, dark wool coat, buckled galoshes and a muskrat hat.

Dressed warmly, Noah would walk to the Town Hall replica that was permanently set up in Winkleman's Grove. He visited it year-round. The site offered him the opportunity to work in his garden, raise bees, tinker with the log structure, cut sod, shovel earth, push a wheelbarrow, target shoot with bow and arrows and rifle, and fire up the cabin's woodstove. He enjoyed every minute of the outdoor work as well as just taking in the day, no matter the season. He was never a man to say he enjoyed vigorous physical exercise, but when it was required or at those times when he saw a plan unfold and achieved satisfaction with the results, he knew his work was worth the effort.

Life is a great web of opportunities consisting of seized chances and of consequences for all partakers. As we live our lives, we leave our mark. Whatever the world may be like a century from now, it will be affected in part by what each one of us has been, done and thought. So WGY radio reporter Enoch Squires, Richard Smith, Oscar Burguiere, Doctors Latimer Sr. and Jr., Jay Gregory, Madeline Dodge, Burton Rondeau, Peggy Byrne, Adolph and Mary Dittmar, logger Harvey Carr, Adirondack Museum supporters Eleanor and Monty Webb and others have collectively and individually helped shape the folk history of Noah's world just as they shaped his life and the lives of people who may read about or see what is preserved about the Cold River hermit.

Courtesy Edward Harmes

Noah's next remarks act as a forward to the 1960 diary. They appear beside a clipping titled "Alright Let's Test Catholic Loyalty." He drew a finger pointing to the last line that reads "A pamphlet is offered free to show test of Catholic loyalty."

Noah wrote: "It's a sure guess not a word there about the holy inquisition. The Massacre of St. Barr in 1572 and not a word about U.S. Catholic soldiers who left the U.S. flag and went to other side when a Catholic priest spoke to them in Mexico."

***

January 27, 1960. Morning sunshine; day overcast. Nebulosity on Mountains. Mid-day snowing at Wilmington, N.Y. I write Orlando, Florida. Young lady call March of Dimes collector.

Noah's Hermitage 1934. Courtesy Gay Prue

February 2, 1960. Groundhog Day. If man kept his nose out of wood-chuck business; the woodchuck would never look foolish; But since man has taken over talk for the woodchuck it looks like a fool woodchuck when it's a fool man.

February 12, 1960. Last night thaw caught cold: Today cold and overcast at Wilmington N.Y. I call at sport shop. [Next to a WISE SAYING by Abraham Lincoln Noah wrote: "Nine of those Wise; wonders are not worth as much as a handful of Joe Stalin's dung." 11 P.M. A mouse tried my trap. It worked. He liked it.

February 16, 1960. Sunshine under much nebulosity-cold air-slightly thaw-ing on edge of macadam at Wilmington, N.Y. Call at sport shop.

March 20, 1960. I call at sport shop, post office. I read and write. Melvin Peck Jr. called and get candy and marbles.

March 22, 1960. More clouds than sun; and cool atmosphere at Wilm-ington, N.Y. 9 AM First chipmunk on snow bank in front of our abode. Snow is beginning to settle, Spring ashen.

March 23, 1960. Cold last night, today perfect sunshine- low 15, high 33 degrees at Wilmington, N.Y. I got some birthday cake. Chipper Peck call me. I label compartments of my filler file.

April 6, 1960. Last night snowed one inch. Today, cold & breezy. 1 P.M. 40 degrees; midday new snow gone. Odd snow flakes, random frolic in the atmosphere. After school, I shoot arrows with Chipper Peck.

April 14, 1960. Thursday. I spade in corn in flower bed and take sunflower stalks to the dump. Chipper Peck helped me. A big boy stole marbles from Chipper Peck and he got away with them. Chipper chased the thief but the thief got away and Mrs. Peck had to chase to bring 7 year old Chipper back home.

April 16, 1960. Sunshine, perfect vernal day at Wilmington, N.Y. I count Chipper Peck's pigs. Five on one foot! Chipper is seven years old. I make a Flower Bed for Chipper; and, I plant some seeds for Him. And Chipper, helped me in my garden. I plant a few Sun Flower seeds; and, transplant lilac bushes. Robins are laughing out loud. Elm trees are budding so their tops brown and dense.

April 30, 1960. Sunrise 5:42 AM Sunset 7:42 PM. At Wilmington, N.Y. Vernal time: late juncos are singing. Trees are growing leaves. A robin is building a nest in plants that were dead and had flowers on their heads. [Noah glued various pictures from packets of seeds.]

May 13, 1960. Quite cloudy, Nice May Day at Wilmington, N.Y. I call on sport shop. Bessie Terry tell me "I will buy no more groceries until I get money from you or Warren Terry. The fact that Warren Terry owes you is nothing to me." At evening dusk the frogs sing clear "NeeDeep" at Whiteface Brook.

May 18, 1960. Perfect May Day, perfect sunshine at Wilmington, N.Y. I call on sport shop. Dandelion Blossoms are at standard best. I see first white butterfly. Bonnie Terry get bokay of dandelions. White Memorial highway to top of Whiteface Mountain open today; twenty-six season.

June 10, 1960. Starlings young and old are raising hell within the house walls.

June 27, 1960. 7:30 P.M. For twenty-five minutes I listened to speech by President Eisenhower. Splendid speech.

June 30, 1960. Quite cloudy at Wilmington, N.Y. I'm sick with a virus cold.

July 7, 1960. Many flowers, daisies are blooming. Birthday cake from Bessie, perfume from Blanche, handkerchief from Chipper and card from all the little Pecks.

August 26, 1960. Sunshine at Wilmington, N.Y. Chipper and me call on Eleanor's Restaurant and get ice cream. I help Chipper clean his yard and take a little wagon load to the dump. And we pull Rag Weeds and broaden the trail.

September 1, 1960. Nice summer day. Bad tooth. No sleep last night.

September 16, 1960. Last night: Frost kill morning glories and squash and cucumbers and potatoes and corn. Today perfect sunshine. At Wilmington, N.Y. I make [code] I help Chipper Peck make a ladder [more code]. I make a batch of ink. 7 P.M. call at Justice Court. Carl come and tell lies.
[Noah's comment next to an advertisement clipping titled: "DO YOU HAVE SOMETHING TO SAY TO THIS?"] "Only one dollar adds your name to a vital letter to Khrushchev! At the same time your dollar helps the Democrats win in November! This is your opportunity to tell Khrushchev: 'America we are free to support the party of our choice. We Democrats are backing our beliefs with our votes and dollars!' Send your dollar to: NYS Democratic Campaign Committee. What an American Fool. To Hell With it and the nerve of it."

One of the original lumber camp buildings at Big Dam.
Courtesy Richard Woods

October 15, 1960. Cloudy morning. The day continue, cloudy and mild. At Wilmington, N.Y. I prepare drills for Batchelor Buttons for 1961. [code] Autumn colors are fading and russet, olive and evergreen is beautiful.

October 31, 1960. Low 33; high 53. Perfect Sunshine at Wilmington, N.Y. I read and write. Halloween trick or treat. I call on Chipper Peck.

November 14, 1960. Calm, mild sunshine at Wilmington, N.Y. I try beauty sleep. Sleep a success, beauty a failure. [Line drawing of a buck with notation:] 12 point buck shot at Big Dam, Cold River 1950. Noah John Rondeau, Adirondack Hermit
  I planted sixteen small onions remediation for next Spring.

November 19, 1960. Cloudy and breezy. Wilmington, N.Y. I scribble and beauty sleep. (P.M. I listen to Welk's orchestra.)

November 24, 1960. Nice Autumn day of sunshine at Wilmington, N.Y. I helped Mrs. Pelkey finish moving my riches. [code] Mrs. Pelkey cooked a Thanksgiving dinner that was not hard to take. I watch New York City parade on T.V.

WAYNE HAMNER BYRNE
46 CUMBERLAND AVENUE
PLATTSBURGH, NEW YORK 12901-1815

January 13, 20000000000

Dear Jay:

Thanks so much for your very nice letter -- it was good
to hear from you, and I hope the next letter will say
how well your book is going.. I've heard great things about
it, but haven't seen it, due to a whole succession of
difficulties with my eyes and other problems. In any case
Noey deserves the best, and I'm so glad you did him proud
-- as I hear. Great!

As to Noey's arrest and trial. I have nothing in writing
and never did because this is my father's story. He went
with a friend to spend a week with Noey once at Cold River
to do some hunting. Saw the famous diary, and did everything human to get Noey to let him have a year's record
printed, but Noey wouldn't lend it. Anyway my father was
so taken with this wonderful man, and had such a great time
there, and came back with such marvelous stories that they
became real friends. And so when Noey landed in the Malone
jail he called John P. Myers in Plattsburgh (a man - my
father -- who later became Chancellor of the New York State
Board of Regents) and told him about the arrest and the
upcoming trial in Malone. Judge Main to be the judge -- a
man whose son or maybe even grandson is another Judge Main
in Malone right now. My father went to Malone for the
trial,and hence the story which he always swore was true,
and being an honorable man I believe it. I have no idea
what records there may be. Maitland DeSormo called me a
liar because he never could find any court records in Malone
(so he said). My own sense is that the trial would have
been -- or was -- so unusual that the Judge may have decided
not to record the trial at all. Do you suppose this was
possible? I never questioned it at all because the story was
so direct from my father to me. If you want to quote me as
giving you a first-hand eye-witness account, feel free....
When DeSormo slapped me down i decided not to argue for a
minute, because I had no possible proof -- my father had
died and I had no way to get to Malone to find out myself.

Now in these days of proof and records etc etc, I'm sure
you need this, and I'm sorry I can't help/ But it was a
first-hand account, and I understood that my father had sat
through the trial right to the finish: that's how the story
went,all through our family.

      End of the Myers account! I wish I could help you
further, but I still believe it!

       All the best with your writing, and let me hear
how the book is going, and what you can make of the trial
even without the record. I bxxx BET the Main family has

(margin, right side, rotated): kept the same story alive in their family -- it's too good to let it die! Sincerely, (?)

in the 1960's Peggy Byrne spoke to Noah about his arrest and trial in the 1920's.
She also learned about her father's (John P. Myers) connection with Noah at that
time. As a result she wrote a story about it in the October-November 1972 *NYS
Conservationist magazine.*

Chapter 32

1961

Monday, January 2, 1961. Calm and perfect sunshine and 20 inches of new snow. Wilmington, N.Y. I stay alone all day. I watch the snow scene in Adirondack Mountains.

"This is the profile of a man who stopped the world long enough to get off. In the chaos of 1913, when lust for life turned into lust for war and ramifications were penetrating even the wilderness, a young man put down barber's clippers, laid aside scissors, folded his linens neatly, hoisted a pack, thumbed his nose at the outside world and quietly walked into the Adirondack forest..." began Barney Fowler in the article that appeared in his 'Strictly Outdoors' newspaper column.

Fowler's 1961 "The Man That Stood Alone" full-page story went on to share the stock outline of the ex-Mayor of Cold River's life. It wasn't the first time he had written a story about Noah, and it wasn't the last. Fowler went on to tell many of the details about the "teller of mountain tales" and "spinner of philosophical theories" that many readers already knew by this time, but a rehashing along with current pictures of Noah kept alive the old boy's reputation and brought folks up to date. "I am a realist," he told Fowler. He would be 78 this coming year. "Things I had in the Flow are now at the Adirondack Museum. I worked a short time at the Whiteface Museum." The extra funds were welcome income. It meant he could buy toiletries, canned food, socks, writing paper and post cards, and other much-needed items to round out his personal needs. "I don't want to be a burden to taxpayers, but a man has to live," he said.

***

January 2, 1961. Calm and perfect sunshine and 20 inches of new snow. Wilmington, N.Y. I stay alone all day. I watch the snow scene in Adirondack Mountains.

January 10, 1961. Last night 10 degrees below. Today; frost pictures on windows. Sunshine and cool Atmosphere. Wilmington, N.Y. I do much sewing of patches on ten year old underwear.

I get letter and seven photos from Alaska.

January 13, 1961. Thawing, very mild. At Wilmington, N.Y. I rest and sleep. Eisenhower will get pension of $95,000 per year. Is that all?

January 17, 1961. Peck of sunshine a bushel of clouds; mild and breezy at Wilmington, N.Y. Ice pictures, garnished with frost feathers on windows. I scribble and read; rest and sleep; get up and eat. 8:30 P.M. I listen to Farewell Speech by President Eisenhower; and on T.V., I look into his Honest Face, although the speech, I comprehend every word and He never provoked me to think of Dexter White; and never insinuation to indicate that Ike is a traitor.

January 20, 1961. Cold and overcast. Wilmington, N.Y. 11:45 A.M. to 1:45 P.M. I watch inaugural doings of bigwigs; and inauguration of President John F. Kennedy I had hoped that a Catholic would never be President of U.S.A.! But today I witness inauguration of Irish, Catholic, spoiled Millionaire Brat. I was born in New York State; I will never take orders from John Fitzgerald Kennedy Or any other Catholic Brat, even as U.S. President. Noah John Rondeau

February 1, 1961. Very cold Atmosphere. R.G. Wiezel call for me at 4 P.M. and we call at Cabins. Met Mrs. Bacon; and I have good visit with Friend Wiezel at his Cabin: subjects Astronomy, Science, Markenville, Black Brook, Moons of Jupiter and We have a bit of Oat over Holt.

Actress Arlene Whelan took Noah on a tour of Paramount Studios in New York City. Courtesy of Richard J. Smith from Noah's photo album

February 4, 1961. Last night and this morning snowed 2 inches. At Wilmington, N.Y. Water pipes froze for the 8th time [code]. 11:30 a.m. I go to White Face Brook to get water; (Friends) come to help me.

February 6, 1961. Temperature below freezing at Wilmington, NY. Al and Tracy Pelky call. Jim and mother Smith from Green Street call. A flock of Blue Jays frolic in the field among old milkweeds.

February 9, 1961. Thawing, Big Breeze, Sunshine and some clouds. At Wilmington, N.Y. I bring in Mother's wash, I cook a pork roast [code].

February 13 - 14, 1961. I open Barrel of Cisco- Style of Peter Rondeau, 1891. I do some reading, writing and sewing. 11:20 p.m. a rat eating cheese from the pan of my trap got caught by the nose. I freshen Cisco to start the Holy Season of Lent.

February 19, 1961. Big Rain last night. Today 2 acres of Sunshine play Peek-a-Boo among Mountains and Vallies. Rain water and Liquidized Snow is running down Macadam. I sew Chipper Peck's glove.

1940 Phil McCalvin with Noah. Rich Smith and Phil were regular drop-ins at Cold River hill. Photo by Richard J. Smith. Courtesy Helen McCalvin Sawatzki

February 22, 1961. A bushel of clouds, a handful of Sunshine. At Wilmington, N.Y. I make two arrows for Chipper Peck and I give him rubber bands to fix his cross gun.

February 28, 1961. First Sunshine after 5 days of gloom.

March 1, 1961. Sun, then clouds- more gloom. I get letter from Lord (Oscar) Burguiere. Corn flower plants are coming up in my flower bed.

April 2, 1961. More clouds than sun. Sunday. I go to Nazarene Church and listen to children speaking and singing, Easter subjects, little tots in Easter bonnets and butterfly skirts were sweet little speakers.

April 8, 1961. Lightly snowed last night. I listen to Lawrence Welk's orchestra; I go back to old Wool after 12 days in long handle cotton.

April 24, 1961. Overcast and cool air. I call in Wilmington City. As I glance about the roadside fields, hills, and mountains; grass is greening,

FAME & $HEKELS

buds are swelling, birds are singing and seeds are geminating. I put keystone between two rocks in flower bed to retain soil.

May 1, 1961. Perfect Sun - Greening Grass. First swallows. I plant 30 sunflower seeds. Jenny Pelkey paint bed frames. Robins laugh out loud. Song sparrows jingle small change. I go back to cotton underwear for second time.

May 7, 1961. Last night rained puddles. I call in City; and confab with Joe Rondeau fishing on east side of Memorial Bridge. Robins cheer-up. Green grass on Winkleman's lawn. Golden sunshine.

June 1, 1961. Welcome June, stay until July. Have a good time. Don't mind the Black Flies.

June 9, 1961. Nice June Day. First daisy. 4 P.M. call on Dr. Spranz. "Check-up." Dr. replies: "Live to be 100 years."

June 16, 1961. I study typing touch method, all fingers.

July 8, 1961. Cloudy morning. Artist Jack Lewis from Delaware call on me. And I poise while he make portrait of hermit in water color.

July 12, 1961. Warm, Sunshine day with breeze To (Adirondack) Museum 9 a.m. Cut more poles and finish museum wigwam. Good crowd 14 states and Canada represented.

July 20, 1961. Sunshine scattered, clouds. Buy a swivel chair from Frank Savage. [code referring to how old it was and the amount he paid.] 10 PM bath. Professor Nye [code].

July 21, 1961. Two coopers put up "Adirondack Hermit" sign on my wigwam. I sold my buckskin bag. Bill Petty sit in my new rocking chair and tell a story about a big bear.

July 24, 1961. A young couple from Pennsylvania call. They took my photo at the North Pole 11 years ago while on their honeymoon. [Noah wrote a note next to an article entitled "The Creation of the World":] "And without Him there was not any-thing made that was made. Yes! And He looked at His work and it was very good; and he blessed it and it don't change. Now, pass the rheumatism and T.B."

August 23, 1961. A deer mouse tried my mouse trap last night at museum and it worked.

August 28, 1961. Sunshine, morning today; sun and clouds. Wilmington, N.Y. Mrs. A. J. Dittmar and four youngest children and Mrs. Menz and two daughters; all call on me at Whiteface Museum.

September 22, 1961. I sleep and watch the weather go by. Then a collector calls a week after I paid the bill in full; and the latest caller has another bill for the same thing. It looks like an American Thief.

November 5, 1961. Very cloudy morning. For first time I wear Fool American license on my back and take my gun for a short hunt in woods at sundown.

November 10, 1961. I receive lies from a liar in the American Welfare.

November 23, 1961. Overcast and mild. I begin shaping my new diary for 1962 by trimming down diary pages and adding 60 clippings.

December 13, 1961. A handful of Sunshine; and a bushel of clouds. Frozen auto tracks and snowflakes in air.

December 24, 1961. I put spruce cones and glitter on Xmas tree. [Following a clipping titled CALL SMOKING SLOW SUICIDE Noah wrote:] "Yes! And while killing slow, Tobacco make feet drag heavy; and Tobacco does not sharpen or keen, but it dulls our fibers so that the fine inspirations are impossible."

Chapter 33

1962

Adirondack history is peppered with examples of woodsmen who, like Noah John Rondeau, listened to the beat of different drummers. Some were destined for roles in the mountains' folklore when they caught hold of the public's attention and took up their banner.

Jennie Pelkey's home was still decorated for the holidays with Christmas lights, tinsel, eggshell glass ornaments, colorful ribbon candy and long strings of cranberries and popcorn strung over Christmas tree boughs when Noah's residence at her comfortable boarding house came to an end.

Monday, January 1, 1962. Wilmington. Warren Terry helping me pack my riches to move from Wilmington to Hazelton.

Noah's diary reveals nothing about why he decided to pull up stakes to re-settle in Hazelton, a hamlet northeast of Wilmington about seven miles from Au Sable Forks. While Noah's diaries show his noteworthy way with words, countless fuzzy diary entries leave many loose ends. These raise questions for those who read his diaries from end to end. I have been able to sat-isfy my curiosity through research and interviews, but I understand Noah's diaries had one purpose only—to record Rondeau's personal observations. Never in his wildest dreams would he have thought they would be used to construct a biography. For that reason, one can only make assumptions based on diary snippets and remarks by those who knew him well.

Barney Fowler said he'd "known Noah before Noah left the woods"— before he became a sensation, when "TV first flickered his image to a na-tion from New York City studios." Had the Internet been around in the 1960s, my guess is Barney would have been a fan of Twitter. His short

Photo by Edward Hudowalski.
Courtesy Grace Hudowalski

updates would have kept followers both updated and informed. Fowler found it amusing that big city "emcees whose wilderness experience consisted of witnessing squirrel battles on the Taconic Parkway" couldn't really get a handle around many of Rondeau's answers simply because they couldn't relate to a man "who dressed simply," who shot deer and bear for meat, subsistence fished and tended a vegetable patch deep in the mountains. Noah's attempt, reported Fowler, "to bring the outdoors indoors...wasn't Noah's way of life. It disrupted his normal living: it was upsetting, heady and exhilarating. For being a hermit, he became a national figure; for living alone in the woods, he became famous."

* * *

January 15, 1962. I read and write. Fourth Payment Last Year's Income Tax Due to Hell with It!

January 19, 1962. Perfect Sunshine. Hazelton, N.Y. 1 P.M. I go to Elizabethtown with Mrs. Terry; and pick up 3 stones in front of county buildings. I go in sheriff's office to commit myself to county jail; and I meet officer Fred Smith; I state my case. The officer was concerned and he called a judge; called welfare office; he went to welfare office; made several phone calls; got me a welfare cheque for January and he promised to make effort to correct.

January 30, 1962. Sunshine and wind blowing. ["WITH GOD ALL THINGS POSSIBLE" was the title of an article Noah read and then made this notation next to it pasted into his journal:]

"God, if it's so god damn easy for you to make all things good; and as you want them; why in hell don't you make contagious good health instead of so many contagious g.d. diseases?"

February 6, 1962. Frosty windows, cute designs. Earl Vosburg [sic] killed in 1959.

February 16, 1962. Cloudy, feeble sun through veil of nebulosity. Hair cut beard trim; Cold River style.

February 20, 1962. A pinch of clouds. Col. Jon Glenn launched in space to find orbit around earth. Glenn again in capsule again gone around the earth and around again and around again. In Atlantic -rescue, the same old Glenn again plus three orbits plus a g.d. finnigan.

March 19–20, 1962. Overcast and cool. Charles Lawrence and family call. I continue to check my riches for insurance. A crow flies north over the mailbox talking to himself crow fashion. A Blue Jay laments outdoors and our parakeet responded from his cage. I read and write. I find pleasure, farming in seed catalogs.

March 25, 1962. Sewer pipes raise hell [code].

April 1, 1962. Last night snowed one inch. Juncos and Song Sparrows called. I feed them cornflower seeds. [Jotted next to a photograph of Cuba's Castro and Soviet Union's Khrushchev both embracing Noah wrote:] "An April Fool Hug."

April 10, 1962. Morning grimaces of Sun. 9:30 a.m. a trembling, vibrating tremor of the Earth shook me modestly as I sit on my bed. I get two gallons of brook water near Washburn's.

April 16–20, 1962. Temperatures playing Tag on both sides of the freezing point. I plant 36 tomato seeds. I have civilization's distemper that people call a cold.

I make bowl of Eternity Tea. I take 12-foot Tag Alder bean poles and give a dead apple tree a hell of a whipping. I get sticks from the river bank, I get 6 poles from willow acres. Water frogs hoarsely grind their teeth in willow marsh.

April 26, 1962. Perfect sunshine and light breeze. I move 10-pound blocks from stump to woodshed. [code] I plant three packages of Aster seed. Leaves on lilacs are bursting out of tiny buds.

U.S. scored first hit on moon 11 A.M. Eastern Standard time with the United States launch of Ranger Four which crashed on the moon's mysterious backside.

Letter from the Essex County Department of Public Welfare:

> Dear Mr. Rondeau,
> Please be advised by the Social Security Administration that you have been requested to appear at the Plattsburg office in determination of your eligibility of your Social Security benefits. You have had two notices to appear. Failure to appear will cause you to be ineligible for these benefits. Your failure to verify eligibility for these benefits will also make you ineligible for old age assistance through this office. We therefore suggest you present yourself to the Plattsburg office without delay.

April 28, 1962. A pinch of morning sun. I get two jugs of water from Kilborn's Brook and ride home with Mrs. Preston. In the hours of sunshine, I see the lawn and lilacs greening. Warren Terry and his Marian return from their vacation. 7 P.M. I go to Terry's to Alfred's back by 8 o'clock. [code]

[The note Noah scrawled on an envelope from the Essex County Department of County Welfare:] "Call at Plattsburg office. Check for Big Riches."

FAME & $HEKELS

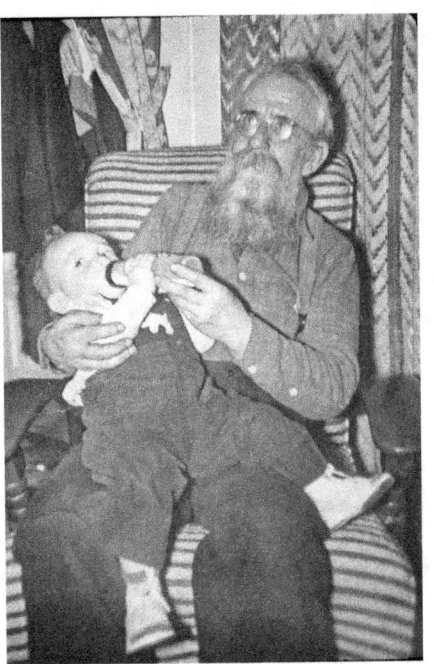

Tending Bar for Gary McCalvin - NJR Noah and Gary McCalvin at Alpine Terrance' Saranac Lake NY. Courtesy Helen McCalvin Sawatzki

April 29, 1962. Clocks advance one full hour. How much am I offered for the daylight that I've saved

May 1–2, 1962. May Day wonderful. The snow is all gone and Vernal green is the lawn. Trees grow new leaves and grekels say: "I'm up a tree." I walk to Saw Mill Road.

I call on Doc Hodgskin. Had a splendid visit. The doc and Warren Terry get notice "Not to Keep Boarders."

May 5, 1962. Overcast all day. I run lawnmower over green lawn. I arrange my riches and go camping. I wash my camping dishes.

May 22–23, 1962. Perfect Sunshine. At Buck Hill. I have my first outdoor fire. I rake dry leaves. 9 p.m. the first Whippoorwill tunes up.

I wind big clock. I do more camp overhauling. At 3 P.M. I call at Patty Conway best ever clump of lilacs. I call at Sumac Clearing and at Strawberry Clearing. I see a 100 Apple and Cherry Trees all in bloom. I get milkweeds from potato patch. I see four week old bear tracks made by a big Bear and one small live pine topped off by a large bear a month ago.

June 1–4, 1962. A nice June morning. Birds are singing at Buck Hill. 10 o'clock I am making Bisquick dumplings. 11 o'clock I'm eating dumplings and I pity the Hermit who is not enjoying a June day and Bisquick dumplings. At dusk a snowshoe rabbit 4 feet from camp.

A Spotted Adder thirty inches (long) come into camp; and I shoot 3 times with 22 cal. rifle. Dead Adder!

Singing birds and Vernal green. A perfect place for a Hermit's vacation. I shoot two more Spotted Adder's six feet from camp. Later I banish them in forest.

June 30, 1962. I have a happy snooze. I have a frankfurter, bread and coffee. Gail Read do the Twist. I have watermelon and I have grape juice. Thanks June for 30 days. Thanks for commencement at schools. Thanks for growing hay. Come again June, next year after May.

July 3–4, 1962. Perfect Summer Day. I have day sleep. I take Gail Read by airplane to Peek-A-Boo Hill. I take the pin curlers off of my whiskers. Comb my whiskers in style. Hurrah! The Fourth of July.

August 1, 1962. Morning Sun at Au Sable Forks. Good morning August. Welcome since July. Stay till September. Don't mind hay fever. Sundown I walk. I start writing my Will and my Won't.

August 24, 1962. I call on Doctor Spranz. Receive letter from Dr. Dittmar. I call at Fleek's Pharmacy.

August 29, 1962. A hot August day at AuSable Forks. 11 o'clock Mrs. Dittmar call for me and take me to Plattsburg. 12:30 we dine with Rotary Club at Cumberland Hotel. 1:50 p.m. I speak "40 Years in 35 Minutes." Good Crowd. 2:30 p.m. Dr. Dittmar extract my last 8 teeth.

September 10, 1962. Overcast then Sunshine. I take Dale and Tracy Pelkey to Peek-Boo-Hill in my airplane. I call at the Tin Can Dump and at Frog Pond. I pick a cup of Juniper berries.

September 15, 1962. Nice September day at North Jay. I put out feed boxes for honey bees. I gather natural herbs for medicine, to make Old People young.

September 25–26, 1962. Frost last night today sun and clouds at North Jay, N.Y. I go with Clifford and we motor over 10 rough miles of woods roads with '29 Ford. Beautiful mountains, hills and vallies. We search for honey bees.

With Peter Pelkey and Smith we take up a bee tree. We take a section of the tree; and the bees, honey, and honey comb, brood comb and embryos. And we take the bee hive and swarm to Smith's home and we set them up near the blacksmith's shop.

October 18, 1962. Nice Autumn Day at Hazelton, N.Y. I whittle and saw on a greenwood cane. Mrs. Hathaway and Mrs. Buckley visit. We confab.

October 27, 1962. Sunshine, breezy, cold air at Hazelton, N.Y. St. Peter and God Almighty set your clock back and notice American wisdom to save "day light".

October 31, 1962. Very cloudy, rain last night and today. Morgan Mountain, full dressed and nebulosity. I call on Dr. Spranz. Call at Rexall Phar. Confab with John Rondeau.

November 5, 1962. At Wilmington to Plattsburg. I make ready to go to Plattsburg with Mr. Robert Anthony. Y.M.C.A. 4 P.M. 5 o'clock I visit library and swimming pool and other parts downstairs. 5:55 P.M. Dr. A.G. Dittmar call at my room. 6 o'clock we go down on second floor and join more than a hundred hungry father and sons; and we move in two lines and pick up dinner cafeteria style. We put a lot of food and coffee out of sight. 7 o'clock Dr. Dittmar introduced me and I speak to fathers and sons. 40 minutes. 8 - 9 o'clock I autograph for sixty boys. I put up for night at Y.M.C.A. room number 9.

December 4, 1962. Perfect Sunshine at Wilmington, N.Y. This day is like a summer day minus black flies and mosquitoes. I call at White Face market

December 17–23, 1962. Snowflakes scattered in breeze make Winter pictures. At Wilmington, N.Y. I write Christmas cards. I receive Christmas cards. Roofs loaded with white Snow, snowplows busy day and night. St. Nick digging like tin roof cat. Santa ready for aerial flight as chimney swallow.

Perfect Sunshine; mild and calm.

At Singing Pines.

Aden Lewis, call and we have ⌐o⊣⊦⌐⊠⅌

[symbols] "⊣A⌇⊁⊁L⌇o⅄" ⊙⊙⊥⊦o "⊙ ⊙,
⊥⊠ ⅄̣ ⊙ ⨉⅃⊦⨉⅄o∈⌶ ⨀⌽⅄ ⊙ ⊁⊣⅃'⊦⊠

And here it is :—

'Ash Wed.' and no ashes to rub on my Fool Head. And no Ciscoes for the Holy Season of Lent. If God find that out — He will raise Hell.

Chapter 34

1963

January 6, 1963. Sunday. Mild and cloudy all day at Wilmington, N.Y. Winter is set: wind, cold and blowing; drifts made by the wind that howled and made the atmosphere so damn cold.

As 1963 began, Noah's peace depended on spending time with friends and neighbors in the Wilmington area—"a common man of fine caliber," is how residents I interviewed described him.

January 6 was a typical "winter weather" day. Noah was back at Mrs. Jennie Buckley's home. His late January description tells: "It's Wintery—Jack Frost is busy inscribing ice pictures garnished with frost feathers on our windows. I eat and sleep and watch the weather go by and sew patches on sleeves of seven-year-old shirt—and the weather is still going by."

Long-time friend Peggy Byrne was still on the trail of writing Noah's life story, but with family commitments and business she did not meet with Noah as much as she would have liked.

The most significant change in Noah's life this year was Noah's living arrangements. Mrs. Buckley would need her spare room she had been renting to him, forcing an unanticipated move. Close by stood Abe Fuller's small rental cabins that lined the AuSable River. Noah arranged a long-term lease of one of Abe's tourist units. It didn't take long before sparks began to fly between the two men.

Richard Smith lived close by. He provided the history.

"Although Noah received some income during his temporary employment at the North Pole in 1950, it was not enough to support him. He had applied for and was given assistance by the Essex County social services department. When his caseworker notified him that his monthly check

Noah did a lot of rocking, reading, and contemplation as he puffed his meerschaum. Pipe, given to him by his friends, the Billy Burgers. Photo by Ed Hudowalski. Courtesy of Grace Hudowalski

from the county would be less because of the income he was making at the North Pole, he balked and decided not to return as Santa the following season. He then lived as a ward of the county for the next thirteen years, boarding in a variety of rented rooms and cabins in the Wilmington - Lake Placid area.

"By 1963 he had hit Adirondack bedrock. I remember seeing the despair in his eyes, and I knew how painful it was for him to endure living in one of Abe Fuller's ramshackle rental cabins on River Road. I saw him often that year because Fuller's cabins were a short distance from my house along the same road. His circumstances were more than I could bear.

"The memories of our Cold River excursions, campfire chats following bear and venison chases, his sourdough pancakes, powerful coffee which could support a spoon upright and our enduring friendship motivated me to do something more for him. He was fiercely independent and didn't want to rely on handouts. It made him feel helpless as his pride and dignity were chipped away.

"I had always wanted a little hunting cabin, and so I bought an acre and a half of woodland in Wilmington and skidded an old chicken coop onto the property. On my off-hours from care taking at several large camps around Lake Placid, I worked on converting the building into a weathertight abode far from the tourist traffic along Route 86. When it was just about completed, I offered it to Noah telling him I preferred to have someone on the property watching over things since most of my time was spent care taking or at my home on River Road. I told him he could live there for as long as he wanted and that he should treat it as his own.

"His despair vanished within twenty-four hours of moving. I was delighted to see my friend happy again, with his dignity restored. I kidded him about his improved smile, but he assured me that it had to do with the new set of teeth Dr. Dittmar had presented him! Offering him the camp, which I had dubbed Singing Pines, was a modest gesture, but the cabin was comfortable and he had regained his independence. We resumed our laughing good times during our once-a-week get-togethers.

"For the next four years he gardened, looked after a few fruit trees, chopped wood and entertained old friends regularly. I remember him commenting, "It's just like Cold River, but nearer to the grocery store and post office.""

* * *

January 20, 1963. I do installment wash on shirt, overalls, two socks and two handkerchiefs.

January 25–26, 1963. It is Wintery Jack Frost is busy inscribing ice pictures garnished with frost feathers on our windows. I eat and sleep and watch the weather go by and sew patches on my sleeves and the weather is still going by.

February 6–7, 1963. Earle A. Vosburg[sic] killed in car wreck in 1959. I receive my cheque for Miserable Existence from "Big Business so called Welfare." [code]

February 10, 1963. Sun and clouds, calm, mild. It is much like Winter, when Winter comes along between Summers.

February 26–27, 1963. Perfect Sunshine, bumps of nebulosity and thawing slightly at Wilmington, N.Y.

I go to AuSable Forks with Clara Hazelton and I call on Dr. Spranz And Fleeks Pharmacy. 4 P.M. ride to Wilmington with Mrs. Hazelton; I take a little nap to 5 P.M. wake up: dizzy, and sickish, not feeling well all evening.

Here it is Ash Wednesday and I did not get Holy Ashes saturated with oil to daub on my head. And, I did not even get a bear or fish for the Holy season of Lent. And, if God ever finds that out He would raise Hell.

March 27, 1963. 450 years ago today: Juan Ponce De Leon discovered Florida. But Florida was not lost to all people. There were enough People in Florida to kill Mr. De Leon with an arrow before he found the "Fountain of Youth" Amen.

April 1, 1963. Perfect Sunshine at Wilmington, N.Y. April, Where in Hell have you been the last 11 months?

April 22–23, 1963. Summertime is here. It's good to see a robin and a green lawn. Snow all gone in vallies. A lot of snow on White Face Mountain. Many Spring and Summertime birds are here; and a few days more will resurrect shrubs that were dead and will dress them with leaves with flowers on their heads. I go back to my cotton underwear.

April 28, 1963. Daylight Savings Time! What a wonder? We have Newspapers, to tell us every year, when to push our clocks ahead and when to push the hands back. Such Wisdom! Sun, Moon and Stars are amazed. Now how much am I offered for the daylight I've saved?

May 4, 1963. I'm packing my riches to move. Mrs. Buckley needs room for her summer customers. [Noah is moving to one of Abraham Fuller's cabins located along the Ausable River on River Road. The location offered ample room for him to garden. It was also near his longtime friend Richard Smith's home on River Road and the village of Lake Placid.]

May 31, 1963. The Spring Time Green of grass and leaves is not a dream; but real is the Vernal Green as the Mountains is high and Vallies Deep.

June 27, 1963. Hot summer day at River Road. Smallest ever bunny is in garden. Daisy blossoms are wonderful. Robins songs are made of chunks of strenuous music. And what singing while blue eggs are incubating.

June 29–30, 1963. I throw potato digger at a rabbit; and hustle him out of the garden.

Thanks June for 30 days. Come again in June next year after May. You're welcome in our front yards. Our Robins need you May to July.

July 1, 1963. Very hot day at River Road. Hi July, where in hell have you been since before last August? Well, for 31 days, have a good time. Don't mind the Black Flies.

I cut 150 suckers off my sweet corn. Abraham Fuller and me go to Lake Placid and Saranac Lake.

July 6–7, 1963. Perfect Sun at River Road. I pay Abraham Fuller $25.00 on July's board and room and Abe has hog argument because He has to furnish fuel to heat my room, when necessary.

My rain buckets are full. I cut MY firewood and charge the labor to Abraham Fuller.

July 10–11, 1963. I examine Abraham Fuller's well water supply. I find a dead animal. Decomposed hardly recognizable. Could be chipmunks or squirrels. Call on Frank Bernard Smith and fill my water jars from a mountain brook.

I make an agreement with Abraham Fuller to pay five dollar rent per month for use of one cabin (drinking) water available and use of latrine; beginning 10 a.m. July 10, 1963 for a time indefinite not specified except I will stay to harvest my garden or leave earlier as I please.

July 18, 1963. Cloudy morning. Sunrise time shower. Early p.m. lightning wink in my electric light bulb over my desk. I look over my Morning Glory plants; and consider my riches.

7 p.m. Abraham Fuller says "Your wood has come." I say "I did not order wood." Then Abe to Wood Man "He has changed his mind again," and Abe rants at my expense.

Noah tending his flower garden. Courtesy Bill Frenette

July 21, 1963. Hot day. Mid Day sprinkle - 1 drop per square foot. Call at mountain brook and get 10 quarts of pure mountain water. In shadows of dusk Midge Gnats tried to devour me as I cut thorn poles. A Robin on a Robin's stump in green lawn is a picture in golden light of sun.

July 28–29, 1963. I call on my garden and, I see a half grown rabbit. Mid afternoon Abraham Fuller call on me and he bring Victor Jacques for a witness. And Victor is a decent old citizen and Abraham Fuller is an American Crook, a Liar and a Dirty Old Hog, not to be depended on and on this occasion Mr. Jacques "is out of place" and makes a sucker of himself for crooked Abe Fuller.

Abraham Fuller is an American Liar. I am preparing to leave River Road since can't get along good with crooked liar.

August 1–2, 1963. Rabbits! Abraham Fuller appear at my door and asked "When are you going to move?" And I say, "Abraham, I will not move for at least 2 months until I can harvest my garden that I got involved into due to your lies, false pretense and dishonesty; and, I will not pay over 5 dollars per month Rent for your little shack accordingly to our agreement of July 10th.

6 p.m. Abe has a sign up which says "Take no more wood."

August 5, 1963. Overcast and showers. River is high. I haul bean poles to camp. Rattle Snake Venom. Emerson Nye call on me on River Road. I say "Nye, you know you are not wanted. Please go away and never come back." Nye replies, "I don't care about your bullshit; if you don't want assistance alright!"

Nye walks to his car,- mumbling about a cheque and he was all gone. This is the day my cheque for August would be issued; I think Nye had my cheque was bringing it personally holding it, to personally bring me to terms; and did not want B.S.

August 7-8, 1963. Last night Rabbits trimmed carrot tops. I water Bachelor Buttons and Cucumber plants.

Courtesy of Richard J. Smith from Noah's photo album

FAME & $HEKELS

65 years ago today I left Jackson Hill. Ran away from home. Left Peter Rondeau and His stick, His Abuse, His religion and His Fool God.

August 16, 1963. Sunshine morning; afternoon scattered clouds. Walked to Lake Placid the length of Wilmington Road later ride to Wilmington P.O. with a French couple. I get my mail and call at White Face market. I have meal at Melvin Peck's. Get letter from Fredrick S. Dennin Abraham Fuller's lawyer.

August 17, 1963. Clouds, sun, showers after sundown at River Road. I cut alder poles in Mr. Porter's forest. Abraham Fuller fanatic builder moved His Freak Shanty, from Mr. Portner's ground, forty feet S near to Abe's potatoes in my garden. 7 P.M. I dig about five pounds of potatoes.

August 20, 1963. Perfect sunshine, scattered clouds, calm. At River Road Abraham Fuller asked for, "Money for your August rent." And I say,- "My rent, you have in advance; and accordingly I will stay until I harvest my garden and you and your attorney are helpless to make it otherwise." And the blab was on Vulgar, Profane, and Nasty. My part appropriate. Abe's part the same lies by the same Liar, Thief, Robber, and American Methodist Abraham Fuller!

August 21, 1963. Perfect sunshine, scattered clouds and calm. At River Road I confab with Mr. Porter at his new well, on his new building lot and walked 200 feet W on newly bulldozed road; thence 100 feet S; then 100 feet through alders and Joe Pye weeds, to slough, where Abe Fuller has a Blue Print to build a Blarney Castle on a Blarney Stone. Sundown: I go to Wilmington with Richard Smith and we stop and see Richard's camp.

August 22, 1963. Perfect Sunshine and scattered clouds continue at River Road. Mid Day: Abraham Fuller is removing small Box Stove from my room; and he installs a larger stove. I wash and dry my red wool blanket. Mr. and Mrs., a young couple, call on me. The man, a Bohemian; the woman, a German.

August 23, 1963. Sun, clouds, light breeze at River Road. Bernard Smith and Howard Peck call on me. Late afternoon: showers. I pay Abe Fuller $3.00 for exchanging stoves and $3.00 for a half cord of Hardwood.

August 25, 1963. Sun and clouds, nice cool Summer day at River Road. Four miles from Lake Placid I read and write and I cook potatoes and squash. Richard Smith build a new cement chimney at Singing Pines [his camp in Wilmington].

August 27, 1963. Summer clouds, nice hot summer day. AuSable Forks - River Road. I gather thoroughwort and other plants. Mrs. Shelby Richardson bring my packbasket, axe, and traps to Sadies. I ride to Wilmington with Myrtle McCasland. Lunch at Peck's ride to River Road with Melvin Peck. While I was away two days someone stole cucumbers from my garden.

August 29, 1963. Overcast, early morning shower at River Road. I use Privet sticks and red loss to mark squash and cucumbers. I make copy of 8-5-'63 letter to Essex County welfare. I prepare to go to Saranac Lake.

August 31, 1963. Early morning shower and a nice day of sun and clouds at River Road. First morning glory bell flower. I visit the garden early morning; Abraham Fuller glue his Fool Face in my window and squint to see what He can snoop.

September 4, 1963. Morning overcast, cool; Evening: clear, cool, ready for frost at River Road; On my plants six Bachelor blossom buttons, ten Morning Glory Bells, 188 Summer Crookneck Squash; about 400 ears of corn; the majority, too young to mature before killing frost. I have 60 new bean poles tied in bundles ready to move from River Road. 7 PM I use three blankets and two coats to cover squash, and cucumbers.

September 6, 1963. Early fog followed by sunshine and scattered clouds at River Road. I pull up thirty bean poles. I hang up gourds to dry. I slat down six quarts of cucumbers. I dig twelve pounds of potatoes. Evening: Abraham Fuller cover his cucumber vines (but) there are no cucumbers on the vines. There has never been any but Abe cover(ed) the vines. Nice vines Abe.

September 10, 1963. Scattered clouds. Perfect sunshine. At River Road I ask Abe Fuller to sign a Receipt for two months rent; I had his cabin July 10 to September 10 at $5.00 per month paid in advance and he refused to sign. Evening: Abe Fuller cover cucumber vines again. No cucumbers yet.

I take Dale and Tracy Peckey to Peek-a-Boo hill in my airplane. I call on the Tin Can dump and at Frog Pond and pick a cup of juniper berries.

September 19, 1963. AM bits of sun; generally cloudy; Mid Day sprinkle two gallons in my rain catcher under eve-spout. At River Road

5 PM I go with Richard Smith and we take a load of my riches to Singing Pines. I set eight mice traps. We have coffee and return to River Road.

September 20, 1963. Mrs. Mendel return my photo album and scrapbooks. A pinch of sunshine and a bushel of clouds. 5 PM Richard Smith come along with a car and trailer and we take another load of my riches to Singing Pines. We go to the spring. 9 PM I'm home at River Road and Richard drive on three doors and he's home. I notice with Flashlight [that] rain water has been emptied from rain catcher and filth put in container; and some green grass covered the filth; and at other end of cabin under the porch, an old suitcase has also been treated to filth and some of my magazines were tossed on the filth.

September 21, 1963. Perfect sunshine. Perfect Autumn colors. At River Road I pack the last of my riches to move to Singing Pines. Today I notice some of my food items are gone missing: 1 pound brown sugar 1 box sardines 1 can red meat, 30 oz. 1/4 pd. bacon 1 jar marmalade.

September 22, 1963. Clouds and Sun. River Road - Singing Pines. 9 AM I help Richard Smith load car and trailer; and we drive 9 miles to Singing Pines camp. I get lunch and Richard work to complete unloading. After lunch Richard saw wood. I wash dishes and write a letter.

September 24, 1963. Frost last night; today perfect Autumn sunshine. At Singing Pines I put nails in studdings and plate and hang up my wardrobe in my New Home. I chop Stovewood and wigwam poles. Autumn colors are at climax best 10 days early. Ferns are red as foxes tales. A few leaves are falling. A splendid time. Cool frosty days full of sunshine.

September 26, 1963. The beauty of Autumn is at hand in mountains and vallies. Trees and shrubbery, flora and fauna all in transcend mutual harmony of change. What a time for a naturalist to walk among the Adirondack hills at Singing Pines. I add poles to my wigwam. 4 PM Richard Smith call and do carpenter work on camp.

September 29, 1963. Overcast, showers, sprinkle and lulls all day. At Singing Pines camp Richard Smith call with Carpenter Tools and he build a door frame, jams and header; wallboard casing; and he made a door of planed lumber and he hung the door with hinges. Quite a perfect job.

September 30, 1963. Perfect sunshine. At Singing Pines camp I put up a clothesline. I chop some stove wood. Thanks September for thirty days. Thanks for poly colors, on mountains and vallies. Thanks for beauty in inexplicable by tongue or pen, or reading in a den, But happy the living who gaze on hills or glens.

October 2, 1963. I write Ward Lumber Co. for a load of wood. 5 PM, R.T. Wiezel from Lake Ontario call on me and we go to Wilmington and Rudy get a bottle of liqueur; and Parker cups; and we park and have, old time spree plus, gab fest; and at dusk we go to Hazel and Bill's Restaurant and we have a good dinner plus more gab.

FAME & $HEKELS

Courtesy of Richard J. Smith from Noah's photo album

October 5, 1963. Soft maple red leaves from Heart Lake [pressed between pages] found between dock and trail to Mt. Jo. Madeline Dodge picked them. 8 o'clock go with Madeline to Keene Valley library, register, meal tickets. 9 o'clock ride to Heart Lake. Visit with Mrs. Abele and others. Leaves pasted in book are from bank at Heart Lake where we baptized my rifle.

October 10, 1963. Perfect October day, calm, mild. At Singing Pines camp I cut poles and put down skids to pile on 16 inch stove wood that will be coming. I pick up two cords of old lumber- four years stranded and I classify most of it for kindling. 4 PM four kids call on me. They want to see the tepee. They are five to eleven years old. Two boys and two girls.

Richard Smith call and make a door and complete wall between S and middle room and we have dinner and confab about "good guns".

October 6, 1963. Sunshine continues shinning. At Lewis, NY. I ride to Elizabethtown with Bruce Mc Phail; and call at county office and I return to Lewis; afternoon go with Roy Hathaway and we call at Cornwrights

Sawmill and we call on Jack Gough and Grover Cornwright. We have a good afternoon visiting with old timers. Ninety-two wore out but what spirit, what yarns. Big, Big Bucks!

October 23, 1963. Calm, mild and sunshine. At Singing Pines camp. I cut two four inch popular; and two five-inch maples; and I cut them in Stove Length Sticks. 9 PM two large skunks are on my door steps. One with short narrow stripe and one with broad long strips.

November 15, 1963. Generally cloudy, two hours sun, mild snow all gone. At Singing Pines I add five poles to wigwam. I cut stove wood for the night. I bottle trappers chowder. I pin licenses to jacket. I arrange big game rope.

November 16, 1963. Clouds and sun. At Singing Pines I chop three maple trees among silver birches. I put American fool trap tags on six traps and prepare packbasket for trapline.

November 20, 1963. Wet leaves froze last night. Today: perfect sunshine. Frozen leaves relax. At Singing Pines. I go to Wilmington. Ride with Denton's. I write Welfare; I write Gary Mc Calvin. I call at Wilmington post office got cheque, two weeks delayed. Returned with Abe Fuller.

November 25, 1963. Cold last night. A half inch of ice on water caught in rain catcher. Perfect sunshine morning. At Singing Pines. 5 PM Mr. Denton and his son, James bring me two pigs heads. Evening I carve and classify cuts of pork.

November 30, 1963. Last night much rain. Today overcast. Snowed two inches. At Singing Pines. 4 PM I go with Harold Peck for a load of wigwam poles to Mrs. Dodge. Thanks November for thirty days; and so far Autumn has been the mildest ever. Evening: I boil and purify brine to cure and keep jowl pork.

FAME & $HEKELS

December 3, 1963. Early morning snowed one inch- mild and overcast all day. At Singing Pines I find the winter scene perfect; the twelve foot spruce ten feet from the cabin door is decked in perfect X-mas style and the caulk white birches among singing pines and the concave of the semi circle of the road is perfect scene for the hermit to view through the little cabin's window.

December 12–15, 1963. Sunshine, snow 10 inches deep. Winter scenes are wonderful. I read and write. I cut greenwood. I start a wash. I write Christmas cards. Mr. Denton from across the road bring me a gift package from Nazarene Sunday School.

December 25, 1963. Mid Day I walk to Wilmington then taxi to Mr. and Mrs. Mackhe. Splendid turkey dinner with Madeline Dodge. 6 PM taxi home.

December 26–27, 1963. I put plenty of wood in Camp. It is nice winter weather. 8 inches of snow cover topograph. Chickadee Birds call for Suet. I prepare a feed House for Birds and I load it with wet Suet pieces, Rice, Cooked Cornmeal and Sunflower seeds. I wash 8 pieces.

Chapter 35

1964

January 1, 1964. Wednesday. Sun and clouds calm and moderate temperatures at Singing Pines. I put out a tree house for the birds. I cook a Slam Bang stew. I put almanac clippings in this diary. First brown-breasted nuthatch calls and partakes of suet with chickadee birds near my window.

Noah John stood beside his Singing Pine's backyard wigwam shortly after dawn. Smelling the mild air, he knew that yesterday's January warm spell would resume once the sun worked higher over the horizon. "Overcast-Very mild Thawing Two glimpses of Sunshine tossed in. Snow, just right to make a Snow Man," he recorded at Singing Pines on Friday, January 3, 1964. "Woodpecker, Nuthatch and Black Cap Chickadees call for Suet. I read and write. I start sour dough to generate yeast to raise my winter Pan Cakes."

The following day Richard Smith arrived. Together they walked through the fresh snow. "It had snowed about two inches," Smith said about that day. Noah recorded it as his "First trip to [the] Spring [for] 1964."

Smith remembers the weekend because of all the ceremonial fuss Noah made over his first homemade pancakes and the robust but flavorful Eternity Tea he brewed, as well as the noticeable enjoyment Noah showed. "The camp hadn't been one hundred percent fine-tuned by then," he told. "There were renovations still to be done, but Noah didn't care all that much about what carpenter projects I still planned to do. From past observations, years ago back at the river during the 1940s, I was convinced he preferred to concentrate on the beauty of his surrounds rather than the

Courtesy unknown

bareness of his accommodations.

"I recall we did a lot of confabbing too. Noah loved birds. At times the red-breasted nuthatches and chickadee birds would fly into camp when we left the door open to carry in armloads of firewood. Noah would put sunflower seeds in the palm of his hand. The birds would feed from his hand. He told me the birds were so passionate about his feeding them that 'the chickadee birds would stop me in the woods and would not let me pass until I'd give them sunflower seeds.' He kept a supply of them in his pocket."

1964 was the time Noah began to reexamine his religious beliefs.

In Noah's self-penned "My 60 Years of Recollections" there is a strong suggestion that his father had respect for work and a bedrock Christian belief. Peter Rondeau "raised his children with a fear of the Lord." Clarence Petty tells it the way he remembers it straight from Noah.

"His folks were highly religious. They were Catholic and that's at least one reason he left home. He told us that his father got the priest to bring him in there [to see the priest]. The priest said, 'You've got to come to church when your father tells you to or I'm going to turn you into a little yellow dog.' That did it right there. Noah said, 'After that I wanted nothing to do with the Catholic religion…' and he was against the whole Catholic religion from then on."

His rejection of the Catholic Church and his resentment of his father caused him to strike out on his own, and he turned to the faith of the Sev-

Courtesy of Richard J. Smith from
Noah's photo album

enth Day Adventists. Petty remembers, "Rondeau observed Saturday as the Sabbath."

It's ironic that Noah embraced the Adventist religion, since many of that faith are vegetarians. Petty continues:

> I recall the only time that Noah offered to do any work at our place was one Saturday. He came to Coreys to help us in the fall of 1922. He had come along for his mail in late afternoon just before sundown, all dressed up in a white shirt and suit coat as we were pouring cement and stones into a form for the foundation of a garage. He stood around and watched us until the sun set, and just as the sun went down over the horizon, he took off his coat and suddenly started working like mad picking up stones and putting them into the fresh concrete foundation. I remember at the time I wondered about it, and later mentioned this to my mother. She said, "You know Noah's Sabbath is celebrated on Saturday and the Seventh Day Adventist does not approve of working that day until after sundown."

Throughout the mid-sixties Noah was frequently visited by Fanny Wolfe, a Jehovah's Witness and her son, Douglas A. Wolfe, from nearby Bonnie View. Fanny and Douglas found answers to spiritual questions using Scriptural basis, not doctrines and traditions, and they encouraged others to examine their own beliefs to find answers to their questions.

In my interviews with Douglas Wolfe, I learned 1964 was the year Noah

renewed his interest in his large family Bible by rereading it. The Wolfes enjoyed talking with him as well as challenging Noah to find answers to questions he raised.

Based on conversation with Doug, I believe Noah concluded that he believed in a higher power, but one who gave him latitude to make up his own mind and make mistakes and learn from them.

Starting a new year called for Noah to express his wish of good luck for another "random scoot around the Sun" and to record nature observations.

Winter did not restrict Noah at Singing Pines as it had locked him in around the Town Hall back at the river. He had time on his hands, time to read, write, study, go places, and visit.

***

January 19, 1964. At Singing Pines. I see plenty of rabbit tracks between camp and spring. A red-breasted nuthatch light on my hand and picked crumbs. Trapper Lewis call. (Decoded: From Mother L grapefruit and oranges.) I walk about Best Pine and apple orchard.

[Throughout Rondeau's 1964 and '65 selected diary entries expert Rondeau code readers and writers, David Green and Adam Pearsall, completed their last decoding of the hermit's chicken scratches. Greene reminded Pearsall that whenever "a sideways Y" appeared it means "I'm writing in phonetic French."

Pearsall shared Greene "had a chuckle" when Rondeau wrote the letters R and P, though Rondeau "commonly swapped out R and P.. not to mention forever trying to figure out if Noah means E or W when it is in the middle of a combination...."

A view of Cold River above the Hermitage.
Photo by author

February 3, 1964. At Singing Pines I split ten large maple blocks and I carry 3/4 cord of two foot wood 75 feet and pile wood between maple trees.

February 7, 1964. Last night snowed 2 inches of plastic snow. Today total overcast and mild. At Singing Pines Five kinds of birds get sunflower seeds near my window. I receive [welfare] cheque for miserable existence from "Big Business" so called Welfare. I shop in seed catalogs.

February 12, 1964. At Singing Pines. Aden Lewis call and we have (Decoded: a picnic. We cut 24 inches pine & 1 13" <plen> & we cut 12 medium trees 6 to 12 inches.) And here it is: Ash Wed. and no ashes to rub on my Fool Head and no ciscaes for the Holy Season of Lent. If God find that out, He will raise Hell.

February 22, 1964. Chilly winter air. At Singing Pines I get stove wood to perpetuate the homefire against the winter temperature.

February 25, 1964. Last night snowed 1". To Day Perfect Sunshine at Singing Pines. Richard Smith call and He get my mail; And (Decoded: 6 gals kerosene have 2 picnics).

March 8, 1964. At Singing Pines. 10 o'clock I measure a 10 inch popular into 24 inch blocks. Richard Smith arrived from River Road and he bring my mail and other items and he saw a cord of 24 inch wood with a chainsaw.

September 10, 1964. Nice summer day. At Singing Pines I do many chores at camp and yard and garden and wigwam. I prepare ground for next Spring planting.

September 16, 1964. Happy day. At Singing Pines I get a special stick from the forest and make a metal hook and ring and articulate them to make a devise to hang a pail of water in summer wigwam.

September 30, 1964. A nice September day. At Singing Pines Thanks September for thirty days. And thanks for a carpet of red and yellow leaves. And thanks for mature fertile seeds. And thanks for the gold on our pumpkins that were green. September, come again next year after August.

[A letter from Oscar Burguiere, an old Cold River friend whom Noah dubbed "Lord" Burguiere was placed in this page. It reads:]

My Dear Grand Old Noble,

...you remember Carolyn is my sister that you gave the fox skin to in 1935. I am happy that you are staying with Richard Smith now. I enclose a little story that I should think you would enjoy.

A man goes to a priest and asks if he would give his dog absolution?

Priest: "Of course not. Go down the street and see the Protestant minister. Maybe he will do it for you."

Man: "Do you suppose he would do it for one hundred dollars?"

Priest: "Why didn't you tell me yours was a Catholic dog?" "Come right in."

Mrs. Rene Sweeney and daughter, Patsey, were asking about you again. So if you don't send them at least a pennie postcard we are going to plant Bermuda grass seed in your pansy bed by way of helicopter, and we are going to get Earl Vosburg's ghost to chase you up and down River Road. Now it would not be fair for you to gilt my baby sister, Helen, for Patsy. Well enough for now.

October 18, 1964. Perfect autumn Sunday. At Singing Pines I read 15 chapters of Revelations by St. John. First Bible Reading in 27 years.

October 20, 1964. A nice October day. At Singing Pines I read seven chapters, finish book Revelation

October 24, 1964. Generally overcast. At Singing Pines I keep Sabbath. First time in 27 years.

October 31, 1964. Perfect sunshine. At Singing Pines 24 children call with false faces and paper bags. "Trick or treat"

November 20, 1964. Nice autumn weather. At Singing Pines I read and write and prepare to keep the Sabbath.

December 2, 1964. Sunshine and freezing temperature. At Singing Pines I read and write. It's wonderful and satisfactory to know that Babylon the Great has fallen; and God's Kingdom rules. Amen.

December 12, 1964. Cloudy morning. After 10 o'clock much sunshine At Singing Pines I keep the Sabbath. After dark Hi Denten bring me a pig's head. 7 to 9 P.M. I wash and carve the pig's head. [code]

December 23, 1964. Sunshine, slightly thawing. At Singing Pines I pile 2 cords of wood. Mid day Mr. Medcalf called with frames for glasses. This is first day of season, the chickadees call for winter rations. And a half dozen chickadees take about fifty sunflower seeds from the palm of my hand. These birds were well trained last winter.

December 24, 1964. At Singing Pines. Chickadees are tending their breadline "sunflower seeds."

Chapter 36

1965

Noah prepared for the 1964–65 winter season in ways he always had, by providing himself with the necessities of life. Where once he had wild meat and the root crops raised in the clearing, he now had an ample stock of store-bought necessities, along with some deer and bear meat provided by Richard Smith and a can of bear grease, "which is an absolute necessity" Noah always pointed out to Smith. Smith would remember his own "hungry smell" of Rondeau's Slam Bang Kettle concoctions. Where once he cached valuables in garbage cans placed among large rocks at the Mammoth Graveyard, he now used padlocks on Singing Pines' doors.

Thursday, January 7, 1965. Sunshine and 5" hard snow. At Singing Pines. 11 a.m. I go to Wilmington –taxi with Benj. Elliott to AuSable Forks. Call on Dr. Spranz, A&P [code] call at Black Brook [code] 4 o'clock [back] at Singing Pines [code].

Starting a new year called for Noah to express his wish of good luck for another "random scoot around the Sun; and come to think; O'Gods! I did not pray." But no matter—"The weather would be as just the same, as if I prayed all the time for dry weather, or all the time for rain."

Winter did not restrict Noah at Singing Pines as it had locked him in around the Town Hall. He had time on his hands, time to read, write, study, go places, visit—a Mr. Metcalf was oft mentioned—and it is left to one's imagination to figure out what he meant when he remarked on January 28, "I make a Hard Wood Dibble."

Noah recorded on February 11: "I read – 'My Moose Creek Trap Line'

Courtesy Bud Smith

by E. J. Dailey in *Fur-Fish-Game*" (a popular sportsperson's magazine). Remarkably, he did not make one comment about the author. Between 1919 and 1928 Dailey and his partner, Richard Wood, had been, to a certain extent, Noah's one-time rival trappers in the Cold River country.

By 1965, there was significant evidence of age in Noah's handwriting and a bit of poor health in his voice, but he carried on as he always had. People who knew him in the Adirondack wilderness and when he lived in the Wilmington area have said they could not help but feel "there was a sense of the presence of God" in Rondeau's being—his struggles, the life-long appeal of an outlying woodland life, his pastoral musings as he viewed breath-taking beauty from a mountain top, the images he saw in clouds against a measureless sky, or what he eyed growing from the forest floor. His friends felt Noah knew God was there.

"Much overcast, light rain; a.m. Freezing Sleet, p.m., Thawing Sleet. At Singing Pines. I buy a 3 gal. Crock from Melvin Peck. 8:30 p.m., Raining," was noted on Wednesday evening, February 10, followed by two long lines of code.

Wednesday, February 12. Perfect Sunshine; Mild and calm at Singing Pines. Aden Lewis call and we have a picnic. And here it is Ash Wed. and no ashes to rub on my Fool Head and no ciscoes for the Holy Season of Lent if god find that out He will raise Hell.

Sunday, March 7. Nice weather at Singing Pines. I read and write; and I prepare order [code] Sundown: Hi Denton and James call. [code] Gary McCalvin and His Lady Friend call at Singing Pines. They feed my Chickadee Birds sunflower seeds out of hand [code].

The following day a "Mr. Winch and Party" took him to AuSable Forks for another appointment with Dr. Spranz.

* * *

March 20, 1965. Overcast and few glimpses of Sun. 4 P.M. Snowed 1". At Singing Pines. 11a.m. at Wilmington and call at Melvin Peck and at White Face Market. [code] a.m. Mr. Metcalf call. p,m, James Denton call [code].

March 25, 1965. Calm, Mold, Sunshine and thawing at Singing Pines. I notch Green Balsom Log, and raise it on WigWam. Harold Peck and Lewis call. [code]

April 11, 1965. A Nice Vernal Day. At Singing Pines. Richard Smith, calls. 11 to 3 we fire chimney, clean stovepipe

April 15, 1965. Cloudy, and sprinkling at Singing Pines. 3a.m., trimming Beard and Hair. Mid Day: Melvin Peck call with my mail.

May 6, 1965. Nice Sunshine on Silver Birches, among Singing Pines. …p.m., I ride to Wilmington with Melvin Peck—Call at P.O. I dine at Eleanor's, Taxi home with M. Peck. I plant 2 Nut Trees. Richard Smith,

Courtesy Dr. Adolph G. Dittmar, Jr.

Bring 15 Trees Shumway and Burpee and Interstate Nursuries. We (backwards) have a picnic.

May 20, 1965. A hot day At Singing Pines. I plant 37 Gladd Bulbs (Gurneys) I work 5 hours in Hi Garden; I plant 3 lbs Canada(s?) Held peas; 2 lb. Blackeye (d?) P: Row 19 and 20 (backwards): I dine with Agnes. I water North Garden. Orchard. Richard Smith, call 7-10P.M. Radio Cabnet

May 29, 1965. Nice Vernal Day At Singing Pines. Miss Joanne Petty, call with Her Cousin, Mr. [Edward] Petty. (Decoded: At Hi's garden I plant popcorn.)

June 4, 1965. Frost last night. To Day: cold, breezy, at Singing Pines. I plant Rows: NO. 31-32-33-3(4?) 2 kinds-Burpee Wax Bean and S. end, Row No. 35-38 Hill. (Pencil Pads-Black Wax.) (Decoded: Agnes bring me milk and bacon. Hattie Bombard born.) Kaiser died 1944.

June 18, 1965. Clouds, Thunder, 4 p.m. Shower at Singing Pines. I water Hi Garden. (Decoded: Broadcast 10 lbs. proso seeds. I dine with Agnes. Victor Jacques dine. I get mail from Wilmington by Agnes.)

June 22, 1965. Sunshine at Singing Pines. I write Richard Smith. (Decoded: Nice graduate. I plant 2 rows onions. Purple top rutabaga; row 3 of turnip. Row 4 turnip.) extra early Milan.

July 6, 1965. Cool after rain at Singing Pines—AuSable Forks. I go to Wilmington, Greyhound to Ausable Forks. Call on Dr. Spranz. Lodge at St. Patrick. [Decoded: The entire page of Noah's written code about black bears he killed need to be translated upside down. He used his "ever other letter" trick in it too. The list appears as Rondeau wrote it.]

Date	Comment
10.27.1927	near Marble Mt.
05.03.1924	minus 3 toes
12.12.1931	8 ner wse wad b no canines
11.07.1923	Jungle Lodge broken jaw [the so-called "lodge" was trapline camp]
10.27.1934	bohemian thief
10.29.1934	above anvil [Anvil camp was a Santa Clara deserted lumber camp high in Ouluska Pass.]
06.08.1953	arrows
11.09.1937	oscar/greer [Oscar Burguiere and Greer Latimer took part in the hunt. See Appendix B.]

Mary Dittmar and Noah fishing Boiling Pond 1943. Courtesy Dr. Adolph G. Dittmar, Jr.

11.02.1938	runt
12.05.1938	aubel [Refers to a small brook in the vicinity of Camp Seward.]
11.11.1940	lord buy hide ["Lord" refers to Oscar Burguiere's handle.
05.21.1931	8 trio hill near camp
10.23.1934	2 paper bag brook [Another stream near Camp Seward. The name originated by Doc Latimer and Jay Gregory when they hung a paper lunch bag there.]
10.28.1934	5 nut cracker [Rondeau's reference to his bear traps.]

July 26, 1965. Hot Sun-Scattered Clouds No rain. At Singing Pines. I work 4 hours at Hi Garden. I use chlordane on Copper Head Grubs. (Decoded: I count 33 tomatoes on plants. I dine with Agnes. I confab with Mrs. Dudley.)

August 17, 1965. Very hot weather. 10 p.m., Lightning-Thunder. 11p.m., Raining at Singing Pines. I walk to Wilmington, Dine at Eleanor's. (Decoded: Confab with Phelps.) I call at Melvin Peck; and at White Face Market.

August 18, 1965. Last Night: Rain ½". To Day: Cloudy Morning Sunshine Day at Singing Pines. Hi Denton, Call, 10 to 12 a.m. I call at Hi Garden, 1 P.M. I picked Wax Beans, Squash and Parsley. I dine with Hi and Agnes.

August 19, 1965. Last night rain ½". To Day: Cloudy Morning. Sunshine Day at Singing Pines. Hi Denton call 10 to 20 min. I call at Hi's Garden, 1 P.M. I pick Wax Beans, Squash and Parsley. I dine with Hi and Agnes. (Decoded: I call at Lee Hind's and I give squash and wax beans. June bug.)

August 20, 1965. Sunshine and scattered Clouds, cool, after rain. At Singing Pines. I stake Gladiolus Plants. (Decoded: A Vt. Man call...and take photo. Agnes help me pick vegetables.) Moses Akey Salad, first blossom, 10 ft. from camp.

August 27, 1965. Clouds and Sun at Singing Pines. I go to Wilmington. (Decoded: Call on Madeline [Dodge] with rhubarb. Plan orchard.) Call on Melvin Peck. (Decoded: Dine at Elanor's.) Call at White Face Market. Taxi home. (Decoded: Victor Jacques has a fool laugh. Bull shit.) Mid Afternoon: Three Men call on me. (Decoded: Victor Jacques nose in.) Blighted Black Ash Seed are falling.

August 28, 1965. 3 to 10 a.m., Showers. At Singing Pines. 9a.m., Miss. Call to get a Photograph. First Heavenly Blue Bells on Morning Glory Vines in Garden. P.M. Bert Cross (Decoded: A Plattsburg Italian man call. 3 fish for guide. 8 to 10 Richard Smith call. Bear eating on dump. Shitbag.)

September 6, 1965. Warm and Nice. Singing Pines-AuSable Forks. (Decoded: 1 stingy bath.) Man in red fabric all. (Decoded: What have you for sale?) I killed Mouse in Seed Can. I carry peck Tomatoes to Wilmington. Dine at Eleanor's. (Decoded: I borrow 20 cents from Mr. Cousin.) I taxi to Madeline Greyhound to AuSable Forks.

September 13, 1965. Morning-two hours Sun, then Cloudy all day; Mid Day sprinkle 1 to 5 p.m., Rain 3/8". At Singing Pines. I pick 6 doz. Pods Snap Beans. (Decoded: And I cut them up and put them in six bags. I cook 20 pods snap beans salt pork.) I put away Rhubarb Sauce.

November 3, 1965. Nice Day Autumn Sunshine. Our snow vanished at Singing Pines. (Decoded: petit ourec bon mongae.) I put Bear Meat on ice. I put a supply of wood in camp. 3 o'clock Hi Denon call. (Decoded: I go stear at racater for Denton. Agnes give me a quart of apple sauce.)

Bette Ohern bushwacking to Boiling Pond, 2007. Courtesy Author's photo

November 4, 1965. A nice Day-Autumn Sunshine. Our Snow vanish. At Singing Pines. I put Bear Meat on ice. I put a supply of wood in camp. 3 o'clock, HI Denton call.

December 5, 1965. Last night: Snowed ¼". At Singing Pines. Richard Smith, call 2 to 7 p.m., (Decoded: lodge hunt. June bug.) Mr. Wolf call from Bonny View. (Decoded: with comnpagnon.)

December 10, 1965. Total cloudy—Snowed ½" at Singing Pines. I first use my New Double roaster and roast Venison Roast. (Decoded: Gift of Bob Bowen. June bug.)

December 18, 1965. Total Cloudy-Snowed ½". At Singing Pines. I first use my New Double-Roaster, and roast a Venison Roast.

December 24, 1965. Last Night-Sprinkle. ToDay: Mild, Snow nearly all gone. At Singing Pines. 9a.m., Dale and Tracy Pelkey, bring me a loaf of

Courtesy of Richard J. Smith from Noah's photo album

Fresh Bread. Mid-Day Walt Denton bring me a Gift Pkg. from Sunday School Class, of Nazarene Church. (Decoded: 1 stingy bath.)

December 25, 1965. Mild-Overcast all day. A.m., Green Christmas p.m. White Christmas. At Singing Pines. 11a.m. I walk to Lee Hinds. Ride with Benji El to Madeline Dodge; and I dine with Madeline. (Decoded: she give me a shirt. I call in orchard. 1 kiss as please a peer visit.) I taxi home. (Decoded: I get gift from Mrs. Jennie Pelkey.)

Chapter 37

1966

January 1, 1966. Saturday. To Day very mild, no snow, sunshine, summerlike at Singing Pines. A brown-breasted nuthatch and several chickadee birds call in my kitchen and ask for a handout. They get sunflower seeds and then in a Christmas tree shucking Pea Nuts "Chickadee dee dee."

On this 1966 New Year's Day, the strong winter winds were not bellowing down through the metal chimney cap on Singing Pines, nor were its outer clapboarded walls muffled in snow. When that happened later on, Noah's snug little home would look as if it had been tucked in to sleep under great white blankets.

Soon the cold and snowy days of winter would come, and life in the middle room of Noah's Wilmington three-room place would change. Today was a day for Noah to lay aside the responsibilities of splitting stove wood and wander the back lot, enjoy a slow-moving day of fine weather, be entertained by birds' antics, and timing how long it took the red squirrels to carry away a buckwheat griddle cake he placed on the Shrine of Holy Pancake feeding stump. The whole day was one to delight an old man who now had the leisure to enjoy it.

The following day's entry was brief: "I arrange two cans for coffee service."

Richard Smith was not one to be idle around the camp. Singing Pines did not require much to remain serviceable, but Smith kept a watchful eye on it. He said, "Weekends, I most often went down to see Noah and to check the camp—mostly to see if one of the large pines had gotten too old to sing and had demolished the place. I had the thought that once

Noah passed I'd use the building as a hunting camp, as the River Road snow comes early, and crunchy snow never made for good still hunting. I also had this crazy idea in the back of my mind that when I retired I might sell the River Road house and move to Singing Pines to live. The taxes would be lower. With no water, sewer or electric, it could be done cheaper to finish out my days as Noah did. But who can give up hot water, an electric toaster, a flush toilet and shower— a cozy home, to go back to camping and roughing it again?"

Smith said it was easy to persuade Noah to amble around the yard at Singing Pines in the unseasonable mild weather. Noah simply liked being outdoors.

"One of Noah's jokes was being able to tell which season it was by which trees he walked around," Smith told me. On their walks he'd reminded Richard just in case he had forgotten, and Richard would always play along. "And how's that again, Noah?"

"Well, the way to make a distinction is ya go around this birch tree one day and tomorrow, well ya go around the pine. That's it right there. That makes a good variety. Well, sometimes back around the corner of time they were some long winters, but I like 'em long. People want to live too fast. And, their time'll all be gone and they won't have a place to turn." Noah's explanation didn't prove what season it was. But, just listening to how he talked was entertaining.

Monday, January 3, 1966. At Singing Pines I catch 60 quarts of rainwater from roof (collected in garbage cans for fire protection). Measure ground and plan vegetable beds for next Spring.

The morning of January 24, Noah awoke to find the wind had discovered fresh snow to pile, and he went out to a land of quiet whiteness, glistening in the morning sunshine. "Last night snowed 6 inches. Today A.M. cloudy. P.M. Sunshine. In last 24 hours a foot of snow fell. ... I broom a foot of snow out of a hundred feet of trail around cabin and to public road. A man from Upper Jay stopped to shoot his camera at me. Real winter scenes are here. The eaves of camp well garnished with

Courtesy of Richard J. Smith from Noah's photo album

Madeline Dodge and Noah. Courtesy of Richard J. Smith from Noah's photo album

Polly Russ learning a lesson about archery from Noah, August 9, 1934. Courtesy of Charley Russ

icicles. Chickadee birds call for food."

As in those bygone years at the river site, one source of hermit recreation was the animals. Noah said he "never attempted to tame wild life.

When I was a youngster, sometimes I'd catch a woodchuck and put him in a cage, you know. Feed him clover and so forth. But that's all—there's a lot a nonsense in it."

* * *

February 2, 1966. Perfect sunshine all day at Singing Pines. I set a trap for a bluejay and in thirty minutes a Jay bird got caught in the trap.

March 16, 1966. Perfect sunshine day after frosty night at Singing Pines. I'm washing fabric. About Mid day a lady called from Essex County welfare.

April 12, 1966. Cloudy At Singing Pines. At midday a rabbit tried to run over me in my garden. I fell 14 trees and cut them up clearing ground to plant fruit trees.

May 11, 1966. Morning sunshine on silver birches among singing pines. The day continues sunshine and a chill in the vernal air. At Singing Pines I soak 4 grape vines, 1 pear tree and 6-in-1 apple tree. I plant them. I also plant 3 blueberry plants, 1 red dogwood and 4 purple lilacs. Lady from Essex County Welfare call on me.

[In addition to a small allotment from the Essex County Social Services, Noah was allotted a Social Security retirement benefit in the amount of $35.00 per month for the period 09/1965 – 08/1967.]

June 5, 1966. Perfect June day of sunshine and purple lilacs. At Singing Pines. At 8 A.M. Clifford Smith call for me and I go to his home for the day near Haystack mountain. And what purple lilacs and old time covered bridge through Upper Jay past Noble Denton's Lilacs and Lilacs and Haystack Mt.

August 15, 1966. Morning overcast, sun 2 minutes for the day. 99 per cent overcast At Singing Pines. Last night my best ripe tomatoes disappeared from plant.

September 1, 1966. Perfect sunshine morning. The day continues sunshine. At Singing Pines. 10 A.M. I set trap for chipmunk. 11 A.M. in trap dead chipmunk. Midday cremation. I pick last tomatoes. Sundown call at refreshing spring.

October 9, 1966. Perfect sunshine at Singing Pines. Mid Day Mr. and Mrs. Wiezel and Mrs. Wiezel's mother and teenager called. We sit among silver birches and singing pines and have a splendid visit.

October 17, 1966. Sunshine all day and cool air. At Singing Pines I make a blue denim bag from a pants leg and bag. 120 very small potatoes mostly early ones.

November 11, 1966. At Singing Pines. Last night a mouse tried my trap and it worked. I darn and patch heels on wool socks.

November 18, 1966. A.M. feeble sun, P.M. overcast. At Singing Pines. Today Curing effect [code]. 5 P.M. I go shopping at Wilmington, every step too much for Old Man. P.M. home.

December 18, 1966. Very mild P.M. Sprinkle at Singing Pines. At dusk Richard Smith fixes stovepipe and puts up my storm windows.

December 19, 1966. Perfect sunshine all day at Singing Pines. 3 P.M. at refreshing spring. 4 P.M. a lady from Whiteface Methodist Church brings me a Christmas package artistically prepared.

December 23, 1966. At Singing Pines, A young man call with package from Salvation Army. At first shades of dusk Walter Denton bring me a package from Wilmington Nazarene Church.

December 25, 1966. At Singing Pines. Last night snow 10 inches. Today total overcast and forest decked in Xmas style. The most beautiful Xmas storm ever. I broom trails about camp and get wood for the night.

FAME & $HEKELS

Chapter 38

February 1967

Wednesday, February 1. Total overcast all day. At Lake Placid hospital. Good sleep last night. Morning - good wash. Breakfast 7:30. Vitamin shot 10 AM. 11 AM Blood test. One bath [code]. Noon luncheon. I write Richard Smith [code]. Melvin Peck called.

Wasn't it just yesterday that Noah had loaded his hermit treasures into burlap bags and hopped into a little red helicopter, on the first leg of a journey to a sportsmen's show in New York City?

That was twenty years ago—a thing of the past—and he said just that to his New Year's Day guest, Richard Smith, who'd stopped in for coffee. Smith recalled that some of their talk revolved around the number of pound cans of Beech-Nut coffee "Mr. Whiskers," a nickname Smith used infrequently, used to buy from Holt's Variety Store right across from the high school on Main Street in Lake Placid, "because he liked his morning coffee."

Over the span of their thirty-three years of friendship, Smith hadn't forgotten the advice Noah had given him the summer of 1934 when Smith told Noah he'd prefer to quit high school and live in the woods like him. Noah explained it was after the house fire at Coreys when he decided to go into the woods permanently. "I had spent three-quarters of my time in the backwoods." Smith recalled Noah always spoke wistfully whenever he talked of learning. "If I could have had a good education when I was a boy, I wouldn't have gone into the woods. I tell people 'Cold River is a good hiding place for a failure.'" Smith said Noah always followed

Noah at Indian Falls lean-to. Courtesy Roger D. Freeman M.D.

with a "soft chuckle." Before he continued. "I just study now because of the satisfaction in it. I figure that if I could live to be five hundred years old, I'd be quite a scholar."

Noah admitted his chosen way of live was hard. He got hungry and felt the cold like anyone else. He admitted, "I guess this way of life wouldn't do for most people but the beauty of nature and life itself were here long before human life was coined and that appeals to me more than the riches of the world.

"I don't know as if I could be any happier under the circumstances. I've got the flowers and the trees, the mountains and the stars. I have nine books on astronomy; I've read them over and over and I still got a lot to learn."

The amateur observer also liked to share his celestial opinions. He'd share, "I've got some ideas of my own I'd like to explain to folks. For instance, too few of them realize that they're living on a round planet that rotates in space and travels rapidly. I see the planets orbit, nine of them that we know of, first as being made perfect and put in line with the sun.

"Then, seems to me like somebody once caught an orbit somewhere, like a hoop or a circle, and pulled one side out one way and the other another way to make a tilt to the sun, and set it rotating in space—that's the Earth."

Alice H. Wood remembered Noah well from the days she worked as a cashier at her father's store: "He would first get some magazines and newspapers, then ask for the large tin of tobacco and some ground coffee. He was a very quiet man. I don't recall any conversation. I would place his purchases in a bag and add it up, tell him what he owed; he'd pay and I'm sure he would say 'Thank you,' pick up his bag and leave. When he left, we would remark that Noah must have run out of supplies."

THURSDAY **6** MAY

[handwritten diary entry with symbolic cipher script]

Courtesy of Richard J. Smith from
Noah's photo album

Speaking of the beginning of 1967, Smith recalled Noah's steps had grown weary over the past year. "You couldn't blame him for how he felt." Richard was referring to Noah's state of health.

"I clearly remember we talked of the passing years and how I came to purchase the Singing Pines property," Smith told me during one of several times he invited me to the camp in 1991–'92.

The hermit's 1967 diary entries appear in *Noah John Rondeau's Unlikely Pilgrimage*, which at this writing in 2022 remains unpublished.

Afterword

February 1947 had been a watershed month for 63-year-old Adirondack hermit Noah John Rondeau following his appearance at the sportsmen's show at Madison Square Garden. His long existence living as a hermit-of-sorts snuggled in Cold River valley in the Adirondack High Peaks for over 30 years was the very thing that propelled him into becoming an instantaneous attraction. The money he earned and the celebrity-like status he gained motivated promoters of the popular sportsmen's show circuit to include his appearance at other events throughout the Northeast.

With the valise of knick-knacks he marketed to audiences, news reports told how he "charmed" urban sophisticates with his special brand of folkish discourse. He addressed them about living at Cold River and fielded repeated questions from lines of people waiting to meet him.

He was busy as a sought-after speaker at numerous business and civic associations, county fairs, and Saranac Lake's Winter Carnival. His diary entries indicate that he was proud of his sudden celebrity status and happy to earn more money in a week than he had in a year as a trapper and guide.

And yet throughout his new life as a public figure it was still the peace he experienced in the wilderness that pleased him best. His circle of friends and acquaintances widened greatly, and his struggle to survive in the woods underwent a revolutionary change. There were more changes on the way, but for now nothing could dim his high spirits and the delight he took in the unexpected turn of his new life outside Cold River.

Noah John Rondeau's Unlikely Pilgrimage by William J. O'Hern is the fascinating story of the final seventeen years of the hermit's celebrated life.

Noah casting in a pool behind Big dam.
Courtesy Richard J. Smith from Noah John Rondeau photo album

Richard said he had to guard Noah because he was pulling a fiddlebow over squeaky strings.
Courtesy Richard J. Smith from Noah John Rondeau photo album

This picture was taken when Richard brought some jam to Noah. He said thank Mrs Bb for me. Courtesy Richard J. Smith from Noah John Rondeau photo album

Noah carrying big bear. Courtesy Richard J. Smith from Noah John Rondeau photo album

Santa's Workshop at the "North Pole"

Courtesy Richard J. Smith from Noah's photo album

* * *

Santa's Workshop, an amusement park located in Wilmington, N.Y, began operations in 1949. It was once heralded as "the No. 1 tourist attraction in the East."

The idea for the village, located a half mile up the Whiteface Mountain highway, which leads off Route 86 at Wilmington, originated with Julian Reiss, a Lake Placid businessman. The design of the park was done by Arto Monaco, of Upper Jay; it was built by Harold Fortune, of Lake Placid, who also owned the site, and helped promote the park.

The park drew immediate media interest, with attendance peaking at 14,000 on September 2, 1951.

The original North Pole children's village consisted of nine stripped-

When not working as Santa, Noah John Rondeau lived outside the entrance of the North Pole. His replica log cabin mirrored the actual building he relied on for his survival in the cold river wilderness. It served as an additional tourist attraction at the theme park. "I remember having my picture taken with Rondeau. These pictures were taken on a Sunday inlet october 1950. My father owned a grocery store in Hudson Falls and only had Sundays off to make the trip to Wilmington. Noah and I had something in common. We were both raised to speak the french language. I spoke only French until I entered school." Courtesy Alice Genthner

Photo with the young girl and Notable Adirondack hermit, Noah John Rondeau was employed to play the role of Santa Claus throughout the late summer and fall of 1950. "I do not remember much about the occasion except that I did not like Santa. I was young and scared. Mother Hubbard is consoling me." Courtesy Alice Genthner pine log houses designed with a Mother Goose motif by Monaco, a former Walt Disney and MGM artist. Among the bright Christmas-colored buildings were Santa's home, his workshop, his blacksmith shop, a church, a post office, and several stores.

Santa's home was made for children to inspect inside and out and talk with him as long as a child wished. Santa's Workshop was manned by gnome helpers, dressed in medieval costumes, making toys. The stores contained their products for children of any age. Toys could be purchased or ordered for future delivery.

In the blacksmith shop, other Santa's assistants worked at the forge. In the post office children were able to sit down at little desks to write a note to Santa or letters to friends and relatives back home. The United States Postal Service designated The North Pole as an official post office in 1953.

A statue of St. Nick looked down from the small chapel and inside behind the altar was the Nativity Scene in miniature.

Harmonizing with the mountain setting were rustic bridges, one of which, beside a huge waterwheel, crossed a little duck pond.

Perhaps the biggest attractions for the little folks, next to Santa himself, were the numerous white-tailed deer, the goats, and the sheep that freely mingled among the visitors, hoping to be petted, and begging for a biscuit which could be purchased from several dispensers stationed about the grounds. Deer didn't care if they were not handed food. Once they saw someone put a nickel in the slot, they knew enough to help themselves. Oftentimes a goat would give a friendly little butt to get one's attention. Shetland ponies were also available for rides.

Reiss later started "Santa's Operation Toylift," which delivered toys and gifts to underprivileged children in northern New York and Vermont. This grew with the provision of a C-46, the "Silver Sleigh," by Standard Oil of New Jersey, to cover 13 States, the District of Columbia and two Provinces of Canada, delivering ten tons of presents to orphaned children. In the Summer 1956 issue of *North Country Life* magazine, "Operation Toylift" features in detail its history.

The long-running Adirondack Mountain business venture is still visited by children and grown-ups as of this writing (2022).

Noah's bear story and Dittmar's On Rondeau. Photo by Author

Left to right: Ditt, Noah, and Mary Dittmar. Noah is recording his bear story at the Dittmar's Silver Lake camp. Courtesy Helen Menz

Camp Seward's True Story of Greer's Bear

On a cloudy yet mild Thursday in November 1937, teenager Greer Latimer left Camp Seward following breakfast, hiking upriver to Cold River City for a get-together. Greer, 17, exchanged greetings with 54-year-old Noah Rondeau and then, following the instructions of the hermit, dropped behind him as Noah took the lead toward a winding forest path.

That's how Greer's day began. The events that followed on that day were heralded in the Deposit Courier the following week. "Two Bears Killed in North Woods by Hunters from Deposit," his hometown newspaper shouted, but the paper didn't tell the entire story. And why not? All the details were not available. Greer chose to remain silent until May 14, 2000. George Latimer, Greer's son, and Greer explain why in the following email of that date:

Dad [Greer Sr.] has always been rather vague about his bear hunt in Cold River. Now at 80 years of age, and cornered on a lazy Sunday afternoon, he has laughingly agreed to reveal the truth about his north woods hunt with Noah John Rondeau in 1937.

On the day in question, Dad had gone off alone to visit Noah while his dad stayed at Camp Seward to do chores and some deer hunting with guests. Dad had no particular thought in mind when he decided to strike off that day other than to take his rifle along in case he came on to a buck. It had been a habit to visit with Noah since he was young. It was obvious Noah enjoyed children and they him. Dad and his brothers CV Jr. and Don had known Noah for years. They liked his little corner of the world as much as the hermit did. Every one of them had listened to Noah tell stories about game wardens who had been snippy and snooty, and it was difficult to accept Noah could be a poacher. They saw him as a person who used the benefits of the deep woods to survive. If that meant taking more than the legal limit, so be it.

Father and his brothers asked Grandfather [Latimer] many questions about Noah and his decision to live in the woods. They were told the hermit actually had a very stable wilderness life. He included reports in letters he wrote us, like 'Chickadees, Juncos, Nuthatches and sparrows feed near my window,' and how he watched 'Butterflies Kiss Blossoms.' They'd all seen the small vegetable patches he tended, listened to him play French-Canadian and American tunes on his fiddle—he actually called it his 'Antonius Stradivarius' violin—and said he always looked forward to my grandfather and his party each year. He didn't like hunters that came into his woods who drank too much. They could ruin the woodland.

When Dad arrived at the hermitage, Noah was standing over his huge black cooking pot cooking up an unlucky rabbit for supper. It was a huge pot. It was suspended over his perpetual cooking fire from chains that hung from a tripod. He called anything that was brewing Everlasting Stew.

After testing the brew's contents, which was excellent, Dad was told to get his rifle and follow Noah. Dad did not question Noah's directions; this was his domain and he was the master. They hiked for less than a mile. During that time he talked about 'the flory and the fauny'—he could tell you everything about what wild plants to eat and whatever you would want to know about the local animals.

Dad loved being with Noah. He was drawn to him partly out of curiosity, but mostly out of the desire to enjoy his company. Since Noah was an experienced woodsman, he let him do most of the talking and was just waiting to see what he had in mind. He figured there was some sort of strategic location he might be going to, or maybe Noah needed his help, so he never interrogated him like: 'Where are we going? What do you have in mind?'

Noah said he had bear traps set around the area—there were three at Dog Orchard, one each at Flat Iron, Seward Pond, Maggot Brook and Bog Orchard. Dad had seen some steel traps Noah hung in a tree near

Kerosene Brook to lose any trace of human scent. Noah kept one trap at Paper Bag Brook behind Camp Seward. In fact, everyone knew about it. The steel trap that was attached to a tree with a heavy cog was covered with twigs and leaves. You wouldn't want to accidently step into it. Dad said his father heard Noah comment about the traps he set all over the mountain. They were a liability for any hapless hunter. Noah's only comment was 'no one had any business stepping into one.'

Stopping after less than a half hour's walk, Noah raised his finger and pointed, telling Dad to look to his left. A very large and angry black bear was caught in one of his steel-toothed traps. How Noah knew beforehand that his trap held the beast, Dad to this day has never understood. He assumes it was just the timing of his arrival. He knew traps needed to be visited each day. Dad was not expecting to see a bear in a trap at that time.

Dad said he felt his eyes enlarge to the size of silver dollars when he spotted the huge bear that he supposed was dead in the trap, but which suddenly came to life when it saw them. The bear acted ugly. Noah was all business. In a matter-of-fact manner, he told Dad you can always catch more flies with honey than with vinegar and that it was true with bears too. He was talking about the scented decoy that appealed to an animal's chemistry, drawing it closer to the steel trap set nearby. As a result, a trapper could end the season with more catches.

With no fanfare, Noah told Dad to shoot the growling bear. 'Kill him! Kill him!' It was not only caught and frightened, it was mad, up on all four feet as best it could be, and intent on getting out. Dad's trembling hands raised his rifle and fired a clean shot to the heart. Noah instructed Dad to fire one more for good measure, which he did. Then Noah and Dad sat on the ground and poked the black bear with sticks for 4 or 5 minutes before attempting to approach the now-still carcass. Dad was told to watch closely for signs of life. 'Watch to see if it winks. You don't want to curl a bear's mustache. It don't make 'em happy,' he was told. Once assured the bear was dead, Noah wasted no time in removing the bear from the trap and gutting the animal.

As the two approached Noah's camp, they were surprised to find Noah's good friend Oscar Burguiere waiting for them. Oscar volunteered to help

Dad pack the head, hide and a little meat back to Camp Seward, leaving most of the meat for Noah. Dad thanked Noah for providing him with his first bear hunt, even if it was a little unethical. To Noah, this was all in a day's work and he found no need to fuss over the hunt. He had constantly matched his wits against any number of trapped animals, and he could relate any number of tales of animals' intelligence in the woods and their ability to sense danger, and how their will to work their way out of a tight place when cornered far exceeded that of man.

Returning to Camp Seward with Oscar was an experience in itself. Oscar shared what he'd learned about bear trapping: bears are continually on the alert, they have a keen sense of smell, no one should ever be misled by the small beady eyes because the eyesight is quite keen as is their ability to hear. It requires great skill to ever approach them.

When Dad strutted into camp with his trophy, my grandfather was very impressed by the hunting experience Dad began to share, but as he finished with the story, my grandfather suggested he omit the part about the trap. I'm not sure to this day why my grandfather made this comment. Perhaps he may have known it was an illegal method of hunting.

Upon returning to Deposit, my dad was surprised to find his adventure had preceded him and the facts had become somewhat distorted in a newspaper story. Everyone wanted to hear more about his adventure with the Adirondack black bear. The local paper wanted to do a follow-up article, and the Rotary Club wanted to have Dad give a blow-by-blow account of the hunt at their next meeting.

Finding himself in somewhat of a pickle, Dad was forced to invent a new version of his hunting trip—eliminating the part about the trap and adding some tall bragging indulged in by some respect to his dumb luck and novice ability. Giving an embellished account of the bear hunt, Dad realized that his story of the exploits of a 17-year-old budding woodsman would have impressed even Noah John.

After all these years, Dad finally decided that it was time to fess up and tell the true story about Noah and the bear. Dad spent many other times with Noah, following winding tracks through the backcountry, but never again did he ever see or shoot another trapped bear.

FAME & $HEKELS

"Grandfather jotted Dad's success in Camp Seward's notebook:

Tues. Nov. 9, 1937: Greer Latimer, age 17. Out hunting with Oscar and Noah killed a 225 lb. black bear on the Flat Iron @ 11 AM. Also in camp was family friend, "Win" Alder. No snow on the ground.

Noah also noted this day's events:

At Meat Wigwam. High water, cloudy, mild. Call at Flat Iron Bear Trap. Reset, plastered with bear limburger [attractant]. Hid gal. Bait. Oscar set Doz. mice traps. Greer go with Bear-darn Law Braker.

Don Lattimer and Noah. Photo by Author

Adirondack Wilds

Acknowledgments

MY SINCERE APPRECIATION goes to all those people who were mentioned as contributors in this book but the research about Noah Rondeau goes a lot deeper. I have talked to hundreds of people who have had a little to a lot of contact with the hermit of Cold River. Too many to acknowledge here....

I will also like to acknowledge Mary L. Thomas who I initially relied on for the first draft and Neal Burdick, my final editor, for suggestions in planning and final organization.

www.ingramcontent.com/pod-product-compliance
Lightning Source LLC
Chambersburg PA
CBHW071631140626
46555CB00022B/2056